Christian Scholarship in the Twenty-First Century

Christian Scholarship in the Twenty-First Century

PROSPECTS AND PERILS

Edited by

Thomas M. Crisp
Steve L. Porter
Gregg A. Ten Elshof

WILLIAM B. EERDMANS PUBLISHING COMPANY
GRAND RAPIDS, MICHIGAN / CAMBRIDGE, U.K.

Published 2014 by

Wm. B. Eerdmans Publishing Co.

2140 Oak Industrial Drive N.E., Grand Rapids, Michigan 49505 /
P.O. Box 163, Cambridge CB3 9PU U.K.

Printed in the United States of America

20 19 18 17 16 15 14   7 6 5 4 3 2 1

Library of Congress Cataloging-in-Publication Data

Christian scholarship in the twenty-first century: prospects and perils /
    edited by Thomas M. Crisp, Steve L. Porter, Gregg A. Ten Elshof.
        pages   cm
    ISBN 978-0-8028-7144-2 (pbk.: alk. paper)
    1. Learning and scholarship — Religious aspects — Christianity.
    I. Crisp, Thomas M., editor.

    BR115.L32C477   2014
    230.07 — dc23

                                              2014008697

www.eerdmans.com

Contents

Introduction

In the spring of 2012, Biola University launched its Center for Christian Thought, whose mandate is to facilitate high-level Christian scholarship on topics of importance to the Christian community and the broader culture, and to translate and disseminate that scholarship to non-specialists in the Christian community and beyond.

What guides the project is the conviction that the Christian intellectual tradition, a wisdom tradition stretching back thousands of years, is a source of considerable insight on perennial human questions about the shape of the good life, human happiness, virtue, justice, wealth and poverty, spiritual growth, and much else besides, and that Christian scholars can do enormous good in the world by bringing the resources of this tradition into conversation with the academy, the church, and the broader culture. But in the evangelical community — and to a lesser extent, the larger Christian community — Christian thinkers tend to be under-resourced: Christian college, university, and seminary faculty have considerably higher teaching loads than their secular colleagues, and by and large, there isn't much funding available for distinctly Christian reflection on culture, art, history, philosophy, literature, science, business, medicine, music, and so on, and their connections to human flourishing. Biola University's Center aims to play a part in changing this, to free up Christian thinkers to reflect on these topics in light of the Christian intellectual tradition, and to make the riches of this tradition accessible to non-scholars in the church and the broader culture.

Note, though, the talk here of "Christian scholarship," "distinctly Christian reflection," "Christian thinkers," and so forth. These terms have a surface clarity to them. "Christian scholarship," for instance: isn't that just scholarship from a Christian perspective? No doubt, but saying exactly what that comes to turns out to be difficult. What is it, for example, to do historical scholarship from a Christian perspective? Or physics, chemistry, psychology? Is there a distinctly Christian approach to studying these topics, and if so, what might that be? What, in short, *is* Christian scholarship? What distinguishes it from other sorts of scholarship? What is it about Christian scholarship that makes it specifically *Christian?* Is it a matter of doing scholarship on certain characteristically Christian topics? Or is it rather that Christian scholarship brings to bear certain specifically Christian sources of evidence on its investigations? Or is it perhaps that Christian scholarship is scholarship done through the lens of distinctly Christian affect, valuing, or feeling? Or is it all of this?

These are questions of first importance for the Christian intellectual community, for if there *are* distinctively Christian approaches to the various academic disciplines, it might be that by approaching them in these ways, we can better manifest the gospel, better image the manifold wisdom and beauty of God, better serve a suffering world. If there are distinctly Christian ways of approaching our scholarship, it would be good to know.

In the spring of 2012, we brought several wise and eminent Christian thinkers together for a semester-long discussion to reflect on the nature of Christian scholarship, which concluded with a conference in May of 2012. This volume comprises ten essays presented at that conference, ten rich and deeply interesting reflections on the nature of Christian scholarship which we are delighted to be able to collect into a single volume. Most of the essays were refined in weekly interdisciplinary discussions around the Center's "round table." These were lively conversations undergirded by growing friendships. Indeed, if one way of doing distinctively Christian scholarship involves doing our academic work in community with others, then these essays are deeply Christian. We offer these essays to the Christian intellectual community with the anticipation that they will help members of that community into deeper understanding and practice of robustly Christian scholarship in their fields.

The first essay, *"Fides Quarens Intellectum,"* by Nicholas Wolterstorff, is a reflection on the general contours of Christian scholarship. Wolterstorff proposes that the Christian scholar will be animated by two types of love. First, the love of craftsmanship, the love of crafting a fine specimen of scholarship. And second, the love of understanding: the love of moving from a state of perplexity to a state of understanding, which the Christian scholar loves both for the wisdom of God it reveals and for its usefulness in the pursuit of shalom.

Wolterstorff then reflects on the question of *how* the Christian scholar will engage his or her discipline, suggesting that the Christian scholar should think and act with a Christian mind in the practice of his or her discipline, and speak with a Christian voice. Speaking and acting with a Christian mind in one's discipline, says Wolterstorff, is not a matter of developing a theology of one's discipline, nor a matter of integrating one's Christian faith with the deliverances of one's discipline, nor a matter of pointing out similarities between Christian doctrines and the claims of one's discipline. Rather, it's a matter of approaching one's discipline with distinctly Christian habits of attention, modes of perception, habits of evaluation, and capacities for delight and love: ways of attending, of perceiving, of thinking, of valuing and loving shaped and formed by the Scripture and core traditions of the church. To speak with a Christian voice is to speak with a voice which always pays due honor to the ones we speak of, and avoids the abusive and demeaning talk so prevalent in the academy. And it's to speak in a voice that can be heard in the academy, that is appropriate to the standards of the discipline and contributes to the discussion of the discipline.

Alvin Plantinga's essay, "On Christian Scholarship," is likewise a reflection on the general contours of Christian scholarship. Christian scholarship, says Plantinga, differs from other sorts of scholarship in its use of the teaching of Christian Scripture in attempting to understand the world. Such scholarship involves two main projects. First, there is cultural criticism: pointing out cultural and intellectual projects that proceed from assumptions inimical to Christian faith and showing where and how they diverge from Christian commitment. And second, there is a positive task, something that goes beyond mere criticism: here the goal is to engage the various topics and projects of non-Christian scholarship, to build theories about them, but to do so from an evidence base that includes those things we know by faith. So, for example, where our naturalist colleagues will theorize about our love of music purely in terms of its evolutionary significance, Christian theorizing about it will go further, holding, perhaps, that our love of music is a gift from God that puts us in touch with beauty, beauty that flows from God and of which God is the chief exemplar. Engaging these projects may come at a cost to the Christian scholar, resulting in a certain amount of disdain from those in her discipline. Facing this requires Christian boldness and courage; the Christian scholar must remember that the main aim is not acceptance by the mainstream of her discipline, but faithfulness to the Lord.

Paul K. Moser's "Toward Christ-Shaped Philosophy" focuses on the discipline of philosophy, on the question of what Christian philosophy is, but his ideas carry over to other sorts of Christian scholarship. Moser thinks that

Christian philosophy should call attention to and uphold the importance of the inward, empowering union with the risen Christ available to those who call him Lord. And it should accommodate two senses of the phrase "doing Christian philosophy." First, the "strict-content sense" of doing Christian philosophy is a matter of doing philosophy that is explicitly Christian in conceptual content, in that it involves claims about Jesus, the Spirit of Christ, reconciliation to God in Christ, and so forth. Second, the "kingdom-enhancement sense" of doing Christian philosophy is a matter of interacting with philosophy, whatever its content, with the aim of clarifying its contributions to a philosophy that is explicitly Christian in conceptual content, and "enhances God's redemptive Kingdom in Christ," where, says Moser, that is a matter of facilitating or perhaps deepening one's inward reconciliation to God and experience of his inward empowerment. Doing Christian philosophy in the kingdom-enhancement sense requires that one restrict one's scholarly energies to projects that thus contribute to the deepening of reconciliation with God. Those lines of philosophical inquiry that don't serve this purpose are not appropriate research programs for Christian thinkers.

Jonathan A. Anderson's essay, "The (In)visibility of Theology in Contemporary Art Criticism," treats what he describes as a vast divide between contemporary art history, theory, and criticism, and religious — in particular, Christian — thought. After exploring the reasons for this divide, he proposes that theological engagement with contemporary artworks can "thicken" our engagement with them, and sketches what a "theological art criticism" might look like, suggesting that it will be criticism that is concerned with providing careful, thick interpretations of contemporary artworks that resonate with the language and standards of contemporary art discourse while bringing theological questions and concerns to bear on its attempt to understand the work.

Dariusz M. Bryćko's "Steering a Course between Fundamentalism and Transformationalism: J. Gresham Machen's View of Christian Scholarship" is a reflection on the brand of Christian scholarship endorsed by Machen, an early twentieth-century Presbyterian theologian and founder of Westminster Theological Seminary and the Orthodox Presbyterian Church. Bryćko compares Machen's approach to Christian scholarship with that of Abraham Kuyper, the great Dutch Reformed theologian and statesman whose views on the nature of Christian scholarship have come to prominence in the American Christian academic scene owing to their influence on thinkers like Alvin Plantinga, Nicholas Wolterstorff, George Marsden, and many others. Bryćko detects a triumphalism in Kuyper's views on Christian scholarship and cultural engagement not present in Machen, and proposes that, though Machen heavily influenced the early fundamentalist and evangelical movements, his approach to Christian scholarship avoids the anti-intellectualism of those movements.

M. Elizabeth Lewis Hall's essay, "Structuring the Scholarly Imagination: Strategies for Christian Engagement with the Disciplines," develops a typology of approaches to Christian scholarship. She begins with a broad definition of Christian scholarship meant to capture a variety of approaches to combining scholarship with Christian faith. Next she develops her typology, dividing types of Christian scholarship by motivation for the scholarship, epistemological assumptions and methodology underlying the scholarship, the content of the scholarship, and the outcomes of the scholarship. She then proposes several factors relevant to selecting modes of scholarly engagement: the scholar's discipline, the level of specificity of the scholarship, and the audience for which the scholar is writing. Hall concludes with a few prescriptive remarks.

Craig J. Slane's essay, "The Cross and Christian Scholarship," comments on exclusionary practices in Christian scholarship in light of the cross. Slane's argument turns on a creative re-reading of Justin Martyr, who has typically been adduced as a proponent of continuity between Greek wisdom and the Johannine Logos. Slane proposes that, for Justin, the main line of continuity between Christ and Socrates is not a similarity of thought, but a similarity of rejection: each was persecuted by those who would resist Logos. By keeping the scandal of the cross in play, Justin provided an admirable example of Christian scholarship capable of deconstructing modes of scholarship that protect Christian institutions by excluding and expelling those deemed a threat to those institutions. Yet in his failure vis-à-vis Jews, Justin also became a prime example of how easily Christians can fall prey to the logic of exclusion and expulsion.

Natasha Duquette's "Dauntless Spirits: Towards a Theological Aesthetics of Collaborative Dissent" is a reflection on a community of women scholars of eighteenth- and early nineteenth-century Protestant dissent who were writing poetry and aesthetic theory from within marginalized Protestant communities. These were doubly marginalized writers, owing both to their membership in non-conformist church communities and to the limits imposed on them because of their gender. Christian scholars, whether writing from their own liminal perspectives or writing on behalf of the marginalized, have much to learn from these women, whose tactics ensured that their views got a hearing from a wide, international audience. Such tactics can be applied by those writing from the margins today.

The next essay, "The Holy Spirit and the Christian University: The Renewal of Evangelical Higher Education," by Amos Yong, reflects from a Pentecostal and charismatic perspective on the nature of Christian higher education. Yong wonders what difference the Holy Spirit makes to the Christian university, and sketches a vision of a Christian academic life empowered by charismatic encounter with the Holy Spirit, imbuing research, scholarship, and teaching with a vitality not possible absent such encounter.

The final essay, "Barth on What It Means to Be Human: A Christian Scholar Confronts the Options," by George Hunsinger, briefly examines Karl Barth's theological anthropology and his critical interaction with naturalist, idealist, existentialist, and neo-orthodox alternatives to his anthropology, then draws three lessons for Christian scholarship from Barth's approach. First, before Barth critically examines alternative anthropologies, he develops criteria of adequacy based on Scripture. This allows Scripture, rather than competing viewpoints, to set the terms of the debate. Second, Barth carefully exposits competing views before attempting an assessment. Sometimes he gives an internal critique rooted in conceptual tensions within the view he is criticizing; other times he gives an external critique based on his theological criteria. And third, Barth examines everything from a center in Christ. Hunsinger puts it well: "It is Jesus Christ who determines what is real and what is merely phenomenal. It is he who conditions our lives as human beings. It is he in relation to whom we live and move and have our being. Our real existence as humans is our being for God in and through him."

Paul instructed those in his churches to "take every thought captive to Christ." In the context of the academy, following this injunction will require careful and sustained reflection on the nature of Christian scholarship. The essays that follow are an example of such reflection, and we pray that they will push forward the ongoing conversation on the prospects and perils of Christian scholarship in the twenty-first century.

THOMAS M. CRISP
STEVE L. PORTER
GREGG A. TEN ELSHOF

Fides Quaerens Intellectum

Nicholas Wolterstorff

Over the years, many students have come into my office to discuss career choices. Should they set their sights on becoming a professor, or should they go into some other line of work? And if they do set their sights on becoming a professor, should they go into philosophy or into some other discipline?

Rather late in my career I took to putting three questions to students contemplating some particular career choice: Do you love it? Are you good at it? And is it worthwhile? I always made a point of adding that they might not find a position that satisfied all three criteria; but they should look for one that does.

I did not suggest that they ask themselves whether they felt *obligated* to go into the career they were considering, for over the years I learned that almost always, when a student felt obligated to go into some career, it was because his or her parents had made him or her feel obligated. And never once in my entire career did I suggest that they ask whether the career they were contemplating was likely to yield fame or fortune. I suggested that they ask whether they loved it — and if they did love it, whether it also fitted their talents and was worthwhile.

Let me begin with some comments about that specific form of love which is love of learning. I know that there are people in the academy who do not love learning — or do not love that particular branch of learning in which they find themselves. But that's not how it should be. What should be is that we who are engaged in learning — scholarship and teaching — are in it for the love of it. From the first half-hour of my first college philosophy course, I found myself in love with philosophy. I remember saying to myself, after those first thirty minutes, that I had no idea whether I would be any good at this stuff, but if I did prove to be good at it, this was it. That first love of philosophy has never grown cold.

What sort of love was that, the love of philosophy that I experienced in that first half-hour? Love comes in many forms. What form of love is love of learning? And what is it about learning that leads some of us to love it?

I suggest that love of learning comes in two main forms. Start by noticing how often those of us engaged in scholarship use the language of *doing* and *making*. We speak of gathering evidence, of constructing theories, of developing arguments, of conducting research, of writing books — all highly activistic language. Love of learning, when it takes this form, is the love of producing something of worth — a well-crafted essay, a new theory. This form of love of learning resembles the woodworker's love of crafting a fine cabinet and the poet's love of composing a fine poem. It's a species of craftsmanship. When talking to students about writing philosophy papers, I often told them to think of it as blending craftsmanship with intellectual imagination. Early on I used a metaphor for craftsmanship: the dovetails should all be tight, I said. But I soon learned that most of them had no idea what a dovetail is.

Love of learning, understood as the love of crafting a fine specimen of scholarship, images the love manifested in God's work of creation.

But this was not the love of learning that I experienced in that first half-hour of philosophy, for the obvious reason that producing philosophical essays was still well in the future for me. Nor was it this form of the love of learning that I discerned in my father, in my grandfather, and in some of my aunts and uncles.

My grandfather was a farmer on the prairies of southwest Minnesota. But he did not love farming; he disliked it, maybe even hated it. What he loved was reading theology. As much as possible he neglected farming and gratified his love of theological learning. But this love did not eventuate in any works of theology — though he certainly talked a lot about theology. So love of learning takes a form in addition to the love of producing worthy pieces of scholarship. More than sixty years after that first half-hour of that first philosophy course, this other love of philosophy remains alive in me. What is this other love of learning?

It's the love of understanding. Previously one was baffled, bewildered, perplexed, or just ignorant; now one understands. Some of us love gaining understanding. I'm inclined to think that we all do, all human beings, though some don't like putting much effort into it.

This second form of love of learning, the love of understanding, is not merely in addition to the love of producing worthy pieces of scholarship. Understanding is the point of the enterprise. Scholarship is for the sake of understanding. We produce works of scholarship in order to articulate, record, and communicate what we have understood.

When I listen to deconstructionists and postmodernists, I sometimes get the impression that they never think in terms of gaining understanding; for them, the academic enterprise consists entirely of producing essays that others will find interesting and provocative. Some take the radical next step of insisting that there is nothing there to be understood; production is all there ever is — though it's worth noting that even those who say this tend to get upset when they think that they themselves have been *mis*-understood! They don't want their own works treated as the occasion for a play of imagination.

It's the love of understanding that keeps scholarship alive. If that love were extinguished, scholarship would die out. What would be the point? More money can be made elsewhere.

For the benefit of those just entering careers as scholars, I should add that this love of understanding carries along with it a dark side — namely, frustration. You are baffled by something. You want to find something out. You want to understand. But you are unsuccessful: reality won't yield its secret; the mystery won't part. So you are frustrated. A good deal of what goes into being a scholar is being able and willing to live with the frustration of wanting to understand that which, for the time being, resists being understood. A blend of exhilaration and frustration — that's the experience of those gripped by the love of understanding.

Why do we human beings long for understanding when we don't have it? Why do we relish it when we do have it?

Sometimes we prize understanding because what we have learned enables us to causally bring about certain things — enables us to change the world and ourselves in certain ways. But this reason, prominent though it is in the modern world, is not the only reason for prizing understanding. It was not the reason my grandfather prized theological understanding. It is not the reason some of us prize philosophical understanding; as the old saw has it, "Philosophy bakes no bread." There are forms of understanding that are to be prized wholly apart from what they enable us to bring about causally.

Why is that? Why prize learning that is not of use for changing things? The only way of answering this question that is available to the secularist is to identify or postulate some factor within the psychological makeup of human beings; Aristotle thought that it's characteristic of human beings just to *wonder* about certain things, to wonder why projectiles fall to earth, for example. For an answer of a very different sort, not incompatible but different, an answer that points away from the self, I invite you to turn with me to the wisdom literature of the Old Testament.

"How great are your works, O LORD!" exclaims Israel's songwriter. "Your thoughts are very deep!" (Ps. 92:5).

> O LORD, how manifold are your works!
> In wisdom you have made them all;
> the earth is full of your creatures. (Ps. 104:24)

Over and over the theme is sounded. The cosmos in which we find ourselves is not just here somehow, nor are we just here; both we and the cosmos were made. We are *works,* works of God, made with wisdom:

> The LORD by wisdom founded the earth;
>   by understanding he established the heavens;
> by his knowledge the deeps broke open,
>   and the clouds drop down the dew. (Prov. 3:19-20)

The response of the Psalmist to this vision of the cosmos and ourselves as works, works of God made with wisdom, is to meditate reverentially on these awesome manifestations of divine wisdom and to praise the One by whose wisdom they were made:

> On the glorious splendor of your majesty,
>   and on your wondrous works, I will meditate. (Ps. 145:5)

> I will sing to the LORD as long as I live;
>   I will sing praise to my God while I have being. (Ps. 104:33)

Not only are we and the cosmos works of divine wisdom; so also is Torah, God's guide for Israel's life. It too is a work of divine wisdom:

> The law [Torah] of the LORD is perfect, reviving the soul,
> the decrees of the LORD are sure, making wise the simple;
> the precepts of the LORD are right, rejoicing the heart;
> the commandment of the LORD is clear, enlightening the eyes. (Ps. 19:7-8)

The response of the devout Jew to this vision of divine wisdom embodied in Torah was to meditate with delight on Torah so as, in this case too, to get some glimpse of the wisdom embodied therein. "Happy are those who do not follow the advice of the wicked. . . ; but their delight is in the law [Torah] of the LORD, and on his law they meditate day and night" (Ps. 1:1-2).

> Oh, how I love your law [Torah]!
>> It is my meditation all day long.
> Your commandment makes me wiser than my enemies,
>> for it is always with me.
> I have more understanding than all my teachers,
>> for your decrees are my meditation. (Ps. 119:97-99)

The orientation that I have all too briefly been describing — of meditating with awed and reverential delight on God's works of creation and redemption so as to get some glimpse of the wisdom embodied therein — has, so far as I can tell, virtually disappeared from the modern world — rejected by secularists, of course, but also neglected by Christians who, if they pay any attention at all to the divine wisdom embedded in creation, turn it into a doctrine that they hold along with other doctrines.

So I invite you to do some imagining. Imagine that those of us who are Christian scholars recovered this vision; imagine that for us it became an orientation toward reality rather than one doctrine among others. Then we would see it as the point of the natural sciences not only to produce theoretical constructs worthy of admiration but to enhance our understanding of the cosmos. And we would regard the cosmos not as something that is somehow just there but as a work of God, infused with divine wisdom. Love of learning, so understood, would lead us to revel in awe at these works of divine wisdom and to praise their maker, some of whose wisdom we had now glimpsed. There is something deeply defective about the student or scholar who has never felt that awe.

Cell biology of the past fifty years is an extraordinary scientific construct — admirable both for its intrinsic worth and for its technological utility. But more than that, it has revealed to us some of the astounding intricacy of this part of creation. In coming to understand that intricacy, we get a glimpse of divine wisdom. We both praise the great achievements of the cell biologists and stand in awe of the divine wisdom that cell biology has revealed.

Some of you will have been asking yourselves whether the orientation that I have been describing and commending is at all relevant to the humanities, those disciplines in which we study not what God has made but what our fellow human beings have made — works of literature, of visual art, of music, of philosophy, and so forth. I have asked myself the same question. Let me offer a suggestion.

There were powerful currents of thought in the twentieth century that urged us to treat texts and works of art autonomously — urged us, for example, not to ask what Augustine said in the *Confessions* but to ask what *the text* says, not to ask what Milton said in *Paradise Lost* but to ask what *the poem* says — powerful movements, in short, toward removing authors and artists from the scene of the humanities. Instead of regarding oneself as engaged with Augustine when reading the *Confessions,* one is to regard oneself as engaged with the text called the *Confessions;* instead of regarding oneself as engaged with Milton when reading *Paradise Lost,* one is to regard oneself as engaged with that impersonal artifact which is the text called *Paradise Lost;* and so forth. Such a removal of persons from the scene, such a depersonalizing of the humanities, has gone hand in hand with the emergence in psychology and sociology of ever-new reductionist accounts of being human. Bach's *Sonatas and Partitas for Solo Violin* are, of course, abstract sound patterns. But they are more than that. They are musical intelligence and imagination of an extraordinary level embodied in sound — wisdom embodied in sound. To listen to them is to engage J. S. Bach. To insist on removing Bach from the scene is to dishonor him.

Here, then, is my suggestion. If one sees the cosmos not as something that's just there but as a work of God made in wisdom, then one will naturally also see poems, symphonies, bridges, churches, and the like, not as found objects but as *works* made by persons with one and another degree of wisdom, made because the maker thought, loved, and imagined, and in so doing imaged God the Creator. Before such embodied wisdom we also stand in awe, as we do before scientific theories — awe at the incredible gifts that God has bestowed on humankind.

I introduced these reflections on wisdom by noting that learning is to be prized both for the sake of what it enables us to bring about causally, and wholly apart from that. Since it is the latter reason that gets neglected in the modern world, given our infatuation with technology, I began with that. But let me now make just a very brief comment about the utility of learning.

Here too the Jewish and Christian believer will have a distinct "take" on things, that distinct "take" being rooted in the conviction that, as creatures of God, made in God's image, we human beings are not just here to act as we please; we have a calling, the calling to be agents of shalom and good stewards of the earth and its creatures. That conviction will guide both the direction of our own learning and our employment of what humankind has learned. We will pursue and employ learning for the sake of authentic development — development of the potentials of creation that promotes shalom. And we will pursue and employ learning for the sake of bringing about justice. We will, in the words of Isaiah, pursue and employ learning

> to loose the bonds of injustice,
> to undo the thongs of the yoke,
> to let the oppressed go free,
> and to break every yoke. (58:6-7)

Obviously, a great deal more could be said — indeed, *cries out* to be said — about the pursuit and employment of learning for the sake of shalom. But I must move on.

I've been talking about the two forms of love that do or should animate the Christian engaged in scholarship: the love of understanding which motivates scholarship and is its yield, and the love of the craft of good scholarship. I want now to move on to some remarks on *how*, as I see it, the Christian engages in scholarship.

Let me proceed by first offering a compact formula and then unpacking its content. Here is the formula: The Christian scholar should think and act with a Christian mind, and speak with an appropriate Christian voice, as he or she engages in his or her particular discipline and participates in the academy generally. Let me begin unpacking this formula with some remarks about how I understand the academic disciplines.

Recently I listened to a talk in which the speaker argued that teaching intelligent design is incompatible with the nature of natural science; if intelligent design is to be taught anywhere in the curriculum, he said, it must be in philosophy courses. In thus arguing, the speaker assumed that natural science and philosophy both have a nature, or essence, and was claiming that discussion of intelligent design is incompatible with the nature of natural science but compatible with the nature of philosophy.

The speaker's assumption about essence is a common assumption, though less common today, I would say, than it was forty years ago. The idea is that natural science came to birth in the early modern period, at the hand of people like Robert Boyle, Isaac Newton, and the like, when the so-called scientific method became established; what preceded it was not science but the prehistory of science. So too for economics, for psychology, for sociology, for "the scientific study of history," and so forth; they all have a Platonic essence that was manifested in history at a certain point after millennia of preparation.

Without arguing the point here, let me say that I think of the various academic disciplines very differently. I think of them as social practices, some, like philosophy, with a long ancestry, and some, like molecular biology, of recent origin. These practices are constantly changing as the result of developments both within and outside the discipline. What happened in the early modern period was not that the essence of natural science, after millennia of preparation, finally put in its appearance in history; what happened was that the long-enduring social practice of forming theories to explain the workings of physical nature underwent a truly dramatic alteration.

A social practice is a tradition. It's a way of doing something that gets handed on to newcomers who are thereby inducted into it. The newcomers learn the goals of the discipline and its framework of concepts; they acquire the skills necessary for engaging in the discipline; and along the way they pick up ways of assessing products of the discipline as better and worse, these evaluations often, but not always, connected to various specific goals of the practice. Social practices are norm-infused.

Often it turns out that newcomers envisage new goals for the practice and new modes of evaluation. When that happens, it will seldom be the case that everybody instantly rallies round those new goals and modes of evaluation; instead, the practice becomes the site of controversy. In the penultimate chapter of his *Essay Concerning Human Understanding,* John Locke makes the point with telling whimsy:

> Would it not be an insufferable thing for a learned professor, and that which his scarlet would blush at, to have his authority of forty years' standing, wrought out of hard rock, Greek and Latin, with no small expense of time and candle, and confirmed by general tradition, and a reverend beard, in an instant overturned by an upstart novelist? Can any one expect that he should be made to confess, that what he taught his scholars thirty years ago, was all error and mistake; and that he sold them hard words and ignorance at a very dear rate? (IV.xx.11)

The social practice that is some particular academic discipline is a *shared human* practice — not a practice reserved for Christians, not a practice reserved for naturalists, but a practice for all of us together. The social practice of philosophy, my own discipline, belongs neither to Christians nor to naturalists but to all philosophers together. And so for all the other academic disciplines: they belong to all of us together, just as the state belongs to all of us together.

The Christian scholar participates in those shared human practices which are the disciplines. He should do so, I said, thinking and acting with a Christian mind and speaking with an appropriate Christian voice.

What do I mean by "speaking with an appropriate Christian voice"? For one thing, the Christian voice, whether within the academy or elsewhere, will always be a voice that pays due honor to the other person. "Honor all human beings," says the writer of the New Testament epistle First Peter (2:17). The Christian voice will be firm and forthright, if that is what the situation calls for; but it will never be abusive. There is a great deal of abusive and demeaning talk that takes place in the academy. The Christian will refuse to engage in such talk. The Christian voice will never demean, abuse, or ridicule fellow scholars — or, indeed, any other human being.

There is another, and more subtle, point to be made here. The voice with which the Christian scholar speaks must be a voice that can genuinely be *heard* by one's fellow scholars in the discipline — a voice such that it contributes to the dialogue of the discipline. Every now and then, when teaching at Yale, I would have a student who did not know how to speak in the voice appropriate to the Yale philosophy classroom. Invariably this was an evangelical student, and always a male. He would ask a question or make a statement in a voice appropriate to a Bible camp rather than to a philosophy classroom, the philosophy classroom, in this case, including non-Christians as well as Christians.

Evangelicals often interpret a hostile response to something they have said as indicating hostility to Christianity — or, more specifically, hostility to evangelical Christianity. Sometimes it does indicate that. But sometimes the hostile response is due instead to the fact that the speaker has not learned to make his point in a voice appropriate to that shared human enterprise which is the discipline in question. He has not learned how to speak in this context.

So that is what I mean by speaking with an appropriate Christian voice. What do I mean by "thinking and acting with a Christian mind" in the practice of one's discipline? Let me introduce my explanation by mentioning some things that do not count as examples of what I have in mind.

Thinking and acting with a Christian mind does not consist of developing some Christian addition to one's discipline. In particular, it does not consist of developing a theology of one's discipline — a theology of music, a theology of sociology, a theology of history, or whatever. These are not bad things; but they're not what I have in mind. Thinking and acting with a Christian mind in the practice of one's discipline is not additive in character.

9

Nor does it consist of *integrating* one's Christian faith with the results of one's discipline. The image evoked by the term "integration" is that of there being two things, one's faith and the results of one's discipline, and these two things then being tied together in some way — integrated. To think and act with a Christian mind in the practice of one's discipline is not to tie together in some way one's faith and the results of the discipline. It is to be guided by one's faith in one's practice of the discipline.

Nor does thinking and acting with a Christian mind consist of doing the sort of thing that Dorothy Sayers does in her book *Mind of the Maker*. Sayers takes R. G. Collingwood's theory of art in one hand, and the traditional doctrine of the Trinity in the other hand, and points out similarities. But that's not thinking and acting with a Christian mind within the discipline of the philosophy of art. With a bit of imagination, one can always point out similarities between some Christian doctrine and certain results of some discipline.

Last, thinking and acting with a Christian mind in the practice of one's discipline is not to be identified with coming up with different views from those of one's non-Christians colleagues; it is not defined by difference. The fact that some of my non-Christian colleagues agree with me on some point does not establish that I was not thinking and acting with a Christian mind in arriving at my conclusions. I should hope for agreement, and be gratified when it emerges.

If thinking and acting with a Christian mind in the practice of one's discipline is none of those things, what is it? The first thing to say is that I am using the term "mind" metaphorically; it carries the same sense for me here that it does when St. Paul speaks of "the mind of Christ." Though it has intellectual content, its content goes well beyond beliefs and doctrines.

We human beings do not just react to what we experience; we interpret it, as we do the experience itself and reality more generally. And to some of our experience we ascribe value of one sort and another, as we do to some of what we experience and to some parts of reality more generally; we *valorize* these. Some of our interpretations and valorizations are innate to us; they are part of our nature. But most are not like that; we learn them, acquire them. And many of these are acquired from our fellow human beings; they are handed on to us.

Consider, for example, our engagement with music. We don't just react to music. We interpret music; and we valorize both the music we hear and our modes of engagement with it, both the interpreting and the valorizing being, for the most part, the consequence of learning. We learn what to listen for, what to attend to. We acquire concepts that apply to what we hear, these concepts not only enabling us to describe what we hear but also shaping our auditory perception, so that we don't just *hear* some passage of music but *hear it as such-and-such* — hear it as a fugue, for example. We learn to evaluate one passage of music as better in certain respects than another passage. We acquire capacities for delight; we learn to love certain works of music. Whereas previously Stravinsky's *Rite of Spring* was an inscrutable cacophony, now we love it.

All of this, and more, goes into our learning to interpret and valorize music. We acquire what I shall call a *musical mind,* or, if you prefer, a *musical formation,* that is, a formation for interpreting and valorizing music and one's experience of music — call it, for short, one's *musical IV-formation.* One's musical IV-formation includes thoughts about music; but as we have just noted, it includes a great deal more as well: habits of attention, modes of perception, habits of evaluation, capacities for delight and love. What we learn, in talking to others, is that one's own musical IV-formation is similar to, but also different from, that of others, sometimes radically different.

Just as we each acquire a particular way of interpreting and valorizing music and our experience of music, so too those of us who are Christians have acquired a Christian mind, that is, a Christian way of interpreting and valorizing what we experience, our experience itself, and reality more generally. We have acquired what I shall call a *Christian IV-formation.* Such a formation includes doctrines, principles, and views. But it is not to be identified with those; in particular, it is not to be identified with what is today often called "a Christian worldview." It's more than that, much more; it includes habits of attention, modes of perception, habits of evaluation, capacities for delight and love. Recall my earlier discussion about the delighted awe experienced in getting a glimpse of the divine wisdom embedded in creation. A Christian mind is like a musical mind.

Just as one person's musical formation is similar to but also different from that of others, sometimes radically different, so too the Christian formation of one person is similar to but also different from that of others. They differ, of course, in the particular interpretations and valorizations that they incorporate. But they also differ in scope.

Some are narrow and constricted in scope, including little more than the embrace of a few Christian doctrines, or little more than valuing the Bible as "the good book," or little more than enjoying listening to praise songs in Sunday worship services. Of the various modes of IV-formation which shape such a person's life as a whole, his Christian IV-formation plays a minor role, nowhere near as influential as, say, his formation as a lawyer or his formation as a devoted follower of the Chicago Cubs.

Other Christian IV-formations are wide in scope, being more influential than any other formation in shaping the person's life as a whole. Of course, never will a person's Christian IV-formation shape her entire life; the life of each of us is also shaped by the formation one acquires as a member of a particular national culture.

Those social practices which are the academic disciplines are likewise ways of interpreting and valorizing experience. To be inducted into one of these practices is to acquire a mind, an IV-formation, which is structurally similar to a musical mind; one acquires the mind of a physicist, the mind of a literary critic, the mind of a philosopher, and so on. The mind of a physicist includes thoughts, of course: theories, ideas for experiments, memories of experiments, and the like. But it too includes habits of attention, modes of perception, habits of evaluation, capacities for delight and love.

My thesis, once again, is that the Christian scholar should think and act with a Christian mind — a Christian IV-formation — when engaging in his or her particular discipline. In propounding that thesis, I am making two controversial assumptions that I must now articulate and defend, as best I can, in the brief space remaining to me.

First, I am assuming that the Christian mind of a scholar is in fact relevant to engaging in his discipline; I am assuming that it speaks to the ways of interpreting and valorizing that take place in that discipline. If it is in fact irrelevant to those ways of thinking, those ways of attending, those ways of perceiving, those ways of valuing and loving, then my thesis assumes that the scholar who is a Christian should *try* to acquire a Christian mind that *would be* relevant to engaging in the discipline.

Why do I assume that a scholar's Christian mind either is or should be relevant to engaging in his discipline? I do so because I believe that the person who is a Christian should seek to conform his mind, his IV-formation — his ways of attending, of perceiving, of thinking, of valuing and loving — to Scripture and to the core tradition of the church; and I believe that a mind so conformed will in fact be relevant to matters that arise within his discipline. Scripture does not just speak about the transcendent, leaving us free to form our interpretations and valorizations of experience as we will. It speaks to our experience and to the reality that we experience.

Defending this thesis requires citing plausible examples; the proof is in the pudding. So let me offer a few. My opening remarks about wisdom provide us with an example. Someone whose Christian mind has been shaped by Scripture will regard the intricacy and immensity of the world that the natural sciences open up to us as God's wisdom embodied in creation; with praise and in awe he will dwell on these glimpses of divine wisdom.

Here's another example of a different sort. Over and over in history, biography, and social theory, one comes across writers who operate on the assumption that religion plays no role in explaining why people act as they do — or on the assumption that, if it does play a role, that role is so insignificant as not to be worth paying attention to. An example: Jean L. Cohen and Andrew Arato, in discussing the anti-Communist revolution in East Germany in their book *Civil Society and Political Theory,* pay no attention whatsoever to the role of religion and of religious leaders in that uprising. The impression one gets is that leaders who just happened to be Christian pastors held meetings in buildings that just happened to be churches and used language that just happened to be religious in order to motivate the people to rise up and get the boot off their necks. Another example of the same point: in his otherwise fine biography of John Adams, David McCullough pays no attention whatsoever to Adams' religion; unless readers know otherwise from other sources, they will come away from the book with the impression that religion played no role in Adams' life. I could give a good many other examples of the same point. A person whose Christian mind conforms to Scripture and the main Christian tradition will not neglect the role of religion in human life and history.

Here's another example of yet another sort. For more than two centuries now, thinking and writing about the fine arts has been conducted within what I have called, in some of my writings, the grand modern narrative of the arts. A prominent component in that narrative is the claim that the act of creating works of art is socially other and transcendent, as are the works themselves. Instrumental rationality pervades modern society and destroys all the old unities. Artists, by contrast, employ imagination rather than instrumental rationality; and the works they create possess organic unity. The social transcendence commonly attributed to art has led a great many writers in the modern period to take the next step of ascribing religious import, of one sort or another, to art. A typical passage is the following from Wilhelm Wackenroder's *Outpourings of an Art-Loving Friar,* written in the late 1700s:

> Art galleries . . . ought to be temples where, in still and silent humility and in heart-lifting solitude, we may admire great artists as the highest among mortals . . . with long, steadfast contemplation of their works. . . . I compare the enjoyment of nobler works of art to *prayer.* . . . Works of art, in their way, no more fit into the common flow of life than does the thought of God. . . .

That day is for me a sacred holiday which . . . I devote to the contemplation of noble works of art.

A person whose Christian mind conforms to Scripture and the main Christian tradition will think highly of art, to be sure, but will not make of it an idol, as Wackenroder does.

Let me move on to the second assumption that I am making when I propound the thesis that the Christian scholar should think and act with a Christian mind when engaging in his or her discipline. I am assuming that there is nothing about a Christian mind, and nothing about the academic enterprise, that obligates the Christian scholar not to do so. This assumption is contested on a number of different grounds.

One ground of contestation is that religion is irrational and should, for that reason, be kept out of the academy; as one of my Yale colleagues once put it, religious people suffer from "a rationality deficit." I cannot, on this occasion, engage this charge. Let me simply say that over the past thirty years or so there have been extensive discussions by philosophers concerning the rationality of religious belief; and I think I can safely say that anyone who has worked through that literature will conclude that the charge of irrationality cannot be sustained. Late in his life, Richard Rorty, after recalling that he along with many others had charged religion with irrationality, remarked that he had changed his mind and that he was then of the view that the charge was pure bunk.

Another ground of contestation is that religion proves always to be a source of intolerance, and that for the peace of the academy, and of society in general, it must be confined to the private lives of people. On this occasion I can also not engage this charge. Let me simply remark that if it were true in general that religious people are less tolerant than non-religious people, we would have to consider whether that would be a good reason for trying to confine religion to the realm of the private. But I know of no careful studies of the matter. For what it's worth: When I look back on my own experience in the academy, and when I recall what others have told me about their experience, it's far from evident to me that religious people are less tolerant of non-religious people than are non-religious people of religious people.

There is a third ground of contestation that I do want to spend some time discussing. Deep in the mentality of modernity has been the assumption that engaging in the academic disciplines is, or should be, an exercise of our generically human rationality. Here, rather than allowing our various religious or comprehensive philosophical IV-formations to shape what we do, we go to the things themselves by employing our shared perceptual capacities, our shared introspective capacities, our shared capacities for apprehending necessary truths, our shared capacities for making inferences, and so on. As John Locke put it, instead of appealing to tradition, we appeal to reason. Parenthetically, a good many writers have noted that Locke's sharp tradition/reason contrast has to be qualified; it's impossible to engage in any academic discipline without being formed by the tradition of one's discipline and without appealing to that tradition.

One is initially inclined to say that, on this view of how the disciplines are to be practiced, we are to work *from* consensus and *toward* consensus. But that can't be right. If some colleague stubbornly hangs on to some favorite theory in the face of mounting evidence against it (recall Locke's learned professor), that cannot be allowed to function as a brake on the endeavors of the rest of us. I think the idea is rather something like the following: In the academic disciplines, we are to aim at basing our views solely on arguments and evidence that all competent practitioners of the discipline would accept if those arguments and that evidence were presented to them, if they understood them, if they possessed the relevant background information, and if they freely reflected on them at sufficient length. It's that sort of counterfactual consensus, rather than actual consensus, that we are to work from and toward.

Let it be noted that thinking and acting with a Christian mind as one engages in one's discipline is not incompatible with conforming to this counterfactual consensus requirement. Suppose that a sociologist is led by his Christian IV-formation to conclude that the understandings of the human person that dominate sociology are all deficient in some important way. He might then try to defend this conclusion with arguments that satisfy the counterfactual consensus requirement. There is no reason, in principle, why he could not succeed in this endeavor. I understand the traditional neo-Thomist position to be that this is what he ought to try to do, namely, satisfy the counterfactual consensus requirement. And I agree that this is what he ought to try to do.

The question I want to press, however, is this: What does he do if he does not succeed? Given the counterfactual character of the requirement, it will often not be easy for him to determine whether or not he has succeeded. Sometimes it will be difficult to determine actual agreement or disagreement. Everybody that I know agrees with me; but how do I know what some philosophers in New Zealand think? Note, however, that even if I do discover disagreement, that does not establish that I have not met the requirement. I have to take the next step of figuring out why they disagree. Might it be that it's because they have not fully understood my arguments and that they would agree if they did understand? Might it be that it's because they lack some crucial piece of background information? Might it be that it's because they have not thought long enough about my line of argument?

We should not overlook the arrogance implicit in judging that one's colleagues are deficient in one or another of these respects. "If you understood my argument, you would agree." "If you were better informed about the relevant background, you would agree." "If you just thought longer and harder about it, you would agree." That's arrogant.

Difficult though it will sometimes be to determine whether one has met the counterfactual consensus requirement, let us suppose that our sociologist concludes that he has not. Try as he did, he did not succeed in finding arguments and evidence that meet the counterfactual consensus requirement. His fellow sociologists have not all rallied around his position; some have, but not all. Yet at least some of those who disagree appear to understand his arguments and evidence, appear not to be ignorant of any relevant piece of background information, and appear to have taken seriously what he said and thought about it at length. Yet they disagree.

So what does he do now? Does he abandon sociology? Alternatively, does he put his own views about the human person in cold storage when doing sociology and go along with one or another of the dominant alternative views? To adopt the latter strategy would make no sense. He understands those alternative views, has thought long and hard about them, and possesses all the relevant background information. But he disagrees. His disagreement is proof that those who espouse those views also have not met the counterfactual consensus requirement. In fact, nobody in the discipline has met the requirement. So what does he do? What do any of them do?

Before I answer that question, let me highlight the fact that our example shows that there have to be sources of disagreement among scholars in addition to those that the counterfactual consensus requirement highlights. Scholars who understand each other's arguments, who have thought long and hard about them, and who share all the relevant background information still disagree. Let me put the point more crisply: Rational, intelligent, well-informed, and reflective scholars often disagree. Recall a comment I made when I was talking about social practices: It is typical of social practices that there are disagreements among competent, well-informed, and reflective participants in the discipline. Such disagreements need not mark a breakdown in the practice, a failure to live up to certain requirements. To the contrary: such disagreements are essential to the vitality of the practice. The counterfactual consensus requirement is not just mistaken; it is deeply misguided.

Given the disagreements within every academic discipline, scholars often disagree because they have different academic IV-formations; they disagree because they have been formed by different schools of thought within the discipline. But I submit that we who are scholars also disagree because of the different IV-formations that we bring to our practice of the disciplines from our lives in the everyday. We bring with us what we've been formed to be: Americans, participants in a capitalist economy, political conservatives, anti-religious, hard-core naturalists, humanists, Christians, whatever.

So, what to do? What else can one do but engage in one's discipline as the person one has been formed to be? With whatever be one's IV-formation, one participates in the dialogue intrinsic to each discipline, listening carefully and openly to serious objections posed to one's interpretations and valorizations, changing one's mind when that seems the right thing to do, posing as compellingly as possible one's objections to alternative interpretations and valorizations, probing the sources of disagreement, sometimes bracketing one's disagreement with another scholar so as to explore together the implications of points of agreement, working out one's own position to see where it goes, doing this, if possible, in cooperation with others. This is how one ought to engage in one's discipline. I call it *dialogic pluralism*.

Let me state my basic theses one last time. It is the calling of the Christian scholar to think and act with a Christian mind, and to speak with an appropriate Christian voice, as she engages in her discipline. *Fides quaerens intellectum*. She does this out of love, both love of the craft of scholarship and love of understanding. And she loves understanding, both for the wisdom of God and of God's human creatures that it reveals, and for its utility in the pursuit of shalom.

On Christian Scholarship

Alvin Plantinga

> We demolish arguments and every pretension that sets itself up
> against the knowledge of God, and we take captive every thought to
> make it obedient to Christ.
>
> 2 Corinthians 10:4-5

What is it to be a Christian scholar? More, presumably, than just being both a
Christian and a scholar. What more? I'll make a few remarks on this subject,
even though, as President Obama once said in a different connection, it's way
above my pay grade.

Ever since Augustine — indeed, ever since Chrysostom — Christians have
spoken of two books of revelation: Scripture, of course, but also nature. Thus
article 2 of the Belgic Confession, one of the great Reformed creeds:

> We know [God] by two means: First, by the creation, preservation, and
> government of the universe, since that universe is before our eyes like a
> beautiful book in which all creatures, great and small, are as letters to make
> us ponder the invisible things of God.

Christians have held that God is revealed in at least two ways: by the book of
Scripture, but also by the book of nature. From Scripture we learn much about
ourselves, our world, and about God himself: in particular, we learn about
the great scheme of salvation — the great things of the gospel, as Jonathan
Edwards calls them — the magnificent scheme involving the incarnation of

the Word, the Second Person of the Trinity, Jesus of Nazareth, by whose life and suffering and death and resurrection we sinful human beings can once more be in proper fellowship with God. In addition, however, there is a quite different book, the book of nature. From this book we also learn much about God the Creator, about ourselves, and about our world.

John Calvin tells us a bit about the relationship between the two books:

> Just as the aged, or those whose sight is defective, when any book, however fair, is set before them, though they perceive that there is something written, are scarcely able to make out two consecutive words, but when aided by glasses, begin to read distinctly, so Scripture, gathering together the impressions of Deity which till then lay confused in our minds, dissipates the darkness and shows us the true God clearly.[1]

The first book, says Calvin, is to be like spectacles through which we may more clearly see and understand the second. According to Calvin, God has created us with a *sensus divinitatis,* something like a natural faculty whereby we human beings can reach a certain knowledge of God independent of the revelation in Scripture. Calvin himself seems to be thinking of those spectacles as gathering and deepening the deliverances of the *sensus divinitatis.* We might also see here, however, a charter for Christian scholarship: In attempting to understand nature, we should employ the Scripture as spectacles, understanding natural phenomena and the book of nature from the perspective of the Christian faith.

But how do we do that? Exactly or even approximately what is involved? It's all very well to speak of integrating faith and learning, bringing faith to bear on scholarship, practicing scholarship from the perspective of Christian belief, and so on; but can we be a bit more explicit? A bit more specific? Here we can usefully consider another long-standing idea, one that also goes back at least to Augustine.

In his magisterial *City of God,* Augustine traces the whole history of humankind, going all the way back to its beginning in the Garden. In fact, he goes further back — back to a time before the creation of human beings, back to the conflict between those angels who aligned themselves with God, and those who rebelled against God. Augustine saw all of human history as dominated by a contest between two implacably opposed forces. On the one hand, he spoke of the City of God; on the other, of the Earthly City or City of the World: the

---

1. John Calvin, *Institutes* I.v.1.1.

Civitas Dei and the *Civitas Mundi*. The former is dedicated, in principle, to God and to his will and to his glory; but the latter is dedicated to something wholly different: self and pride. And human history is really the story of the contest between these two cities.

Augustine is right. The history of philosophy, the history of scholarship, and, indeed, human history more generally are dominated by a few great perspectives, a few basic and fundamental ways of thinking about God, ourselves, our world, our place in the world, and what we must do to live the successful life. Or, to use an older but more precise terminology, what is the Summum Bonum for human beings? The contest between the two cities is still waged in contemporary life: the contemporary Western intellectual world is an arena in which rages a battle for men's and women's souls. There is indeed a contest between the City of God and the City of the World.

At present, in our part of the world, there is the Christian perspective, the *Civitas Dei*, currently on the defensive in Western academia, if not in the world at large. And of course there is also the City of the World. The current version of the *Civitas Mundi* is divided into two boroughs, or perhaps two townships. On the one hand there is *naturalism*, the position that there is no such person as God or anything like God. On the other hand there is something harder to characterize: perhaps we could call it "autonomism," or "relativism with respect to truth." I'll say a word about each.

First, naturalism. Naturalism is stronger than atheism: you can be an atheist without rising to the full heights of naturalism. On some interpretations, perhaps the young Hegel, or Plato, or the Stoics were atheists without being naturalists. To be a naturalist, one must do more than deny the existence of God: one must also deny the existence of anything like God. And according to naturalism, the heavens are empty; and we human beings are mere cogs in a giant cosmic machine that proceeds in majestic indifference to us and to our hopes, needs, and aspirations. Naturalism goes back to the ancient world, to the philosopher Epicurus; it finds magnificent expression in Lucretius's poem *De Rerum Natura*. Naturalism was mostly in eclipse during the Christian Middle Ages; the Enlightenment brought the French Encyclopedists — Baron d'Holbach and others — as early modern exponents of this way of looking at the world.

Naturalism has by now very much come into its own; according to the philosopher John Lucas, it is at present the orthodoxy of the academy. Contemporary naturalism relies heavily on evolution and Darwinism; it aims to understand us human beings and our behavior in terms of our evolutionary history back there on the plains of Serengeti, when the human race was developing. It hopes to explain our distinctively human traits and qualities as arising by way of their contributing to survival and reproduction, or by way of being related to such traits.

Among the more vociferous proponents of naturalism are the so-called New Atheists, the dreaded four horsemen of atheism — not the four horsemen of the Apocalypse, or even the four horsemen of Notre Dame, but the four horsemen of atheism: Richard Dawkins, Daniel Dennett, the late Christopher Hitchens, and Sam Harris. They are intent on trampling Christianity — and, indeed, any religion — into the dust. Or rather, since Harris displays a decided list toward Buddhism, we might have to say that only three of the four horsemen qualify as proper naturalists. In any event, these horsemen are certainly vocal; classical restraint and understatement are not their strong suit. Dawkins says that anyone who doesn't believe in evolution is "ignorant, stupid, insane, or wicked." Daniel Dennett goes him one (or two) further: Anyone who so much as has *doubts* about evolution is culpably ignorant. At least Dawkins gives skeptics a chance: they could be ignorant, *or* stupid, *or* insane, *or* wicked. Dennett is made of sterner stuff: If you even doubt evolution, you are *both* ignorant *and* culpable — that is, wicked. You wake up in the middle of the night; you think about evolution, this grand and ambitious theory; a vagrant doubt crosses your mind as to whether this is in fact the way God created the living world; and — Bam! You are culpably ignorant!

Naturalists are committed to the thought that there is no such person as God or anything like God; and naturalism is indeed widespread in the academy. The fact is, of course, that its influence goes far beyond the academy, to the elite world in general. But is it really the orthodoxy of the academy? Perhaps not; for there is another borough of the City of the World. This borough is a bit harder to characterize. An early manifestation can be found in the declaration of the fifth-century B.C. Sophist Protagoras, who declared, "Man is the measure of all things, of those that are, that they are, and of those that are not, that they are not." It's not entirely clear what Protagoras had in mind by that oracular statement, but things became much clearer in the eighteenth-century Enlightenment.

One strand of the Enlightenment involves a rejection of the authority of the king and the church, a rejection, so it was thought, of the dead hand of the past. A more radical wing of the Enlightenment, however, really involves a sort of exaltation of humanity and the human condition, and a sort of exaltation of human *autonomy* — autonomism, as we might call it. On this way of thinking, human beings are not beholden to any other powers; they are not subject to anything or anyone. It is as if the rejection of the authority of church and king assumed a kind of momentum, a kind of functional autonomy, and spread from there to a rejection of anything standing between humanity and its apotheosis.

One version of this view received magnificent if obscure expression in Immanuel Kant's *Critique of Pure Reason*. Kant's writing is not a model of lucidity; but according to the most influential interpretation of Kant, it is we, we human beings, who confer structure on the world we live in; it is we who are responsible for its fundamental nature and lineaments. Kant does not deny, of course, that there really are such things as mountains, horses, planets, and stars. Instead, his characteristic claim is that their existence and their fundamental structure have been conferred upon them by the conceptual activity of persons — not by the conceptual activity of a personal God, but by *our* conceptual activity, the conceptual activity of human beings. According to this view, the whole phenomenal world — the world of trees and planets and dinosaurs and stars — receives its basic structure from the constituting activity of mind. Such fundamental structures of the world as space and time, object and property, number, truth and falsehood, possibility and necessity — these are not to be found in the world as such, but are somehow conferred upon the world and constituted by our own mental or conceptual activity. They are contributions from our side; they are not to be found in the things themselves, the *dinge an sich,* as Kant liked to call them (or it). We *impose* them on the world; we do not discover them there. Were there no persons like ourselves engaging in noetic activities, there would be nothing in space and time, nothing displaying object-property structure, nothing that is true or false, possible or impossible, no kind of things coming in a certain number — nothing like this at all.

As you can see, this is quite a promotion for us human beings. And the contrast with naturalism, on this point of the human condition, the human place in the world, could not be greater. According to naturalism, we human beings are just another animal with a peculiar way of making a living. According to Kant, we human beings are the architects of the universe! This is indeed a step up; it is also a claim to impressive autonomy. Etymologically, autonomy is being a law unto oneself. I am autonomous if the laws that apply to me find their origin in me. And on this Kantian picture, this is just how it is for us human beings.

This Enlightenment lust for autonomy is displayed in more than one way, and in a way it is something that perhaps we all understand. We want to be top dog, at least in our own lives. We want some privacy; and we don't like the idea of being held accountable. A very distinguished contemporary philosopher I know says he is an atheist, and adds that he doesn't *want* there to be any such person as God. That is because with God there is at the very least an insufferable invasion of privacy. You can't even think a thought without God's knowing about it, and indeed knowing that you will think that thought before you actually do so. There is perhaps just a hint of this sort of discomfort in one of my favorite psalms, Psalm 139:

> You hem me in, behind and before,
>> and lay your hand upon me. . . .
> Where shall I go from your Spirit?
>> Or where shall I flee from your presence?
> If I ascend to heaven, you are there!
>> If I make my bed in Sheol, you are there! . . .
> If I say, "Surely the darkness shall cover me,
>> and the light about me be night,"
> even the darkness is not dark to you;
>> the night is bright as the day,
>> for darkness is as light with you.

Perhaps this lust for autonomy reaches its zenith with the German philosopher Martin Heidegger, who, at any rate, according to Richard Rorty, said he felt *guilty* for existing in a universe he did not himself create. Now there's a tender conscience! I can imagine Heidegger apologizing to his friends: "I am so sorry. Here I am, existing in a universe I didn't even create. Please forgive me. I promise it won't happen again!"

But autonomism is not the end of the story. First, on this Kantian picture, it is we, the thinkers of categorizing thoughts, who are responsible for the fundamental lineaments of reality; in the words of Protagoras, again, "Man is the measure of all things." But a rather different moral can be drawn from some of the same considerations. Suppose you think our world is somehow created or structured by human beings. You may then note that human beings apparently do not all construct the same worlds. Richard Dawkins does not seem to live in the same world as, say, Billy Graham. Your *Lebenswelt* may be quite different from mine; which one, then (if either), constitutes the world as it really is? Here it is an easy step to another characteristically contemporary thought: the thought that there simply isn't any such thing as objective truth, or an objective way the world is, a way the world is that is the same for all of us. Rather, there is my version of reality, the way I've somehow structured things, and your version, and many other versions: and what is true in one version need not be true in another. As Marlowe's Dr. Faustus in effect says, "Man is the measure of all things; I am a man; therefore I am the measure of all things."

On this view, there isn't any such thing as the truth *simpliciter*. There is no such thing as *the* way the world is; there are instead many versions of reality, each at bottom as acceptable as any other. The idea is that there really isn't any such thing as truth itself — truth with a capital T, as relativists like to put it. Thus the late Richard Rorty: truth is "what our peers will let us get away with." It's not easy to say just precisely what he meant by this; he also said that he preferred an informal, conversational way of putting his philosophical points. Taken at face value, it would suggest an easy way to deal with such social ills as poverty and sickness: get our peers to let us get away with saying there is no sickness; if they do, it would be true that there is no sickness, in which case there would be no sickness! No doubt Rorty is not to be taken at face value here. At the least, however, the idea seems to be that truth is a social construct; it isn't independent of us; it is something we human beings create; truth is relative to individuals or social groups. This relativism with respect to truth is perhaps the most widespread contemporary manifestation of this borough of the City of the World.

These two ways of thinking — naturalism and autonomism or relativism — dominate contemporary elite culture. They dominate *elite* culture: academia, the media, medicine, law, politics, and so on. In the U.S., they do not dominate contemporary non-elite culture to the same extent; polls suggest that most of the non-elite are Christian believers, or at least believe in God. As someone once remarked, India is the most religious country and Sweden the most secular; and the United States is a country of Indians ruled by Swedes.

As I pointed out, naturalism and autonomism also differ enormously with respect to the place of human beings in the world. According to autonomism, we human beings are exalted indeed: we are responsible for truth itself, and truth depends on what we do. According to naturalism, we are no more than animals with an unusual way of making a living — fairly successful, on the whole, but not as successful as bacteria. (The bacteria of the world, taken together, outweigh all of the rest of the living world, taken together.) Perhaps we should think of naturalism and autonomism as having mascots, like the Fighting Irish of Notre Dame, or the Fighting Illini. Maybe the mascot for Autonomism should be Superman; like the University of California at Santa Cruz, perhaps the naturalists could be the Fighting Banana Slugs!

The basic Augustinian idea is that human history essentially involves these two kingdoms. Now, how does this bear on the project of Christian scholarship? What if anything should the Christian scholar do about this? In the above epigraph, St. Paul gives in effect a charter for Christian scholarship. He proposes, first, that we "demolish arguments and every pretension that sets itself up against the knowledge of God. . . ." How do we do that? Clearly enough, by contesting and disputing the various arguments and scholarly projects that are designed to promote and expand projects based on and promoting the kingdom of the world — that is, naturalism and relativism with respect to truth. According to Calvin, we must use the spectacles of Scripture in order to see clearly the book of the world. But there are other spectacles as well: for example, naturalism and relativism. These are distorting spectacles; they warp and deform and obscure the truth. Part of the job of the Christian scholar (more exactly, of the Christian scholarly community) is to show how and why these perspectives do indeed distort the truth. Christian scholars must be aware of them and point them out to their students and others. More important, because a bit more subtle, they must point out the various projects and ideas that are connected with these master narratives. Of course, I can't here give anything like a complete list; I'll just mention a couple.

At present, for example, and in the Western world, there is a sort of enormous emphasis upon tolerance, to the degree that many people go so far as to urge that it is intolerant or arrogant to hold beliefs you know others don't hold (and where you don't think you could convince those others of what you believe). Many people seem to hold that the only real sin, the only thing that is intolerable, is intolerance itself — of lifestyle, moral belief, or whatever. This way of thinking is clearly connected with the strand of relativism with respect to truth that is so widely popular today. Suppose you think there really is no such thing as truth, or suppose you endorse a near relative to the effect that maybe there is and maybe there isn't, but even if there is, no one knows what it is: then you may be inclined to see tolerance as a virtue of paramount importance, and intolerance as a very serious vice, perhaps the only vice. Of course, there is a bit of a problem here: If there is no truth in this neighborhood, or if no one knows what it is, then presumably the same goes for the idea that tolerance is the main virtue and intolerance the main vice. No matter; this is indeed a substantial eddy in the current cultural current; and it is the job of Christian scholars to examine and evaluate this idea from the perspective of Christian theism.

Second, there is the widespread idea that science is a sort of oracle, that its deliverances trump any other purported source of knowledge, and that they are to be treated as the sober truth. There is the children's game "Simon says"; now we have the game of "Science says." Of course, the fact that science regularly changes its mind makes it a bit dicey to rely wholeheartedly on what science says; still, the idea is that when it comes to fixing belief, current science is the gold standard. Now this implies that in any conflict between science and, for example, Christian theology, it is always religion or theology or religious belief that must give way. But can Christians think that's right?

Third, there is evolutionary psychology, which is connected with naturalism. Evolutionary psychology has become orthodoxy within the discipline of psychology. The basic aim here is to interpret all of our characteristically human traits — our art, humor, sense of adventure, love, sexual behavior, love for music, moral sense, and religion itself — in terms of our evolutionary development, back there on the plains of Serengeti. With respect to ethics and our moral sense, for example, Michael Ruse and Edward O. Wilson declare that "ethics is an illusion fobbed off on us by our own genes to get us to cooperate; thus morality ultimately seems to be about self-interest."[2] They also claim that "humans function better if they are deceived by their genes into thinking there is a disinterested objective morality binding upon them, which we should obey."[3] Why so? Individuals with our moral intuitions will be likely to cooperate with each other; groups with our moral intuitions will therefore do better, from the point of view of survival and reproduction, than groups that lack those intuitions. So the function of our moral sense is not to disclose moral truths to us — there aren't any — but rather to enable us to cooperate in groups, thereby enhancing our reproductive prospects.

This is obviously mistaken from a Christian point of view. In other cases there is incompatibility or tension, but at a more subtle level. Consider music — an outstandingly important part of human life all over the world. What's most important about it, and how should we understand it? Not, as a Christian might think, as a gift from God that puts us in touch with beauty, a beauty that flows from God, and of which God is the outstanding exemplar. No. The evolutionary psychologist Stephen Pinker, in addressing a group of musicologists, told them that music has no evolutionary significance, is just a bit of auditory cheesecake, and is therefore merely trivial.[4] Others dispute this. According to Steven Mithen, music does too have an evolutionary significance; it's associated with marching, rhythmical motion, and war.[5] (Bach's B-minor Mass? Mozart's Ave Verum Corpus?) Still others claim that music arose in the context of sexual

2. Michael Ruse and Edward O. Wilson, "The Evolution of Ethics," in *Religion and the Natural Sciences: The Range of Engagement,* ed. James Huchingson (San Diego: Harcourt Brace, 1993), p. 310.

3. Michael Ruse and Edward O. Wilson, "Moral Philosophy as Applied Science," *Philosophy* 61 (1986): 179.

4. As reported by Rodney Clapp in *The Christian Century,* 10 February 2009, p. 45.

5. Steven Mithen, *The Singing Neanderthals* (London: Weidenfeld & Nicolson, 2005).

selection: musically adept individuals were more attractive to the opposite sex and did better in the evolutionary derby. Each of these is an attempt to tell us what the ultimate significance of music is; and each is completely unsatisfactory from a Christian point of view. One project of Christian scholarship, then, is what we might call cultural criticism: pointing out, laying bare, and criticizing current ideas and trends of thought that are incompatible with a Christian perspective.

But Paul goes on: " . . . and we take captive every thought to make it obedient to Christ." Here we can think of the apostle as going beyond criticizing or commenting on elements of culture inconsistent with Christian belief; he is instead suggesting something positive, something along the lines of Calvin's suggestion that we look at the book of nature through the spectacles of the book of revelation. Here the idea would be to consider the many and various topics and scholarly projects engaged by the scholars, and to consider them from the point of view of Christian theism. Now in some areas, Christian theism doesn't make a difference, or at least doesn't make an obvious difference. If the project is that of measuring the distance from earth to the nearest star, or of arguing that no finite axiomatization of arithmetic contains every arithmetical truth, Christian theism seems to have little bearing. If we're thinking of engineering or chemistry, it is hard to see how a Christian scholar would approach the subject in a way different from a secular scholar. The whole area of mathematics would seem to be neutral, at least for the most part. Of course, philosophy of mathematics is a horse of an entirely different color: here Christian theism is deeply relevant in several different ways.

So some scholarly projects are ones to which religious perspective seems to make little difference. Others, however, are very different. These areas — areas where Christian theism makes a difference — are especially evident in the human sciences. Evolutionary psychology, for example, tries to situate and understand characteristically human phenomena by seeing them as essentially related to survival and reproduction: reproductive fitness. The ultimate significance of these human phenomena is always to be seen in relation to our evolutionary origin. But shouldn't Christian psychologists look at the same phenomena from an entirely different perspective? They won't merely criticize the various projects of evolutionary psychology from a Christian perspective; they will also pursue similar projects from a different point of view. Just as evolutionary psychologists understand literature, for example, in terms of its evolutionary origin and the contribution it made to reproductive fitness, so Christian psychologists can or may or should understand the same phenomenon from the perspective of Christian theism. What's involved here is our love of stories, and our love of beauty. And presumably a central notion here is that of the image of God: God has created us in his image; we resemble him in certain important respects; how does our love of stories and of beauty fit in? How exactly should this be done? I'm not a psychologist; I don't know the answer to that question; but I'd urge Christian psychologists to consider and try to answer this and similar questions. This wouldn't be an alternative to the sort of empirical work that psychologists like to do; it would rather be a context for it. And it might indeed suggest different empirical studies from those suggested by the evolutionary paradigm.

We might think that physics is an area where a Christian perspective makes little difference. I think this would be a mistake. Consider, for example, the interpretations of quantum mechanics. At least one of them, the "many worlds interpretation," doesn't fit well with Christian belief. Here the basic idea is that there are a multitude of worlds in the universe in addition to the world we seem to find ourselves in. Consider a given physical system: it will have a wave function evolving over time. For a given future time, there will typically be many possible outcomes of a collapse of the wave function at that time. According to the many worlds interpretation, each of these possibilities gets actualized — in different worlds. So the world is constantly splitting into myriads of other worlds. You and I are in many of these worlds. But then what *am* I? On this view there are many copies of me: each of them is me, or has as good title to be me as any other. But then this is essentially an anti-realism with respect to persons. How, for example, should we think of Incarnation along these lines? Are there in fact several distinct Jesuses? If so, which of the many Jesuses is the Second Person of the Trinity?

But can scientific work, whether in the human sciences or the physical sciences, ever properly proceed from or assume propositions one takes to be known by faith? What about methodological naturalism (MN)? According to Judge Jones in the Dover trial, treating intelligent design as science "violates the centuries-old ground rules of science by invoking and permitting supernatural causation." There is a lot to quarrel with in this statement, but this much seems right: contemporary science as ordinarily pursued involves a sort of constraint. MN must be distinguished from ontological naturalism; MN is a proposed condition or constraint on proper science, not a statement about the nature of the universe. (Of course, if philosophical naturalism were true, then MN would presumably be the sensible way to proceed in science.) The rough and basic idea of MN, I think, is that science should be done *as if*, in some sense, ontological naturalism were true. According to Hugo Grotius, in working at science, we should proceed *as if God is not given*.

Suppose we try to state MN a bit more exactly. First, following Bas van Fraassen, we note that for any scientific theory there is its *data set,* or *data model;* roughly speaking, we can think of this as the data or phenomena that are to be explained by the theory in question. The data must be presented or stated in terms of certain parameters or categories; it could include, for example, the results of certain experiments, but will not (ordinarily) include alleged information described as hearsay. According to MN, furthermore, the data model of a proper scientific theory will not refer to God or other supernatural agents. Thus the data model of a proper theory could include the proposition that there has been a sudden outbreak of weird and irrational activity in Washington, D.C., but it couldn't include the proposition that there has been an outbreak of demonic possession there. Second, there will also be constraints on the theory itself. The theory can properly employ categories or parameters not permitted by the data model. For example, the data might include a deep depression in a Siberian forest; the theory but not the data might posit a meteorite that struck there. (Of course, in another context the meteorite and its effects might be part of the data.) But according to MN, the parameters for a scientific theory are not to include reference to God or any other supernatural agents. Suppose your data set includes that recent outbreak of irrational behavior in Washington, D.C. MN says you can't try to account for that data by a theory according to which there has recently been increased demonic activity there.

But there is a third and very important side of MN. Any given inquiry will be carried out with respect to an *evidence base,* a set of beliefs used in conducting an inquiry. The evidence base for a scientific inquiry will include mathematics and logic, some current science, and a lot of commonsense beliefs. In any given context, there are of course a vast number of possible scientific theories, most of which don't rate a second (or even a first) thought; others are a bit more sensible, but too implausible or improbable to take seriously. It is the evidence base that determines the initial plausibility or probability of a proposed scientific theory. Say that my car won't start. One hypothesis is that a mischievous junior demon is trying to annoy me. Given my evidence base, that hypothesis will be discarded as vastly too improbable. But a Brazilian tribesman, with a very different evidence base, might evaluate that hypothesis very differently.

And the point is that MN also constrains the evidence base for a scientific investigation: the evidence base for a scientific investigation must not contain any propositions entailing the existence of God or other supernatural beings, and can't include propositions known only by faith. Accordingly, if you reject the many worlds interpretation of quantum mechanics on the grounds that it doesn't fit well with the Christian claim of Incarnation, your rejection won't, according to MN, be scientific. In the same way, if part of your reason for endorsing a theory or hypothesis in psychology is that it fits well with a Christian understanding of anthropology, the result won't be science. Still further, the whole idea of starting with a Christian perspective in pursuing a scientific project is ruled out by MN.

Well, what does MN have to be said for itself? Not a whole lot. Taken in a mild form, MN is perhaps a sensible rule of thumb: it's certainly a good idea to avoid too quickly reverting to God's agency in a scientific theory. Taken in the strong form given above, however, there is little to recommend it. And if it is claimed that MN is just part of the very definition of science, then those who advocate a Christian science can simply restate their position: What is wanted, they can say, is a Christian *schmience,* where schmience is just like science except for the MN constraint.

A better objection to the idea of a Christian science — better, because it provides an actual reason why that idea is questionable — is offered by Thomists such as Étienne Gilson. The complaint is that if as a scholar you start from what you know by way of faith, then your results will really be *theology* rather than philosophy or psychology or physics or whatever. Theology in, theology out, as the computer literati might say. Why think a thing like that? Why does the Thomist think it is important to have an economics or psychology that is unspotted by theology? Why is the distinction between theology and philosophy or psychology important? The Thomist will say that what you know by way of reason has a cognitive advantage over what you know by way of faith. That is because what you know by way of faith is really known by *testimony* — if only the testimony of the Holy Spirit. Testimony is indeed important, and we couldn't get along without it. As Thomas Reid puts it, "If I had not believed my parents before I could give a reason for my belief, I had to this day been little better than a changeling."[6] Still, what you know because you have come to *see* that it is true is something that has greater positive epistemic status for you than what you know by way of testimony. You tell me that there is no set of all sets, or no finite axiomatization of arithmetic; I believe; and I am epistemically better off than I was before. But now I come to understand a proof of these things; I see that they follow from propositions that are self-evident, that I see to be true. I grasp and understand the proof and see for myself that the

---

6. Thomas Reid, *An Inquiry into the Human Mind on the Principles of Common Sense,* ed. Derek R. Brooks (University Park, Pa.: Pennsylvania State University Press, 1997).

proposition in question is not only true, but couldn't be false. Then I am even better off epistemically. What I know by reason has higher epistemic status for me than what I know by testimony.

What shall we say? Here the Thomist, I think, neglects the fact that self-evidence or intellectual intuition comes in degrees. I know that that $2 + 1 = 3$ by way of reason; it's self-evident for me, and has maximal positive epistemic status. But there are many other propositions I believe by way of intellectual intuition that have some degree of self-evidence. Consider, for example, the proposition that there aren't any things that don't exist. (You might object: What about Pegasus? Pegasus doesn't exist; so there are some things that don't exist. But the reply is obvious: There *isn't* any such thing as Pegasus.) Consider many of the propositions that form the stock in trade of philosophy: these will be propositions one doesn't know by way of testimony or perception; they are known by way of reason or intellectual insight. But many of them aren't known nearly as well, nearly as securely, as $2 + 1 = 3$. And some of them, I should think, aren't known as well as some things that I know by way of testimony. Pace Meinong and others, I know that there aren't any things that don't exist; but aren't there some things I know by way of testimony that I know better? For example, that my name is Alvin Plantinga and that I live in Michigan? Or that there is such a country as China, or such a city as Chicago? The problem with the Thomist objection, here, is that it's far from obvious that what one knows by way of testimony has less epistemic status than that which one knows by way of reason and perception.

One final objection. We could put it like this. Someone who practices Christian scholarship in the way suggested above will not be able to play nicely with other scholars. She won't be starting from the same basis; as reasons for her conclusions she will put forward propositions not accepted by her scholarly peers; she will not be able to work with other scholars unless they too are practicing Christian scholarship. And this objection seems to me to have a bit more force than the others. But how much force does it really have? Many scholars today aim to give naturalistic accounts of this and that — naturalistic accounts of religion, morality, music, love of beauty, and much else besides. Would it be sensible to criticize them for not being able to play nicely with us Christians, or other theists, or other non-naturalists? I don't think so. Consider Freud's famous account of belief in God as wish fulfillment. There is much to criticize here; for example, there are many atheists who hope that there is no such person as God; and there are some theists who are far from delighted with the idea that there is. But would it make sense to criticize Freud for engaging in a project he can't expect Christians to join? Again, I don't think so. Those who set out to offer a naturalistic account of religion can't expect theists to join with them in this project; but how is that a serious criticism? The thought that no one should engage in any project that takes for granted or assumes what others reject has little to recommend it. This thought completely overlooks the deep pluralism of the human spiritual condition — a pluralism recognized by Augustine and many others. Freud is convinced that theism is false. Why shouldn't he try to give an account of what from that perspective is a puzzling phenomenon: the fact that so many people all over the world and, as far as we can tell, for most of human history, have thought there really is such a person as God or something like him? And in doing this, he is not necessarily, at any rate, addressing theists and hoping to convince them.

Of course, in other contexts Freud may wish to take part in projects that do not in this way start from atheism: the interpretation of dreams, for example. Here Freud's naturalism plays no particular role, and here he and people with very different ultimate commitments can nicely work together. And in still other areas, Freud may be trying to convince believers in God that they are mistaken. I don't know that he does this — for the most part, as far as I know, he simply assumes that belief in God is a mistake and then tries to explain why this mistake is so prevalent; but that would be a perfectly sensible course for him to follow.

And why can't the same be true for Christian scholars? The Christian scholar is a member of at least two quite different communities. On the one hand, she is a member of the Christian community, and in her work she addresses members of this community. When addressing them, it is perfectly proper for her to assume and take for granted what the members of this community do assume, and go on from there. On the other hand, she is a member of the scholarly community defined by her discipline; here, given contemporary conditions, she can't just take for granted what she and other Christians believe.

I say that the Christian scholar is a member of two different communities; the fact is that she is a member of several, more than two. She is a member of the Christian scholarly community, but also a member of the community of Christian scholars that practice her specific scholarly discipline: and these two communities have to be addressed differently. But she is also a member of the Christian community more generally, whether scholars or not; and again, this community has to be addressed in a way different from either of the above. She is a member of the scholarly community that practices her discipline; but she is also a member of the broader scholarly community, a community that includes Christians and non-Christians, those who practice her discipline, and those who practice some other. And finally, she is a member of contemporary society — she is, say, an American citizen. There may be still more communities that should be mentioned; as Ockham taught us, however, one should not multiply communities without necessity, so I will stop with these.

And a Christian scholar may very well address each of these communities. The Christian scholarly community, furthermore, will presumably be addressing all of them. And, once more, what is needed is wisdom and discernment, to be clear as to which community one is addressing, and what the proper and appropriate tone and assumptions are for addressing that community.

But the main point here is that in addressing any and all of these communities, the Christian scholar is a follower of Christ. She will be engaged in projects of different sorts. On the one hand, there are projects that fit into her contemporary discipline, whatever it is; here her audience will be predominantly secular, and she can't sensibly assume or start from what she knows as a Christian. On the other hand, there are projects that are given by her position as a specifically Christian scholar. Here she can and indeed should employ all that she knows, including what she knows as a Christian. Pursuing projects of this latter kind may earn her a certain amount of disdain and hostility in some quarters; that just goes with the territory. Here she may need a certain amount of boldness and courage, remembering that the main aim is not that of achieving a great name, nor that of currying favor with the mainstream of her discipline. The main aim, of course, is to be faithful to the Lord, and to let the chips fall where they may. The chips may not fall precisely where she would like them to fall; in some areas there are penalties for faithfulness. But there are also rewards; indeed, faithfulness to the Lord is its own reward, and it is reward enough.

In sum, we Christian scholars must not remain content with being scholars who also happen to be Christian; we must strive to be Christian scholars. And we must pursue our calling with boldness, integrity, courage, imagination, and Christian wisdom.

Toward Christ-Shaped Philosophy

Paul K. Moser

A Christian philosophy should incorporate and be guided by the subversive Christian message that the outcast Galilean *"Jesus* is Lord" (1 Cor. 12:3; see Acts 2:36). In its talk of "Lord" *(kurios),* this message assigns authority to Jesus Christ, even the authority proper to God (see, for instance, Phil. 2:9-11). The claim that Jesus is Lord figures not only in who counts as a Christian (namely, the one who receives Jesus as Lord), but also in which philosophy counts as Christian (namely, the one that acknowledges Jesus as Lord). A philosophy can be theistic or deistic without being Christian, because it can acknowledge that "God" exists without affirming that Jesus is Lord. In this essay I want to clarify the nature of "Christ-shaped" philosophy, distinguishing two senses of "doing Christian philosophy" and identifying the importance of one's knowing God without reliance on an argument.

A Philosopher for Christ

Following Jesus, the apostle Paul is the most profound advocate of a Christ-shaped philosophy. Christian philosophy, in his approach, depends on God's

For comments on this essay, I thank David Bukenhofer, Richard Davis, Roberto Di Ceglie, John Greco, William Hasker, Michael McFall, Graham Oppy, Steve Porter, Clifford Williams, and Tedla Woldeyohannes. I also thank the audience at the 2012 Biola University (Center for Christian Thought) Conference on Christian Scholarship, including Tom Crisp, Doug Geivett, Joe Gorra, Steve Porter, Gregg Ten Elshof, and Todd Vasquez.

New Testament translations in this essay are taken from the New Revised Standard Version.

Spirit, and the Spirit in question is Christ-shaped, being the Spirit of Jesus Christ. The Spirit of Christ always points to the volitional struggle of Gethsemane, particularly to the struggling *Jesus* in Gethsemane, where Calvary was challenged but sealed. In doing so, this Spirit promises to lead us, noncoercively, from death to resurrection life as lasting, reverent companionship with God. This story is Good News, but it rarely gets a serious hearing from philosophers. A key lesson will be that Christ-shaped (or Christian) philosophy should be joined with Christ-formed philosophers.

Paul's letter to the Colossians offers a striking portrait of Christ-shaped philosophy, but gives a warning: "See to it that no one takes you captive through philosophy . . . and not according to Christ" (Col. 2:8). Paul here contrasts philosophy and Christ. Philosophy outside the authority of Christ, according to Paul, is dangerous to human freedom and life. The alternative is philosophy under Christ, and this involves a distinctive kind of wisdom. If philosophy is the love and pursuit of wisdom, *Christian* philosophy is the love and pursuit of wisdom under the authority of Christ, which calls for an ongoing union with Christ, including one's belonging to God in Christ.

Paul illuminates wisdom under Christ. He prays that the Christians at Colossae be filled with "spiritual wisdom [*sophia pneumatikē*] and understanding, so that you may lead lives worthy of the Lord, fully pleasing to him, as you bear fruit in every good work and as you grow in the knowledge of God" (Col. 1:9-10). "Spiritual wisdom," in Paul's approach, is wisdom intentionally guided and empowered by the Spirit of Christ. It therefore yields "lives worthy of the Lord, fully pleasing to him." No merely theoretical or intellectual wisdom has the power to guide such lives intentionally, and thus Paul refers to *spiritual* wisdom, which amounts to *Spirit-empowered* and *Spirit-guided* wisdom. The redemption of humans calls for an intentional guide or agent who leads and empowers receptive humans inwardly, in accordance with God's character, even when rules and arguments fall short.

Paul reports that he has been commissioned by God to make God's word fully known, and he identifies God's word with "the mystery that has been hidden throughout the ages . . . but has now been revealed" (Col. 1:26). Paul speaks of "the riches of the glory of this mystery, which is *Christ in you* [plural], the hope of glory" (Col. 1:27, my italics). This mystery prompts him to "teach everyone in all wisdom," in order to "present everyone mature [*teleios*] in Christ," being "rooted and built up in him" (Col. 1:28; 2:7). God's main mystery, according to Paul, "is Christ himself, in whom are hidden all the treasures of wisdom" (Col. 2:2-3). This inward Christ is *alive* and *interactive* with God's wisdom and power, seeking to renew humans at their deepest place.

Paul offers a cosmic picture: God created all things *for (eis) Christ* (Col. 1:16), so that Christ might be pre-eminent in everything (Col. 1:18). If Christ is to be pre-eminent in everything, then he should be pre-eminent in philosophy and in every other academic discipline, too. In Paul's grand portrait, God wants "everyone [to be] mature [or complete] in Christ." Accordingly, God wants everyone, even every philosopher, to cooperate reverently with the authority of Christ, and this is not a merely external or juridical authority. Instead, the authority seeking maturity in Christ aims for a mysterious *inward union* (or communion) between the exalted Christ and the people yielding and belonging to him as Lord. This inward union stems from God's aim that all people become Christ-like in moral and spiritual character, anchored in reverent companionship with God as Father. It demands that one be an intentional agent who freely appropriates the life-giving power of Christ as Lord.

Gethsemane Union

Paul identifies the Colossian Christians as having "clothed yourselves with the new self, which is being renewed in knowledge [*epignōsis*] according to the image [*eikōn*] of its creator" (Col. 3:10). They are "being renewed" in "the image" of God and hence of Christ, who himself is "the image [*eikōn*] of the invisible God" (Col. 1:15; cf. Phil. 2:6; 2 Cor. 4:4). The renewal of humans in the image of God in Christ is no purely external matter. It is personally inward owing to an inward *agent-power* (rather than a mere event-power), as follows: "I have been crucified with Christ; and it is no longer I who live, but it is Christ who lives in [*en*] me. And the life I now live in the flesh I live by faith in the Son of God, who loved me and gave himself for me" (Gal. 2:19-20; cf. Gal. 1:16).

The agent-inwardness of Christ fits with Paul's statement to the Galatian Christians that "I am again in the pain of childbirth until Christ is formed in [*en*] you" (Gal. 4:19; cf. Rom. 8:10).[1] It also fits with Paul's pointed question to the Corinthian Christians: "Do you not realize that Jesus Christ is in [*en*] you? — unless, indeed, you fail to meet the test!" (2 Cor. 13:5). His earlier question to them was this: "Do you not know that you are God's temple and that God's Spirit dwells in [*en*] you?" (1 Cor. 3:16; cf. 2 Cor. 6:16; Phil. 2:13; Ezek. 36:26-27). We will clarify "the test" for the inward power of Christ.

---

1. See also H. R. Mackintosh, *The Doctrine of the Person of Jesus Christ* (Edinburgh: T&T Clark, 1912), pp. 332-36; James S. Stewart, *A Man in Christ* (New York: Harper, 1935), pp. 169-72; F. F. Bruce, *Commentary on Galatians* (Grand Rapids: Wm. B. Eerdmans, 1982), pp. 212-13.

Christ lives in Paul, but Paul does not suggest that he himself becomes extinguished or depersonalized by Christ. Instead, he affirms that he himself lives by faith in Christ. If Christ's agent-inwardness extinguished or depersonalized Paul himself, Paul would not be able to live by faith in Christ or to have any faith at all. The Christ-human union, then, does not obliterate human selfhood, and hence does not entail an *absorption mysticism* of no personal distinctions. As a result, Paul does not — and would not — say, "I am Christ." Instead, he honors Christ as the Son of God who created him, loved him, forgave him, and redeemed him with inward divine power. The key feature of Paul's idea of "Christ in you" is the inward agent-power of Christ working, directly at the level of psychological and motivational attitudes, toward a cooperative person's renewal in God's image as God's beloved child. We may call this appeal to the inward agent-power of Christ the *Gethsemane union* approach to "Christ in you."

Paul's approach to human union with Christ resists a reduction to shared ethical commitments, even when divine love commands are centrally present. Ethical commitments and commands do not yield the inward agent-power of Christ that is central to human union with Christ. Paul explains to the Corinthian Christians that "[Christ] is not weak in dealing with you, but is powerful in [*dunatei en*] you. For he was crucified in weakness, but lives by the power of God" (2 Cor. 13:3-4). No mere ethical or juridical account of union will capture the inward agent-power of Christ mentioned by Paul. One can have all of the right ethical or juridical commitments but lack the power of Christ to carry out those commitments.[2]

The power in question corresponds to Paul's talk of a "test" of whether "Jesus Christ is in you" (2 Cor. 13:5). The test is for an inward agent-power characterized by Paul as follows: "Hope [in God] does not disappoint us, because God's love [*agapē*] has been poured into [*en*] our hearts through the Holy Spirit that has been given to us" (Rom. 5:5; cf. 2 Cor. 4:6). Paul would say that *faith in God* does not disappoint us either, but passes the test for the same reason: in receptive faith, we have been flooded in our deepest experience by the presence and power of God's personal *agapē*, courtesy of the Spirit of Christ. An appeal to the "testimony of God's Spirit" will fall short, cognitively and existentially, if it omits reference to the experienced flood of this Spirit's *agapē*. It then will be too remote from God's actual, self-revealed moral character in

---

2. See Mackintosh, *The Doctrine of the Person of Jesus Christ*, pp. 332-40; and H. R. Mackintosh, "*Unio Mystica* as a Theological Conception," in H. R. Mackintosh, *Some Aspects of Christian Belief* (London: Hodder & Stoughton, 1923), pp. 99-120.

Christ. Christian philosophy should highlight this unique vital flood of God's *agapē* in Christ, despite its widespread neglect of such religious experience.[3]

Faith *in God* is neither mere assent to a proposition ("even the demons believe") nor a leap in the dark. Instead, it is the *responsive* commitment of oneself to the God who sends his Spirit with *agapē* and forgiveness for the sake of Gethsemane union with Christ. Faith in God includes one's ongoing resolve to receive God's moral character and power in Christ inwardly, and to belong to God, in the reverent, self-sacrificial attitude of Gethsemane. God calls first by showing us (his moral character of) divine *agapē* for us, and human faith responds with cooperative self-commitment to this God who intervenes in our experience and calls for the self-sacrifice characteristic of *agapē* (see John 15:12-13). When we remove the needed human resolve from faith in God, we end up with faith that lacks a vital human struggle to make Christ pre-eminent in our lives. We then have dead faith, however much philosophy and theism we have.[4]

Strikingly, divine love comes to God's *enemies,* including us (Rom. 5:6, 10; Col. 1:21), and therefore we can test for God's love in us by testing for inward love and forgiveness of our enemies, including our intellectual enemies. To the extent that we resist inward enemy-love, we resist God himself, however shrewd our arguments and theories for theism. To that extent, we also resist God's aim that "the love from Christ urge us on," even toward forgiving and blessing our enemies (2 Cor. 5:14). There is nothing abstract or amorphous about this test for the inward Christ and his salient power. Minimal honesty here reveals our desperate need for divine grace and renewal in the image of Christ as God's beloved children. Such renewal will have a beginning but then will be experienced as a process of one's experiencing what God experiences in having divine love and forgiveness. Jürgen Moltmann has highlighted this process by citing Luther's view that "a Christian's *being* is in *becoming*," and adding, "His becoming is a continual repentance, a continual new start in a new direction. It is a new start from sin to righteousness, from slavery to freedom, from doubt to faith, and from past to future. That is why the Christian's being is still hidden in the womb of the divine future . . . (1 Jn. 3:2)."[5]

Paul identifies an inward agent testifying, or bearing witness, to God's

---

3. I have tried to give such experience its due in my books: *The Elusive God* (Cambridge: Cambridge University Press, 2008); *The Evidence for God* (Cambridge: Cambridge University Press, 2010); and *The Severity of God* (Cambridge: Cambridge University Press, 2013).

4. For elaboration, see Moser, *The Severity of God,* chaps. 2-3; and H. S. Holland, *The Fourth Gospel* (London: John Murray, 1923), pp. 154-57.

5. Jürgen Moltmann, *Experiences of God,* trans. Margaret Kohl (London: SCM Press, 1980), p. 4; cf. Phil. 3:12.

redemptive love: "When we cry [or shout], 'Abba! Father!' it is that very Spirit [of God] bearing witness with our spirit that we are children of God . . ." (Rom. 8:15-16; cf. Gal. 4:6; 2 Cor. 1:22, 5:5). Paul is well aware of false spirits that oppose the Spirit of God, and therefore he gives real substance to his approach, beyond vague talk of a divine spirit. He gives form or shape *de re* to his Spirit-talk by means of the *life*, including the inward life, of the crucified and risen Christ, not just by means of *de dicto talk* about his life. The actual *de re* life of Christ differs from *de dicto* talk about this life because the former has a distinctive agent-power not possessed by the latter. Christ is a personal agent with intentional power, including *agapē* and forgiveness; talk is not. The agent-power in question stems from the inward life of Christ (who, Paul says, intentionally loved him and forgave him), and it shapes how God's Spirit witnesses to God's reality, love, forgiveness, and faithfulness.[6]

The agent-power of divine *agapē* in Christ enables the kind of witness mentioned in Romans 5:5 — that is, God's love *(agapē)* poured into *(en)* our hearts. This is God's self-giving love for his children, including for Jesus as God's pre-eminent Son. Such humanly experienced *agapē*, not to be confused with mere information, prompts the filial cry immortalized by Jesus: "Abba! Father!" Accordingly, the witness of God's Spirit with our Spirit is based on agent-power, anchored in God's flooding a receptive human heart with his distinctive love of the kind shown in his pre-eminent agent, Christ. In that case, we may think of a human as experiencing, and thus sharing in, what God experiences. Moltmann remarks,

> If a person experiences in faith how God has experienced, and still experiences, him, [then] for that person God is not the abstract origin of the world . . . ; he is *the living God.* He learns to know himself in the mirror of God's love, suffering, and joy. In his experience of God, he experiences fragmentarily . . . something of God's own experience with him. The more he understands God's experience, the more deeply the mystery of God's passion is revealed to him.[7]

The life-changing power of divine *agapē* and the corresponding test for it go beyond mere truth, knowledge, understanding, or explanation. In addition,

---

6. For relevant discussion, see Mackintosh, *The Doctrine of the Person of Jesus Christ*, pp. 314-20.

7. Jürgen Moltmann, *The Trinity and the Kingdom* (San Francisco: Harper & Row, 1981), p. 4.

one can receive this power even if one has a very limited understanding or explanation of it. Paul exalts this power above mere faith, hope, knowledge, prophecy, and self-discipline (1 Cor. 13; cf. 1 Cor. 8:1). Prior to Paul, Jesus himself had indicated that the power of *agapē* underwrites being his disciple under "Abba, Father" and being known as such (see Matt. 5:43-48; John 13:35).

Paul thinks of the power of *agapē* within Christians as the power of the inward Christ, the living intentional Christ within Christians. The power in question conforms to and sustains the pattern of the life of Christ. Paul writes, "I want to know Christ and the power of his resurrection and the sharing of his sufferings by becoming like him in his death, if somehow I may attain the resurrection from the dead" (Phil. 3:10-11). Similarly, Paul remarks, "While we live, we are always being given up to death for Jesus' sake, so that the life of Jesus may be made visible in our mortal flesh" (2 Cor. 4:11). We are to live out in our own lives, over time, the pattern of the self-giving life of Christ, who empowers us with divine *agapē* from within as long as we are receptive and cooperative. If we have been united *(sumphutoi)* with Christ in his death, according to Paul, we are to live now in the newness of life with the risen Christ (Rom. 6:4, 5, 11, 13; cf. Col. 3:1).

Paul characterizes divine *agapē* as cruciform, as moved by and conformed to the divine self-sacrificial motive that led to the cross of Jesus. He urges the Philippian Christians, "Let the same mind be in you that was in Christ Jesus, who . . . humbled himself and became obedient to the point of death — even death on a cross" (Phil. 2:5-6, 8). This calls for cooperation with the "God who is at work in [*en*] you, enabling you both to will and to work for his good pleasure" (Phil. 2:13). Christ's self-giving obedience, according to Paul, shows God's distinctive love for humans: "God proves his love for us in that while we still were sinners Christ died for us" (Rom. 5:8). This death manifests the faithful obedience represented in Gethsemane, where Jesus cried "Abba! Father!" and then obeyed God with everything he had (Mark 14:36). He humbled himself, obediently and reverently, in yielding his will and his life in self-sacrifice to God's perfect will.[8]

Although the death of Christ is "for us," we should ask how this event becomes powerful *to us in the pattern of our lives.* Christ's death is an event of ancient history, roughly datable to a Friday in April of A.D. 33. The historical cross of Christ must not be left as *merely* historical, however, if it is to motivate

---

8. For relevant discussion, see Michael J. Gorman, *Inhabiting the Cruciform God* (Grand Rapids: Wm. B. Eerdmans, 2009).

Christians adequately today.[9] The Good News therefore calls for the Gethsemane union of all Christians, even today, with the risen Christ who obediently suffered the Roman cross in ancient times. If we omit this union, the cross of Christ loses its divine redemptive power for today, however attentive and even emotional one's response to it is. The message of the cross would then be reduced to so much talk and emotional response, and Christians would lose their divine motivation from Gethsemane union with Christ.

Gethsemane union is not limited to an instant of time, because the full volitional redemption of humans requires ongoing, diachronic union with the risen Christ. This is compatible with the plausible requirement that there be a starting point for the redemptive process in humans. Even so, humans habitually resist God and his love commands, and therefore an *ongoing* powerful but non-coercive antidote is needed. An event from history, even one's own personal history, will not supply the needed antidote, because no such event offers current *intentional guidance with power*.

Unlike a past event, an inward agent can serve the purpose of divine redemption for humans. The provision comes from the inward Spirit of Christ, who invites and encourages a receptive person to cry "Abba! Father!" as Christ himself did in Gethsemane. The direction of this prayerful cry was, and is, to yield one's will to God's perfect will, and this cry is a repeatable episode, as needed by humans habitually alienated from God. The ongoing importance of Gethsemane, then, is not just as a moral context where humans obey a divine command. Instead, Gethsemane becomes a repeated context where the risen Christ invites, encourages, and empowers one to yield into self-sacrifice, reconciliation, and reverent companionship with God as one's ongoing "Abba, Father." Every occasion of human decision-making, including every opportunity for self-sacrifice for good, can become a Gethsemane context, courtesy of the inward Christ, who values process (the *how*) as well as product (the *what*). This, however, is no claim to human perfection in this life (see Phil. 3:12).

Gethsemane union with Christ, although volitional, is grace-centered, because it revolves around God's unearned offer and sustenance of companionship with receptive humans. One must "work out" this union for salvation (see Phil. 2:12), but such "working out" is volitional cooperation with God that differs from "works" as a means of earning or meriting salvation (cf. Rom. 4:4). Accordingly, Paul describes himself as struggling according to all of the energy that God empowers in him (Col. 1:29). No Pelagian threat will arise here, as

---

9. See Mackintosh, *The Doctrine of the Person of Christ*, pp. 310-13, and Arthur Vogel, *The Power of His Resurrection* (New York: Seabury Press, 1976), chap. 3.

long as we distinguish the terms for *offering* a gift (as completely unearned) from the conditions for *appropriating* the gift (as cooperation of receptive humans with God). A requirement of active human cooperation with God, after the model of Jesus in Gethsemane, does not entail a requirement of human earning, despite widespread confusions in this area.[10]

Gethsemane Philosophy

A Christian philosophy should call for Gethsemane union with Christ. Paul remarks that "knowledge puffs up, but love builds up" (1 Cor. 8:1), and he could have added that *philosophy* puffs up, too. Accordingly, he reports that he does not trade in "eloquent wisdom, so that the cross of Christ might not be emptied of its power" (1 Cor. 1:17). This suggests that a philosophy can empty the power from the cross of Christ. Paul has in mind the *redemptive* power of the cross, as he immediately mentions the cross as "the power of God" for "us who are being saved" (1 Cor. 1:18). How, then, can a philosophy empty the redemptive power of the cross of Christ? It can do so in *many* ways, given that there are many ways to mislead and obstruct people regarding God.

Paul has in mind, at least, the tendency of the world's wisdom and philosophy to obscure or divert attention from the reality of "Christ [as] the power of God and the wisdom of God" (1 Cor. 1:24). One such diversion occurs when a philosophy, even one called "Christian," ignores the redemptive importance of Gethsemane union with the inward Christ. If attention is directed away from such union, as with most philosophy, one easily can neglect the importance of such union for human redemption. A test question arises for any proposed Christian philosophy: Does the philosophy uphold the importance of one's obediently dying with Christ (to everything anti-God) under the guiding agent-power of God as "Abba, Father"? If not, the philosophy misses the mark as a Christian philosophy. Most philosophy fails this redemptive litmus test, because most philosophers ignore redemption as being saved into life with God, and thereby fail to honor God's unique Mediator, the inward Christ.

Aside from the diversionary dangers of philosophy, Paul acknowledges that "among the mature we do speak wisdom, though it is not a wisdom of this age" (1 Cor. 2:6). He would add that among the mature we Christians do offer a philosophy, though it is not of this age. He has in mind the era of the risen Christ, whose Good News is that people of all nations are called

---

10. For details, see Moser, *The Severity of God,* chap. 4.

by God into the lasting life of union with Christ. A philosophy of the era of Christ is distinctively Christian, because it gives pre-eminence to the risen Christ with whom people are to share Gethsemane union. This pre-eminence includes giving primacy to Christ and hence to redemption in Gethsemane union with him. The neglect of such pre-eminence entails neglect of a Christian philosophy.

Doing Christian Philosophy

A Christian philosophy should accommodate two senses of the phrase "engaged in (or doing) Christian philosophy." One sense, which we may call "the strict-content sense," requires interacting with philosophy that is explicitly Christian in conceptual content, involving positive claims regarding Jesus Christ, the Spirit of Christ, reconciliation to God in Christ, inward transformation by Christ, and so on. Another sense, which we may call "the Kingdom-enhancement sense," requires interacting with philosophy (whatever its content) for the purpose of bringing out its contributions (or lack thereof) to a philosophy that is Christian in content and that enhances God's redemptive Kingdom in Christ, under the Good News of God in Christ and its divine love commands.

The relevant Kingdom-enhancement can contribute either to new reconciliation to God or to deepened reconciliation with God, including a deepened appreciative understanding of God's redemptive ways. Given that the desired reconciliation is under divine *agapē* and its love commands, we may understand Kingdom-enhancement in terms of the expansion or the deepening of God's kingdom of *agapē*. Such Kingdom-enhancement depends on the power of divine *agapē*, which can exist and work apart from explicit Christian content. Otherwise, the Spirit of God would be unable to prepare people in advance of their coming to consider and to receive Christian conceptual content.

It would be unduly narrow and short-sighted to prohibit doing philosophy in the Kingdom-enhancement sense. In addition, such narrowness conflicts with the way that various contributors of wisdom literature in the Old Testament engaged with, and borrowed from, non-Hebraic wisdom traditions. If God is the ultimate ground of all wisdom, then genuine wisdom is valuable wherever it emerges, even outside the people or church of God. So, we should not expect or advocate for a Christian ghetto with a monopoly on wisdom.

It does not follow that "anything goes" in Christian philosophy; nor does it follow that all philosophical truth or sound argument is intrinsically valuable or even worthy of human pursuit. The Kingdom-enhancement sense sets a definite boundary with this standard: enhancing God's redemptive Kingdom in Christ, under the Good News and its divine love commands. Mere truth-acquisition, even for philosophical truth, does not meet this standard. Some truths contribute to Kingdom enhancement; others do not.

We humans have finite resources, including finite time, in this life under the divine love commands, and therefore we should adopt a triage approach to the matters we pursue in Christian philosophy (as in Christian life generally). So, we should distinguish between (1) the philosophical questions we may engage, if only briefly, to find out their positive relevance, or lack thereof, to Kingdom enhancement, and (2) the questions we may pursue as a research focus in a Christian life, as an evident means of Kingdom enhancement. Any new question may be fair game for the first category, but the second category is much more exclusive. In terms of research focus, Christian philosophy (and Christian inquiry in general) should be attentive to the second category in a manner that is often neglected, owing perhaps to the false assumption that any philosophical inquiry or truth is intrinsically valuable or otherwise worthy of human pursuit.

Divine Self-Authentication

Christian philosophy joins Gethsemane union with a religious epistemology oriented toward the Spirit of God and Christ. We should find knowledge of God, like human redemption, to stem from divine grace rather than human earning. In particular, a Christian philosophy must acknowledge that the things of God are taught by God's Spirit, the Spirit of Christ, and not by "human wisdom." Paul states that "we have received . . . the Spirit that is from God, so that we may understand the gifts bestowed on us by God" (1 Cor. 2:12). In making Christ pre-eminent in all things, even in wisdom and philosophy, God does not allow the world to know God by its own wisdom. Paul remarks that "in the wisdom of God, the world did not know God through [its] wisdom" (1 Cor. 1:21). Instead, according to Paul, "Christ Jesus . . . became for us wisdom from God, and righteousness and sanctification and redemption" (1 Cor. 1:30; cf. Col. 2:3). The latter treasures are offered by divine grace, but are appropriated by us only in the struggle of Gethsemane union with Christ.

Gethsemane union with Christ as Lord is no mere correct belief that something about Christ is true. Instead, it calls for volitional cooperation and companionship with Christ, who empowers and guides *how* we think, not just *what* we think. The divine fruit of the Spirit of Christ — love, joy, peace, patience, gentleness, and so on — should apply even to Christian thinking and thinkers, who must receive such fruit from God. Divine redemption values the inward process of human cooperation and companionship with Christ as much as any objective reality. Christian philosophy should follow suit, under the pre-eminence of Christ as Lord. It also should acknowledge that communing with and obeying God can awaken one to otherwise neglected realities and evidence of God, as God emerges more clearly as "Abba, Father" in one's experience.

In Christian philosophy, God as the supreme, perfect authority ultimately testifies to God, via the Spirit of the risen Christ, God's own image. Neither claims nor subjective experiences are self-attesting, but God as an intentional causal agent is self-authenticating in being self-manifesting and self-witnessing regarding God's and Christ's reality and character (see Rom. 10:20; John 14:23). This self-authenticating fits with the biblical theme of God's confirming God's reality, given that God inherently has a morally perfect character and cannot find anyone or anything else to serve this purpose. (See, for instance, Gen. 22:16-17; Isa. 45:22-23; and Heb. 6:13-14.) This position has major implications for Christian epistemology, and may be called, following James S. Stewart, *the divine self-verification of Christ in conscience:* "This is a very wonderful thing which happens: you begin exploring the fact of Christ, perhaps merely intellectually and theologically — and before you know where you are, the fact is exploring *you,* spiritually and morally. . . . You set out to see what you can find in Christ, and sooner or later God in Christ finds you. That is the self-verification of Jesus."[11] Christian philosophers should welcome this experienced reality, and re-orient Christian philosophy accordingly.

Through the Spirit of Christ, God manifests the divine character of *agapē* in (the experience of) receptive humans, pouring God's enemy-love into our hearts. This is something only God can do; mere humans and counterfeit gods, including imaginary gods, lack the needed power and character. Being *sui generis* here, God should be expected by us to be self-attesting and self-witnessing. No other agent has the self-sufficient *agapē* character of enemy-love needed for the task; so, no other agent is worthy of worship or divinely self-manifesting. God's self-attesting yields a corrective reciprocity in our receptive experience, particularly in our conscience, whereby we are challenged

---

11. James S. Stewart, "Who Is This Jesus? (2)," in James S. Stewart, *The Strong Name* (Edinburgh: T&T Clark, 1940), pp. 87-88; cf. Mackintosh, *The Doctrine of the Person of Jesus Christ,* pp. 317-20; Moser, *The Severity of God,* chap. 3.

to move toward enemy-love and forgiveness, away from our destructive self-ishness and pride. Ultimately, then, Christians do not convince people regarding God; *God* does, and we contribute by being in union with God in Christ, thereby manifesting the power (beyond the mere talk) of God's own character.

For redemptive purposes, God wants people to know God directly, in an I-Thou acquaintance relationship, without the dilution or the distraction of philosophical arguments. Accordingly, God wants the self-commitment of a human agent to *God*, not (in this context) to an inference or a conclusion of an argument. This fits with the biblical theme that God alone is our foundation, rock, and anchor, including our cognitive foundation regarding God's reality (see Ps. 18:2, 31; Ps. 28:1; Ps. 31:3; Isa. 44:8; cf. 1 Cor. 2:9-13). God wants to be one's sole evidential foundation for believing in God and for believing that God exists, and hence does not want an argument to assume this role. The evidential foundation is *God in God's self-manifesting interventions* in one's life, including in one's conscience. This upholds God's vital existential significance for human inquirers. We can put ourselves in a position to apprehend divine self-manifestation by being sincerely and willingly open to receive and to participate in redemptive self-sacrifice, the hallmark of God's perfect moral character.

An argument can obscure the importance of directly knowing God, and many uses of arguments by Christian philosophers actually do this. In addition, when familiar theistic arguments come under heavy fire, even justified fire, many critics take this fire to underwrite their agnosticism or atheism. This is dangerously misleading. We can represent foundational evidence for God in a sound first-person argument, but such an argument cannot exhaust or replace the underlying experiential evidence from divine self-manifestation.[12]

Nondiscursive Evidence

Christian philosophers often overlook the central importance of a nondiscursive manifestational witness to God's powerful redemptive reality, as they over-emphasize the role of discursive, intellectual reasons. This deficiency may be the residue of a dubious kind of epistemic coherentism that lacks the needed resources of a modest experiential foundationalism. Alternatively, it may stem

---

12. On this matter, see Moser, *The Elusive God*, chap. 2; and Moser, "God without Argument," in *Is Faith in God Reasonable?*, ed. Corey Miller and Paul Gould (London: Routledge, forthcoming).

from a confusion of the conditions for one's either having or manifesting evidence and the conditions for one's giving an argument. We do well, however, not to confuse evidence and an argument. If all evidence is an argument, we face a devastating epistemic regress problem.[13]

An evidential component is *discursive* if and only if it uses assertive language to express a state of affairs. The New Testament category of "witness" *(marturia)*, however, is broader than that of discursive evidence. A witness to God's redemption may include discursive evidence, but it need not. A *nondiscursive* mode of human existing or relating can be a witness to God's redemptive character in virtue of manifesting certain properties of God's character, such as divine *agapē*, without making an assertion. This neglected point bears on an aim to manifest one's reasons for acknowledging God, even to manifest a reason for the Christian hope within one (1 Pet. 3:15). Even when a witness to God includes a discursive component, that component need not be an argument. It could be a descriptive testimony to what God has done in one's life.

Foundational reasons or evidence need not be discursive, but can be non-propositional character traits supplied by God's Spirit: love, joy, peace, patience, kindness, gentleness, and so on (see Gal. 5:22-23). Accordingly, John's Gospel portrays Jesus as announcing that his disciples will be known by their *agapē* for others (John 13:35). Jesus did not mention or use any philosophical arguments in this connection, or in any other connection. The same is true of his followers represented in the New Testament. This noteworthy fact, moreover, does not qualify as a deficiency in their actual reasons or evidence. Talk is cheap, and therefore many inquirers will wonder whether an argument has support from a corresponding nondiscursive witness, which can have power and cogency irreducible to statements and arguments.[14]

A serious problem stems from the frequent divorce of Christian philosophy from the foundation of the inward Christ and Gethsemane union with him. The result is correct intellectual belief without the needed divine power, guidance, and companionship from the inward Christ. In that case, even if one talks voluminously of Christ, one's moral agency does not underwrite that talk by witnessing to the powerful *agapē*-character of Christ within oneself. People

---

13. For details, see Paul K. Moser, *Knowledge and Evidence* (Cambridge: Cambridge University Press, 1989).

14. On a nondiscursive witness in *personifying evidence* of God, see Moser, *The Evidence for God,* which raises doubts about the arguments of natural theology and various attempts to achieve knowledge of God by reason alone; see also Moser, "Gethsemane Epistemology," *Philosophia Christi* 14 (2012): 263-74; Moser, "Natural Theology and the Evidence for God," *Philosophia Christi* 14 (2012): 305-11, and Moser, "God without Argument."

are left, then, with a conflicted witness at best — that is, with talk in the absence of the corresponding agent-power of *agapē*. Christians thus begin to look and act a lot like the world, regardless of their elaborate talk to the contrary.

Christian philosophy cannot be *merely* academic or impersonal, because it cannot ignore questions about our deepest motives and our personal standing before God in Christ. Some philosophers object to bringing Gethsemane union into Christian philosophy on the ground that we should keep philosophy personally *impartial,* and not make it confessional in any way. The philosophy classroom, in this view, is no place for personal confession or redemption. This view is puzzling, however, because it suggests that we should do Christian philosophy without attending to the redemptive *reality* of being Christian in union with Christ. Impersonal talk, however, is too cheap and easy for Christian wisdom and philosophy. It leaves Christian philosophy as impotent as secular philosophy. Philosophy needs redeeming, and that by God in Christ.

A Christian philosophy may prompt an inquirer to ask *why* one lacks evidence reported by some Christians, such as the evidence of the inward flood of *agapē* from God's Spirit. This question will invite motivational issues about one's desires and intentions with regard to God, such as these questions: Am I *willing* to yield reverently with Christ to God in Gethsemane? Have I hardened my heart to God in Christ? Do I welcome the offered inward flood of God's *agapē* in Christ? If not, why not? Am I truly willing to cooperate with the authority of divine *agapē* in Christ, even if my academic peers take sharp exception and offer ridicule? If we avoid the latter question of Christian authority, we will not accommodate the religious epistemology in Christian philosophy.[15] A philosophy can be more or less Christian, but if it omits the pre-eminence of Christ and the redemptive power of union with Christ, it is Christian in name only. So, the fact that a Christian produces a philosophy, even about God, does not make the *philosophy* Christian.

Human reflection can stem from motives contrary to the divine *agapē* exemplified in Christ. In that case, we will lack Christian philosophy, even if we have an intellectual skeleton of the true article. Christian philosophy must stem from and be continuous with the content of the Good News of God in Christ. If, however, one pursues philosophy just to understand, acquire truth, or show off one's intellectual skills, rather than from and for the honor of God in Christ, one is not doing Christian philosophy, anchored in Christ-like, Gethsemane motives and prayer. We have, then, an indispensable moral and spiritual standard for Christian philosophy, courtesy of the Christ who is

---

15. See Moser, *The Severity of God,* chap. 3.

our wisdom, righteousness, and redemption from God. In him we find both *how* Christian philosophy is to be done (anchored in the Gethsemane prayer to "Abba, Father") and *what* (better, *whom*) it should regard as pre-eminent (God's Christ of Gethsemane union).

Gethsemane Spirituality

Christian philosophy depends on Christian spirituality, because it requires our discerning God in Christ for our ultimate authority, even in philosophy. This discerning is not casual or speculative, but requires volitional communion with God, which in turn depends on Christ's Gethsemane prayer: "Abba, Father, . . . not what I want, but what you want" (Mark 14:36). If we fail to make this prayer our own, we fail to enter into Christian philosophy and even Christian life. As exemplified by Jesus, this prayer has its origin in obedience to the primary divine love-command.

The idea of God's offering, as a gracious and powerful gift, what the divine love commands require of humans is central to the Good News of God's redemption as "the power of God for salvation to everyone who has faith [in God]" (Rom. 1:16). This idea fits with the Jesus' emphasis on God's gratuitous provision toward humans (Matt. 20:1-16; Luke 15:11-32). The provision acknowledges that the divine love commands require a kind of power among humans that only a perfectly loving God can provide. The love commands of Jesus call for *fellowship relationships* of unselfish love between oneself and God and between oneself and other humans. Such relationships go beyond talk to attitudes and to volitional fellowship, companionship, and communion between and among personal agents, with God at the center as the source of power for *agapē*. Moving beyond right action, the love commands identify who we are and how we exist in the presence of God in Christ. They correctively judge humans by calling us up short by a morally perfect divine standard, and thereby calling us to obedient redefinition, including "new creation," by the divine gift of companionship with God in Christ. Willing humans move beyond discussion, then, to personal transformation via obedience, in a relationship of reverent companionship with God.

Philosophy in its normal mode, without being receptive to authoritative divine love-commands, leaves humans in a discussion mode, short of an obedience mode under divine authority. Philosophical questions naturally prompt philosophical questions about philosophical questions, and this launches a regress of higher-order — or at least related — questions, with no end to philosophical discussion. Hence, the questions of philosophy are, notoriously, perennial. In contrast, as divinely appointed Lord, Jesus commands humans to move, for their own good, to an obedience mode of existence relative to divine love commands. He thereby points humans to his perfectly loving Father, who ultimately underwrites the divine love commands for humans, for the sake of divine-human fellowship. Accordingly, we need to transcend a normal discussion mode, and thus philosophical discussion itself, to face with sincerity the personal inward Authority who commands what humans need: faithful obedience and belonging to the perfectly loving God. Such obedience and belonging of the heart provide the way that humans are to *receive* the gift of divine love. Insofar as the discipline of philosophy becomes guided by that gift on offer, it becomes kerygma-oriented in virtue of becoming an enabler of the Good News of God in Christ.[16]

Many philosophers ignore or oppose Jesus because he transcends a familiar, self-centered discussion mode and demands that they do the same. Philosophical discussion becomes advisable and permissible, under the divine love commands, if and only if it honors those commands by compliance with them. Accordingly, our use of time becomes accountable to God. Jesus commands love from us toward God and others *beyond* discussion and the acquisition of truth, even philosophical truth. He thereby cleanses the temple of philosophy, and overturns our self-promoting tables of mere philosophical discussion. He pronounces judgment on this long-standing self-made temple out of genuine love for its wayward builders. His corrective judgment brings us what we truly need to flourish in lasting companionship with God and other humans.

A Christian philosophy teacher should use discernment by listening for guidance from the Lord he or she represents. It is, after all, the living God who is being represented, and this God can be subtle and elusive, for good redemptive reasons.[17] Sometimes we desire clear-cut recipes that specify exactly when and how to represent God discursively. We do not have such recipes, however, and this lack may serve our own redemptive good. It may prompt us to listen for guidance in our particular situations of teaching as Christian philosophers. Differences in audiences and settings can matter importantly in serving God's redemptive purpose. In this regard, the university classroom is no different from an audience outside the university. In both contexts, a Christian teacher needs discernment regarding how to proceed and how much to reveal discursively, given the readiness of his or her audience to receive or

16. See Moser, *The Elusive God,* chap. 4.
17. See Moser, *The Elusive God.*

not to receive. A nondiscursive manifestational witness of *agapē*, however, can typically proceed apace, as a powerful antecedent to a potential opportunity for a discursive witness. Such a nondiscursive witness can be effective preparation for a testimony to an audience.

The need for discernment in Christian teaching that involves the Good News calls for a larger undertaking. The apostle Paul points us in the right direction as follows: "Do not be conformed to this world, but be transformed by the renewing of your minds, so that you may discern what is the will of God — what is good and acceptable and perfect" (Rom. 12:2). I have referred to the needed transformation as an "undertaking" because it includes intentional action on the part of Christians. Accordingly, the discernment in question is not passive.

Paul identifies the relevant intentional action, in terms of a kind of redemptive self-sacrifice, as follows: "I appeal to you therefore, brothers and sisters, by the mercies of God, to present your bodies as a living sacrifice, holy and acceptable to God, which is your spiritual worship" (Rom. 12:1; cf. Col. 1:24). A role for such sacrifice rarely emerges in contemporary writing on Christian philosophy, knowing God, spiritual transformation, or discernment of God's will. Similarly, a crucial role for the spiritual transformation of Christian teachers, including teachers of Christian philosophy, is neglected in much contemporary discussion. An excessive focus on relevant intellectual content may account for these deficiencies. In any case, a correction is needed.[18]

In order to discern God's will, Christian philosophy teachers need a spiritual transformation that requires our self-sacrifice to God (as a way of sharing in Christ's perfect sacrifice by the obedience of faith in God). This includes dying to our selfishness and pride in order to flourish in life with God, who seeks to kill selfishness and pride (cf. Rom. 8:13). We must undergo the crisis of Gethsemane daily, yielding our will to God's perfect will, in order to be in a position to discern divine guidance for teaching in particular cases. This Gethsemane experience is the core of our needed redemptive self-sacrifice to God, as we share in the exemplary sacrifice by Christ to God for us.

Paul's ideas of spiritual discernment and sacrifice may seem too messy for some philosophers who clamor for cut-and-dried principles, arguments, and recipes. Such a worry should subside, however, when we consider that our ultimate audience is not a logical principle or an argument, but a personal di-

---

18. I pursue this matter in "Divine Hiddenness and Self-Sacrifice," in *Hidden Divinity and Religious Belief: New Perspectives*, ed. Eleonore Stump and Adam Green (Cambridge: Cambridge University Press, forthcoming).

vine Spirit who is inherently self-sacrificial. This God reveals that the cardinal human failing is alienation from God whereby we fail to commune with God in a manner that shows us how to love God and others as God does. Accordingly, we should not identify the cardinal human shortcoming with a failure to have or accept a conclusive argument for God's existence or even a Christian "worldview." The challenge for us is much deeper when we face a purposive, interactive God's reality and intervention.

As suggested, contrary to some familiar trends, the teaching of Christian philosophy need not assume that people should endorse a particular argument for God's existence. Instead, such teaching should acknowledge and attend (if indirectly and with subtlety) to the most vital human need: to receive divine love in communion with God and thereby to learn to love God and others as God does. Accordingly, Christian philosophers should steer clear of any smarter-than-thou pride and any tendency to mock, harass, badger, or otherwise belittle people who do not honor, accept, or debate certain "apologetics" arguments on offer. The latter tendency, unfortunately, is common in certain sectors of Christian philosophical "apologetics," but it has no place in the redemptive practice of Christian philosophy or teaching. It gives the false impression that certain philosophical arguments are crucial to reasonable Christian commitment. Instead, the experienced crisis of Gethsemane is crucial.

Conclusion

Christian philosophy should leave adequate room for God's self-authenticating work among humans. God does not have to wait for philosophical arguments to advance redemption among humans. Christians, including Christian philosophers, are to manifest God's presence in the power of divine *agapē*, and this witness is more profound, existentially and experientially, than any inferential chain or argument. It manifests the power, and hence the reality, of God's own probing (= proving) Spirit, who seeks to pour life-giving *agapē* into the heart of any receptive inquirer, with or without inferences and arguments (Rom. 5:5). We do well to re-orient the doing and the teaching of Christian philosophy accordingly, in order to welcome this Good News. The remaining question for us is volitional: Are we now *willing* to participate in the powerful life of God in Christ, in God's unselfish love even toward enemies, even come what may?

The (In)visibility of Theology in Contemporary Art Criticism

Jonathan A. Anderson

The Rift between Religion and Contemporary Art

For a variety of reasons, Christianity — and "religion" more generally — did not fare very well in the course of twentieth-century art, neither in the making of it nor in the scholarly discourse about it. The textbooks of twentieth-century art history, theory, and criticism, as well as major museum collections, readily testify to the fact that the institutional "art world"[1] regards Christianity as having made negligible contributions to the fine arts during the twentieth century (which, unfortunately, is a judgment that is easy to agree with). But the reverse is also true: for the most part, the church has little regard for the canons of twentieth-century art as having made any significant contributions to the development and deepening of Christian thought. For most of the last century, the worlds of contemporary art theory and Christian theology developed into distinct cultural configurations that have been remarkably disengaged from each other — in fact, often to the point of mutual unintelligibility. By 1979, renowned art theorist Rosalind Krauss had gone so far as to refer to the relation between "the sacred" and "the secular" as one of "absolute rift."[2]

---

1. While the term "art world" is controversial because it presumes singularity, I agree with James Elkins that we need some such designation to refer to the networks and institutions that produce and support "whatever is exhibited in galleries in major cities, bought by museums of contemporary art, shown in biennales and the Documenta, and written about in periodicals such as *Artforum, October, Flash Art, Parkett,* or *Tema Celeste*" (James Elkins, *On the Strange Place of Religion in Contemporary Art* [New York: Routledge, 2004], p. 1).

2. Rosalind Krauss, "Grids," *October* 9 (Spring 1979): 54.

The reasons for this rift are numerous and complex, tangled up in the sweeping narratives of Western secularization. In Krauss's account, modern artists found themselves "participating in a drama that extended well beyond the domain of art" into politics, philosophy, and especially science, which found itself increasingly (and with increasing success) doing "battle with God."[3] In this context, art was reconfigured and re-theorized as alternative to religion: "In the increasingly de-sacralized space of the nineteenth century, art had become the refuge for religious emotion; it became, as it has remained, a secular form of belief."[4] Up to this point, Krauss's formulation is essentially a restatement of Nietzsche's famous dictum: "Art raises its head where religions decline. It takes over a number of feelings and moods produced by religion, clasps them to its heart, and then becomes itself deeper, more soulful. . . . Feeling, forced out of the religious sphere by enlightenment, throws itself into art."[5] Krauss, however, identifies a further stage in this development, one in which points of contact have been gradually, though decisively, disabled: "Although this condition could be discussed openly in the late nineteenth century, it is something that is inadmissible in the twentieth, so that by now we find it indescribably embarrassing to mention *art* and *spirit* in the same sentence."[6]

This discursive "inadmissibility" forms a twentieth-century backdrop against which talk about "religion" in today's art discourse is notable — and notably problematic. Over the past two decades, artists and scholars *have* begun to use art and spirit in the same sentence again, and there has been much renewed interest in exploring the pressures and bearings that religion and contemporary art might exert on one another. We might even echo Sally Promey in asserting that there has, in fact, been a "return" of religion to the art discourse.[7] But it's a return that has been riddled with problems and confusions: Krauss's rift remains, and it stifles discussion with what James Elkins has called "a complex structure of refusals."[8]

In general, Christians are still learning how to work thoughtfully and creatively in this situation. In what follows, I will try to articulate the primary

---

3. Krauss, "Grids," p. 54.

4. Krauss, "Grids," p. 54.

5. Friedrich Nietzsche, *Human, All Too Human* (1878), trans. Marion Faber with Stephen Lehmann (Lincoln: University of Nebraska Press, 1984), §150, p. 105.

6. Krauss, "Grids," p. 54.

7. Sally M. Promey, "The 'Return' of Religion in the Scholarship of American Art," *The Art Bulletin* 85, no. 3 (Sept 2003): 581-603.

8. James Elkins, "The Art Seminar," in *Re-Enchantment*, ed. James Elkins and David Morgan (New York: Routledge, 2009), p. 171.

contours and logic of these refusals, offer some assessments and suggestions for how we might think about the return of religion to the contemporary art discourse, and then offer some constructive thoughts about moving forward.

The Invisibility of Religion in Contemporary Art Criticism

In 2004, James Elkins, a prolific and well-known art historian at the Art Institute of Chicago, published his controversial book *On the Strange Place of Religion in Contemporary Art*, in which he attempted to understand and diagnose the chronic gridlock between contemporary art discourse and devoted religious belief. Early in the book, he echoes Krauss in his articulation of the problem: "Contemporary art, I think, is as far from organized religion as Western art has ever been, and that may be its most singular achievement — or its cardinal failure, depending on your point of view. The separation has become entrenched."[9] From the outset, his stated task is irenic: he wants "to see if it is possible to adjust the existing discourses" enough to include religious content and religious points of view.[10] Ultimately, however, he reluctantly concludes that such an adjustment remains unlikely: art theory and "religion" are simply structurally incompatible in their current forms.[11]

So, what's his argument? As I read Elkins, the central problem in the art and religion discourse is not reducible to a modernist secularization theory, nor is it simply attributable to the deliberate ideological suppression of religious voices (though he admits this as a reality);[12] rather, it has much more to do with the structure of modern and contemporary visual *hermeneutics*. To distill his argument a great deal, the "strange place of religion in contemporary art" is that the trajectory of art theory and criticism for the last 150 years makes it impossible for religious content to be mediated with any kind of directness,

9. Elkins, *On the Strange Place of Religion in Contemporary Art*, p. 15.

10. Elkins, *On the Strange Place of Religion in Contemporary Art*, p. xi.

11. In his conclusion to *On the Strange Place of Religion in Contemporary Art*, Elkins voices his objection to this state of affairs: "Religion is so much a part of life, so intimately entangled with everything we think and do, that it seems absurd it does not have a place in talk about contemporary art" (p. 115). And yet simply objecting is not enough; overcoming this absurdity requires discussions that are "very slow and careful" (p. 115). Despite the best efforts in this direction, he feels compelled to close his book on an unresolved chord: "It is impossible to talk sensibly about religion and at the same time address art in an informed and intelligent manner: but it is also irresponsible not to keep trying" (p. 116).

12. As he states elsewhere, "There *are* strong attempts at prohibition and exclusion in the academic discourse on art" ("The Art Seminar," p. 174).

clarity, or sincerity of expression, thus effectively precluding it from having any compelling presence in the *interpretation* of artworks. Thus, in Elkins's view the rift exists not in artistic production per se but in the academic writing about art.

In the book and in the various conferences and publications surrounding it, Elkins repeatedly identifies an asymmetry between the spheres of contemporary art-making and the spheres of contemporary art interpretation: "There are separate-but-equal kinds of art, but there are not really separate-but-equal kinds of writing on art. . . . Worlds of art, yes; worlds of art writing, no."[13] In fact, he contends that the most "powerful, well-articulated, convincing accounts of contemporary art" are produced by a "fairly small" academic world of art writing which has "produced the single viable account of what art in the last hundred and fifty years has been about."[14] Of course, he recognizes the flagrant elitism of this kind of claim, but he finds it an inescapable description of the circumstances: "It is an account on which everyone else depends. If you think you're writing freely on art, and that you're beholden to no one in particular, you are virtually certainly beholden to Greenberg, Adorno, Krauss, and not too many others."[15] And he continues to name names: "in North America and Anglophone countries in Western Europe, virtually all major, active art historians are deeply indebted to *October*."[16]

As a shorthand reference for this world of elite art-writing, Elkins repeatedly points to the journal *October*, which he (probably correctly) considers to be the most influential academic journal devoted to contemporary art criticism and theory. Co-founded in 1976 by Rosalind Krauss (the pronouncer of "absolute rift"), *October* has been responsible for constructing and developing — perhaps more than any other single publication — the most formidable methodological machinery available in contemporary art theory over the past four decades.[17] As Matthew Milliner has quipped, "In the intellectual climate of the art world, it's always October."[18]

13. James Elkins, "James Elkins Responds," *Books & Culture* 15, no. 3 (May-June 2009): 25.

14. Elkins, "James Elkins Responds," pp. 24-25. This is of course a dramatic simplification for rhetorical purposes; he handles this claim with more subtlety elsewhere: see James Elkins, *Master Narratives and Their Discontents* (New York: Routledge, 2005).

15. Elkins, "James Elkins Responds," p. 25.

16. Elkins, "James Elkins Responds," p. 25.

17. This was indeed the intention from the beginning: "*October*'s structure and policy are predicated upon a dominant concern: the renewal and strengthening of critical discourse through intensive review of the methodological options now available" (Jeremy Gilbert-Rolfe, Rosalind Krauss, and Annette Michelson, "About October," *October* 1 [Spring 1976]: 3).

18. Matthew Milliner, "A Tale of Two Art Worlds: October and Its Others," *The City* 3, no. 2 (Fall 2010): 5.

So, what are these critical methods that have so persuasively dominated the world of art writing? In 2004 (the same year that Elkins's book was published), *October*'s four most renowned contributing editors — Hal Foster, Rosalind Krauss, Yve-Alain Bois, and Benjamin Buchloh — published their two-volume *Art Since 1900*,[19] which opens with four introductory chapters devoted to articulating the primary critical methods that have framed the modern and contemporary art discourse. Four methods are identified and articulated in these chapters:[20]

(1) *Psychoanalysis:* systematically exegeting the unconscious energies, forces, and effects at play in the making and viewing of an artwork, specifically regarding the operation and repression of desire, fear, trauma, abjection — either at the individual or the collective level

(2) *[Marxian] Social Art History:* attending to the social, political, and economic power-structures framing, supporting, and functioning within the production and reception of an art object — particularly "within the field of ideological production under the rise of industrial capitalism"[21]

(3) *Formalism and Structuralism:* seeking to clarify the material structure of an artwork, both in terms of its formal construction and the semiotic functions of its forms (i.e., analyzing "significations apart from their content"[22])

(4) *Poststructuralism and Deconstruction:* addressing the invisible presuppositions and "institutional frames" that structure how an image or form is designated, discussed, and valued within a social system — for the purpose of exposing and challenging these frames

There are, of course, numerous other configurations and mobilizations of these models — feminist criticism, postcolonial criticism, and so on — but the im-

19. Hal Foster, Rosalind Krauss, Yve-Alain Bois, and Benjamin H. D. Buchloh, *Art since 1900: Modernism, Antimodernism, Postmodernism* (New York: Thames & Hudson, 2004).

20. These models are identified in the preface and in the titles of the introductory chapters, but it should be noted that all four authors comment in their chapters about the difficulty of concisely defining these theoretical models (and they generally avoid doing so), which have all become extremely complex and contested fields in themselves. The summaries given here are my own attempt at concision while allowing for a breadth of positions contained in each.

21. Foster et al., *Art since 1900: Modernism, Antimodernism, Postmodernism*, p. 22. Social art history isn't necessarily Marxian, though it generally functions as such in academic art theory, as it does for the *October* editors — for example, Foster simply refers to it as "Marxian social history" in the roundtable discussion at the end of volume two (p. 679).

22. Roland Barthes, quoted in Foster et al., *Art since 1900: Modernism, Antimodernism, Postmodernism*, p. 33.

plicit argument in *Art since 1900* is that these are the four primary threads from which "an increasingly complex weave of methodological eclecticism" is woven.[23]

Before returning to Elkins's argument, it's important to understand the ways these models work in art criticism, and why they have been such compelling devices in the construction of the canons of twentieth-century art history. In his introductory chapter, Buchloh contends that "all these models were initially formulated as attempts . . . to position the study of all types of cultural production (such as literature or the fine arts) on a more solidly scientific basis of method and insight" in order to "generate a verifiable understanding of the processes of aesthetic production and reception" and "anchor the 'meaning' of the work of art more solidly in the operations of either the conventions of language and/or the system of the unconscious."[24] In other words, the central task of these critical models is to engage the art object as a *cultural* artifact whose meanings are generated by and suspended within existing social, historical, and psychic systems that are *public* ("scientific" and "verifiable") rather than private, and materialist in the scope of their evidence base and explanatory appeal. This is a somewhat helpful explanation, but a more forthright genealogy of these methods might identify them as the mature children of Marx, Nietzsche, and Freud. These methods are the honed and developed "hermeneutics of suspicion."[25]

Central to each of these methods is a suspicion that artworks (and cultural activity in general) are operations of "ideology" — meanings in the service of power. Beneath and behind the surface appearance of any human activity, there is always a more basic (material) explanation — generally centered on either biology or social power — which these suspicious critical methods endeavor to unmask.

It's important to note that these critical methods weren't simply imposed upon modernist and contemporary art but arose along with it. A concrete example from the birth of modern art might help illustrate. Manet's famous

---

23. Foster et al., *Art since 1900: Modernism, Antimodernism, Postmodernism*, p. 22. Feminism, for example, plays prominently in Foster's chapter on psychoanalysis and Krauss's chapter on poststructuralism — and perhaps more than anything it simply is a form of social art history. As such, it isn't distinguished as a fifth critical model if it primarily implements and particularizes the other four methods (whereas it would be difficult to argue that it works the other way around).

24. Foster et al., *Art since 1900: Modernism, Antimodernism, Postmodernism*, p. 22.

25. See Paul Ricoeur, *Freud and Philosophy: An Essay on Interpretation*, trans. Denis Savage (New Haven: Yale University Press, 1970), pp. 32-36.

Luncheon on the Grass (1863) — widely considered one of the most significant early progenitors of avant-garde art — is at first a baffling and scandalizing painting: a starkly lit, seated nude woman stares out at the viewer from a rural picnic in which two fully-dressed male dandies blithely converse with each other about the woman. The landscape recedes towards a second woman wading knee-deep in a river in the background, but the space recedes quite awkwardly: the light logic and perspective are contradictory and inconsistent at multiple points, making it feel more like a collage of disparate scenes than a contiguous space. It's obvious from several passages in this painting (and from Manet's career as a whole) that Manet is a perfectly competent technician, but he has allowed so much incongruity into this work that it hardly hangs together as a whole. Efforts to make sense of the painting's subject matter, or even to admire its artistic construction, are stubbornly unproductive and frustrating — and all the more so given its large, self-aggrandizing scale. This is, by traditional standards, simply a failed painting; and it was rejected as such by the Salon jury of 1863.

However, everything begins to shift once we recognize that the painting's consistent effect is to draw unexpected attention to the *conventions* of representational painting itself: here we have a landscape painting, a nude, a still life, even a bather, all mashed into a large pictorial scale generally reserved only for the prestige and grand pronouncements of history painting. Manet has mingled all the normative devices of the French academy together such that the whole assembly collapses into a bizarre, conspicuously self-reflexive image. The painting sharply points to itself and to its own interpretive "frame" — the historical and social contexts in which it is situated and in which it will be understood. Thus, what is primarily on view here is not a lewd rural picnic (the subject matter seen "through" the medium) but the medium of painting itself and the social systems invisibly operating "around" or "beneath" or "behind" it to make it intelligible and grant it value.

One can see how paintings like this one (and the entire modernist project that would follow from it) focused extraordinary and unfamiliar pressures on interpreters of the work. Viewers who attempt to engage works like Manet's *Luncheon* through a traditional pictorial hermeneutic (passing through the medium to contemplate well-organized subject matter) are going to find themselves not only missing the point but, in fact, coming under its critique: *they are the dandies* staring at and disinterestedly discussing "the nude" who stares back at them from within the painted object. For many artists and critics, paintings like this cast doubts over the assumptions that governed traditional interpretive methods — doubts that would steadily swell over subsequent decades and would become compounded by the proliferation of mechanically reproduced photography. The early twentieth-century avant-garde extended Manet's strategies by increasingly foregrounding the materiality of the artistic medium and the conventions that governed the viewing of art objects. Indeed, in Robert Storr's words, the defining characteristic of such work is that it takes itself as its primary subject: "Before modernist art is about anything else — an image, a symbol, the communication of an experience — it is about the logic and structure of the thing that carries meaning, and about how that thing came into being."[26]

And thus we see why the alternative critical methods eventually outlined in *Art since 1900* (and hammered out in the pages of *October*) would develop and flourish: they are all means for rigorously interpreting an artwork from an "askance" point of view that self-consciously places both the work and our response to it under scrutiny.[27] These models operate on an intensely suspicious hermeneutic that deprioritizes artistic intentions, subject matter, and pictorial composition in exchange for the conspicuous disclosure of the *cultural situatedness* of the art object and the ideological systems at play behind and beneath "the processes of aesthetic production and reception."

Two observations need to be made here. First, it's important to note the ways these four models each (in their own ways) make claims on *all possible artworks* by virtue of the fact that artworks function in human culture in ways that are necessarily psychological, social, political, linguistic, and so on. None of these models will provide an exhaustive account of any given art object, or even the most important account, but they do each claim to account for at least one dimension of any possible art object. The psychoanalytic critic, for example, presupposes that the systems of the unconscious are operative in all human endeavors (art not least among them), and, accordingly, any artwork can legitimately be placed on an interpretive horizon — or is always already on this horizon — in which the orienting questions and points of reference are oriented toward understanding the role of unconscious systems in the production and reception of artworks. Similarly, the Marxist exegetes the axes of social and economic power running through

26. Robert Storr, *Modern Art despite Modernism* (New York: Museum of Modern Art, 2000), p. 28.

27. In fact, Johanne Lamoureux argues that "there has been no theory of avant-garde without a critical project. All discourses on the avant-garde acknowledge the central role of criticality, even if they do not agree on the object or target of that criticality" (Lamoureux, "Avant-garde: A Historiography of a Critical Concept," in *A Companion to Contemporary Art since 1945*, ed. Amelia Jones [Malden, Mass.: Blackwell, 2006], p. 207).

a work; the structuralist examines art objects as intrinsically formal and semiotic; the poststructuralist interrogates the power relations necessarily involved in signification; and so on.

Second — and here we're able to return to Elkins's thesis — one can see how these models would have precisely the effect of precluding serious religious thought from communicating with any kind of directness, clarity, or specificity. Not only is organized religion too much a part of the very social orders that the avant-garde was constructed to interrogate, but more profoundly — and I take this to be the central point of Elkins's book — religious content is unable to survive the suspicious interpretive operations of avant-garde theory and criticism. Subjecting, for example, a pictorial religious allegory to a psychoanalytic or Marxist or deconstructive reading will produce extremely disorienting effects for the devout allegorizer as the image is reappraised as an endless play of sublimated desire, social hierarchies, and institutional power. And such readings simply can't be counteracted with an appeal to an artist's (religious) intentions, because intentions, after all, are precisely what these critical models hold under suspicion. An artwork conceived as a "vehicle" for religious meaning will find itself interpretively derailed and destabilized before the vehicle even gets going — or, more commonly, it will simply be ignored as unworthy of serious engagement. And, interestingly, this dynamic doesn't only preclude religious subject matter: Elkins rightly devotes a chapter to articulating why art that has an *anti-religious* message to deliver is disqualified by the same principle.[28] Religious and anti-religious art alike — and really any work with a "message" to deliver — simply misunderstands and is ill-suited for the contemporary art discourse.

Elkins thus considers whether there might be more sophisticated, nondidactic ways for religious meaning to survive and operate in the context of contemporary art theory and criticism — though ultimately he remains ambivalent about all available options. He notes, for example, how often modern and postmodern art discourses construe aporias and failures in representation in terms of sublimity, a kind of sacredness that outstrips human capacities to cognitively and linguistically contain it. As such, he suggests that the "postmodern sublime has a history of functioning as a placeholder for otherwise unacceptable discourse about religion,"[29] in the sense that it provides "an opportunity for writers in the largely secular culture of the art world to speak

28. Elkins, "Brian's Story Explained: Art That Is Critical of Religion," *On the Strange Place of Religion in Contemporary Art*, pp. 65-75.

29. Elkins, "The Art Seminar," p. 165.

about concepts that used to be studied only by theologians."[30] More specifically, he situates these concepts in relation to the traditions of apophatic or "negative" theology, in which the ineffable Otherness of God is approached by way of negation and cancellation: speech about God that occurs most profoundly in the failure of speech.[31]

However, the problem in all of this, as he sees it, is that artworks and art writing that function in this way never really connote "religious" meaning with any kind of clarity or specificity. In reference to a work by Bill Viola, for instance, Elkins asks, "What, exactly, is religious about recordings of the ambient noise of cathedrals? It is a question no one quite knows how to answer."[32] And thus, in the face of this ambiguity, the most persuasive critical writing proceeds through the prevailing default methods without ever really confronting a work's "religious" questions with any great degree of specificity.

So, for Elkins, it is still unclear how religious content might be able to survive the critical operations of the *October* fourfold with any kind of theological particularity. Religiously oriented art seems to find itself in a double bind: either it speaks directly, at the risk of disqualification from the rubric of contemporary criticism, or it operates indirectly (self-critically) and risks self-negation. Thus Elkins concludes that "committed, engaged, ambitious, informed art does not mix with dedicated, serious, thoughtful, heartfelt religion. Wherever the two meet, one wrecks the other . . . either the art is loose and unambitious, or the religion is one-dimensional and unpersuasive."[33] And thus, as he remarks elsewhere, "The moral would be: find a source of doubt, become an unbeliever, and then come back and make art!"[34]

Religion might very well be reappearing in contemporary artworks in compelling and serious ways, but until there are rigorous critical methods for accounting for it, this reappearance will remain problematized — or simply functionally invisible. The problem is not simply a lack of religiously potent artworks but the lack of compelling, well-informed *interpretations* of artworks that are able to engage the theological significance of the work. Elkins thus believes that "the exclusion [of religion from contemporary art] is an effect of

30. Elkins, *On the Strange Place of Religion in Contemporary Art,* p. 96.

31. Elkins, *On the Strange Place of Religion in Contemporary Art,* pp. 82-113, especially p. 107. For a helpful study of negative theology, see Denys Turner, *The Darkness of God: Negativity in Christian Mysticism* (Cambridge: Cambridge University Press, 1995); see particularly page 20 for a definition similar to the one given here.

32. Elkins, *On the Strange Place of Religion in Contemporary Art,* p. 93.

33. Elkins, *On the Strange Place of Religion in Contemporary Art,* p. 115.

34. Elkins, "The Art Seminar," p. 162.

discourse," which will change only with "changes in the sum total of people who give us our best accounts of art."[35] And with that he leaves the rift open but re-marked as a space that religious critics should regard as working space.

The Return of Religion

So, what might it mean for religion to be "returning" to this discourse, which it appears to be doing? What does it look like for "religion" to provide questions, concerns, and points of reference for a critical engagement with contemporary art, and to do so within or in proximity to the prevailing critical models?

In the scholarly world, the most significant return of religion to contemporary art has been through the fields of religious studies and visual culture studies, which have over the past two decades begun to analyze the formative power of "material religion" or "religious visual culture" in the structure and direction of twentieth-century art. Scholars such as Sally Promey, David Morgan, S. Brent Plate, and others have shown that the available constructions of social art history have been truncated by their exclusion of religion from the study of art in a society deeply shaped by religious beliefs, histories, and institutions. Thus, in Promey's words, the aim of the return of religion in visual studies is "to recuperate a closer approximation to the historical whole, to include within scholarly purview the full range of practices that make images work."[36] This adjustment to the discourse of art history and criticism is not necessarily an adjustment to the critical methods employed; rather, it is an adjustment to the boundaries of what is allowed into the critic's interpretive evidence base and fields of reference.

Essentially, visual culture scholarship argues that religion must be accounted for in any sufficiently "thick" interpretation of the social significance of art. Inherited from anthropologist Clifford Geertz, the notion of a "thick description" of any given cultural object or phenomenon requires that one attend to and attempt to unpack the densely "stratified hierarchy of meaningful structures" in which the object or phenomenon has been "produced, perceived, and interpreted."[37] The production and reception of an artwork, for example, is always situated within (and thus meaningful in relation to) multiple social and

---

35. Elkins, "James Elkins Responds," p. 24.

36. Promey, "The 'Return' of Religion in the Scholarship of American Art," p. 589. See also Sally M. Promey, "Situating Visual Culture," in *A Companion to American Cultural History*, ed. Karen Halttunen (Malden, Mass.: Blackwell, 2008), pp. 279-94.

37. Clifford Geertz, *The Interpretation of Cultures: Selected Essays* (New York: Basic Books, 1973), pp. 6-10.

historical contexts, and our understanding of the work thus becomes increasingly "thick" as we carefully consider it in relation to these multiple contexts. This includes seeing the artwork as an object (or event) that is always already enwoven into systems of formal composition, language, personal and collective histories, various academic and popular canons, psychological affect, economics, politics, institutional power, societal norms, and so on. The rather modest contention of visual culture scholars is that religion has played, and continues to play, a formative role in the ways that objects and images are meaningful in this society; accordingly, any adequately *thick* interpretation of our artworks must also account for religious frames of reference.

This scholarship has been extremely valuable, offering persuasive re-readings of a variety of images and objects, ranging from religious kitsch to the canons of "high art." However, we must also note its limited scope: the questions that have animated these studies are organized almost entirely along historical, sociological, and ethnographic lines. In other words, the particular practices and theological commitments of the religions in question are taken seriously as sociocultural forces, but they generally aren't taken up as practices or beliefs that one would want to hold as a scholar interpreting an artwork.[38] A consistent "methodological naturalism" is protocol in this field, by which interpretation proceeds "with the detachment of the observer rather than the attachment of the adherent."[39] To borrow a metaphor from C. S. Lewis, visual culture scholars have begun carefully "looking at" the streams of religious thought running through twentieth-century visual culture, but they rarely consider it a viable option to really be "looking along" them.[40]

In many ways, this limitation has been productive. Religion certainly *is* a material, historical social phenomenon, always concretely embedded in the same "piled-up structures of inference and implication"[41] within which artistic artifacts are produced, perceived, and interpreted. And ushering religion

38. As David Morgan says, "There are scholars and writers who will make the journey [into the 'spiritual' content of an artwork] as scholars, not believers, but they study something not strictly defined as 'art' — the history of images, visual culture, religious artifacts, the ethnography of visual practice" (*Re-Enchantment,* ed. James Elkins and David Morgan, p. 18; cf. p. 168).

39. Gordon Graham, *The Re-Enchantment of the World: Art versus Religion* (Oxford: Oxford University Press, 2007), p. 53. And for him this detachment has had huge consequences: "Though firmly focused on religion because of a belief in its human significance, the science of religion also contributed importantly to disenchantment of the world."

40. C. S. Lewis, "Meditation in a Toolshed," originally published in *The Coventry Evening Telegraph* (17 July 1945); reprinted in *God in the Dock* (Grand Rapids: Wm. B. Eerdmans, 1970), pp. 212-15.

41. Geertz, *The Interpretation of Cultures,* p. 7.

back into visual studies in this way enables us to see both religion and art as thick practices that can be (or already are) situated along several of the same interpretive horizons — thus permitting interpretive moves in one to have potential "inference and implication" for the other.

However, we must also question whether there isn't still a remarkable interpretive thinness here, a reductive handling of religion that collapses its potential significance for art criticism. After all, the inclusion of religion into visual cultural criticism doesn't necessarily move us beyond or outside those interpretive axes already heavily theorized in the *October* models; it merely adjusts the range of social phenomena allowed into their interpretive field of vision. And it's precisely for this reason that Harry Philbrick can declare, "When religion is broached, it is within some other critical context: heaven as a sociological construct; Mary as a gender symbol; Jewishness as a cultural condition."[42]

And this perhaps brings us closer to the heart of the matter: it's not *religion* per se that is disallowed in the art discourse — it is *theology*. The "strange place of religion in contemporary art" is that religion appears viable for critical engagement only when stripped of theological depth. Visual culture has helpfully brought religion back into critical purview but has mainly done so by simply placing religion on (and confining it to) the interpretive axes of social art history. As a consequence, this development has relatively little impact on Elkins's thesis, simply requiring that his terms are reformulated a bit: When we speak about religion having no interpretive voice in contemporary criticism, what we are really referring to is the absence of a substantive *theological* voice in contemporary criticism. Religion has indeed reappeared throughout contemporary art, but there are not really any functional theological categories operating in contemporary art criticism with which to interpret its content in a theological register — or at least not with any rigor or rhetorical power.

A broader umbrella under which the discussion of religion and contemporary art has begun to operate — and one that may allow theological perspectives into the interpretative process — is the discourse of "re-enchantment." This phrase serves to loosely incorporate several threads of thought that challenge the finality of Max Weber's famous thesis about the "disenchantment" of the world via the forces of modernization.[43] There is much to like about

42. Harry Philbrick, "Creating Faith," in Christian Eckart et al., *Faith: The Impact of Judeo-Christian Religion on Art at the Millennium* (Ridgefield, Conn.: Aldrich Museum of Contemporary Art, 2000), p. 15.

43. Weber borrows the phrase from Schiller and further theorizes it: "The fate of our times is characterized by rationalization and intellectualization and, above all, by the 'disenchantment

the various kinds of scholarship associated with re-enchantment — it has, for example, helpfully critiqued the extent to which the *October* models have often assumed and relied upon a closed, disenchanted (deeply modernist) materialism. The difficulty of the re-enchantment dialogue, however, is a high level of theoretical generality and/or vague privatized spiritualism[44] that quickly dissolves conversation into confusion.[45] The term has, in fact, become so spacious and pliable as to accommodate contradictory usage from scholars as diametrically opposed as T. J. Clark and Suzi Gablik.[46]

The openness of this designation might serve to make space for the general readmission of "spirituality" or "transcendence" into the interpretive categories of contemporary art, but as art critic Joseph Masheck warns, these terms might be entirely too vague to really be constructive: "In the realm of sophisticated artistic commitment we may sometimes really want (need!) something more authentically religious — which probably entails more specifically religious — than the 'spiritually' one-size-fits-all."[47] Indeed, it seems that criticism interested in re-enchantment doesn't attain any particular interpretive grip on actual artworks until it gets religiously specific — or, more to the point, *theologically* specific: rooted in (and thus accountable to) a particular theological framework, grammar, and history.

---

of the world,'" in which we have come to believe that "there are no mysterious incalculable forces that come into play, but rather that one can, in principle, master all things by calculation" (Max Weber, "Science as a Vocation," in *From Max Weber: Essays in Sociology*, trans. and ed. H. H. Gerth and C. Wright Mills [New York: Oxford University Press, 1946], pp. 155, 139).

44. The various lines of thought about "spirituality" and "re-enchantment" in contemporary art have often been routed through Suzi Gablik's *The Re-Enchantment of Art* (New York: Thames & Hudson, 1991): "Re-Enchantment, as I understand it, means stepping beyond the modern traditions of mechanism, positivism, empiricism, rationalism, materialism, secularism, and scientism — the whole objectifying consciousness of the Enlightenment — in a way that allows for a return of soul" (p. 11). Gablik argues that this "return of soul" necessitates a "connective, participatory aesthetics," requiring "new myths" and "new forms emphasizing our essential interconnectedness rather than our separateness" (p. 9).

45. In 2007, James Elkins and David Morgan chaired a conference/publication in Routledge's "Art Seminar" series on the problem of religion and contemporary art, to which they assigned the multivalent title *Re-Enchantment* (New York: Routledge, 2009). The volume is lively and illuminating; but in the end, Morgan rightly summarizes it as "a noisy, meandering, unintegrated conversation that does not easily admit of resolution" but rather "disarray, even cacophony, which sometimes makes the conversation all but impossible" (p. 19).

46. James Elkins makes a similar point in *On the Strange Place of Religion in Contemporary Art*, p. 82, and in *Re-Enchantment*, p. 111.

47. Joseph Masheck, review of *On the Strange Place of Religion in Contemporary Art* by James Elkins, *Art & Christianity* 44 (October 2005): 13.

The Theological Axis

But this question remains: Should theology really be counted within the "stratified hierarchy of meaningful structures" necessary for adequately thick interpretations of contemporary artworks? How and in what cases should theology be accorded a place in art criticism?

Fundamental to anything properly called theology is the question of the relations of human persons, societies, and materiality itself to the presence or absence of God (or gods) — this is perhaps *the* theological question. And once this question is asked, it opens a theological horizon of meaning along which any facet of the world might be examined. Aquinas seems to have had something like this in mind when he defined theology as "a unified science in which all things are treated under the aspect of God."[48]

But we should note that in its barest form this interpretive horizon is kept open simply by the *question* of God's relationship to the world, not necessarily by affirmative answers to that question. In other words, we might take the term "theology" in its minimal sense to refer to that effort of interpretation that occurs wherever any given cultural entity is questioned in relation to any given understanding of God. In this sense, Mark C. Taylor's efforts to think about art through a postmodern "a/theology"[49] or Thierry de Duve's fascinating (and profoundly agnostic) meditation on the unending deferment of resurrection in Manet's *Christ with Angels*[50] are examples of theological interpretation within contemporary art criticism, albeit in forms oriented around divine "absence." My theology is structured differently than Taylor's or de Duve's, but we are each acknowledging the extent to which particular artworks are always already begging questions of world-in-relation-to-God and thus operating against some kind of theological horizon.

And it is the acknowledgment of this "some kind" of horizon that provides grounds for believing that the neglect of such questions in some sense diminishes the interpretive thickness of the art discourse. Such questions *are* live concerns throughout the art world, even if they are rarely critically engaged with much patience or rigor *as* the theological questions that they really are. In

48. Thomas Aquinas, *Summa Theologiae* 1.1.7.

49. See, for instance, Mark C. Taylor, *Refiguring the Spiritual: Beuys, Barney, Turrell, Goldsworthy* (New York: Cambridge University Press, 2012); *After God* (Chicago: University of Chicago Press, 2009); *Disfiguring: Art, Architecture, Religion* (Chicago: University of Chicago Press, 1992); and *Erring: A Postmodern A/Theology* (Chicago: University of Chicago Press, 1984).

50. Thierry de Duve, *Look: 100 Years of Contemporary Art*, trans. Simon Pleasance and Fronza Woods (Brussels: Palais des Beaux-Arts/Ludion, 2001), chap. 1.

this light, a critic who risks treating contemporary artworks "under the aspect of God" might do so for the sake of thickening the accounts of what is going on in the arts today. And the success of this enterprise would then rest on (1) its ability to open artworks into compelling and warranted interpretations that would otherwise be inaccessible, and (2) the capacity of these interpretations to in some way enrich the accounts of how an artwork is meaningful within a given cultural context. Thus, the premise for "theological art criticism" — if that's what it might be called — is that artworks are in some way already theologically meaningful and that our criticism thus benefits from — and is thicker because of — attending to this meaning.

But under what conditions might this actually be the case? There are three distinct situations that come to mind in which theologically oriented criticism may be more or less desirable, listed in order of increasing precariousness: (1) contemporary artwork that is making overt religious references in its form, subject matter, or title (whether the artist is personally religious or not); (2) artwork of any subject matter made by a person of religious faith; and (3) artwork specifically dealing with subjects of interest to a theological tradition (e.g., the human condition, the problem of suffering, and so on).

Artworks That Make Overt Religious References

Within this category I don't see that it makes much difference whether an artist is personally religious or not. If the work specifically draws from or alludes to subject matter that historically has been theologically charged, then the work has already placed itself on some kind of theological horizon and should be interpreted as such. Here's one example: in a 1999 exhibition, Los Angeles-based artist Tim Hawkinson exhibited (among other works) a room-sized sculptural installation entitled *Pentecost*. After reading many reviews of the exhibition, art critic John O'Brien noticed that in everything written about this work there was never more than a sparse half-sentence explanation given of the biblical reference — usually something along the lines of "named for the Bible story in which the 12 apostles 'spoke in tongues' "[51] — and the theological significance of the New Testament text to which it refers was ignored almost entirely.[52]

Regarding this kind of critical refusal, Elkins makes the obvious point:

51. Jeffrey Kastner, "Tim Hawkinson: Ace Gallery," *Sculpture* 18 (July/August 1999): 70.
52. John O'Brien, "The New Zeitgeist," *ArtScene* (May 2005).

"It does seem awkward to be unable to speak about the religious meaning of works that clearly have to do with religion."[53] Yes, indeed; but it's not only "awkward" — it's poor criticism. To be sure, Hawkinson's handling of this biblical subject is highly unconventional[54] and thus critically demanding, but it is also a deeply substantive handling and one that will simply be missed if there are no critics willing (or able) to consider the theological content of the biblical Pentecost in their considerations of Hawkinson's *Pentecost.*

And indeed, there are numerous major artists working today who have made artworks explicitly referencing religious subject matter — Francis Alÿs, El Anatsui, Robert Gober, Ann Hamilton, Damien Hirst, Anish Kapoor, Anselm Kiefer, Wolfgang Laib, Kris Martin, Sherin Neshat, Cornelia Parker, Kiki Smith, and Bill Viola, to name only a handful — and the absence of theologically informed criticism with regards to these theologically informed artworks has (quite obviously) resulted in truncated understandings of these works. Or, put the other way around, in cases where artists are engaging theological material (from whatever perspective or agenda and with whatever results), we should expect that the inclusion of theological reflection in the discourse would provide better — thicker — interpretations.

Artworks Made by Artists of Religious Faith

The example of Tim Hawkinson is of further use to us in this category in that Hawkinson professes a specifically Christian faith.[55] (He is one of the relatively few internationally acclaimed artists working today who does.) This creates something of a dilemma in the criticism done about his work: to what extent

---

53. Elkins, *On the Strange Place of Religion in Contemporary Art*, p. 22.

54. Hawkinson's *Pentecost* is a sprawling tree form constructed of air ducting and commonplace home-building materials. This "tree of life" is hollow, filled with air (or breath/wind), which conducts the rhythmic sounds of twelve humanoid figures, each drumming on the tree with a different mechanized body part. Though the rhythm of each individual is unremarkable, the collective sound of all twelve striking their respective branches creates complex rhythms that fill the tree and the gallery with a percussive glossolalia — a startling image of the Pentecost event.

55. Hawkinson is generally reluctant to discuss *how* his faith shapes his work (preferring to allow interpretations to remain open on multiple levels), but he has frankly said that his faith *does* shape his work: "I am a Christian, and I strive for a closeness with God and to find God in my life. I don't want to be dogmatic about it. I guess it just has a presence in my work because it's — you know, it's part of me" (*All Things Considered*, "Profile: Tim Hawkinson's Art with Moving Parts," National Public Radio [Washington, D.C.: 16 August 2005]).

does a thick understanding of his entire oeuvre — beyond works like *Pentecost* which have overt religious references — make demands on our abilities to encounter it in theological terms?

We need to be wary of placing unjustifiable weight on artistic intention (the artist's voice simply cannot preside with any final authority over the "piled-up structures of inference and implication" in which the work is produced, perceived, and interpreted as meaningful); but we also need to be wary of dismissing the artist entirely. Curator Howard Fox offers one example of attempts to actively restrain Hawkinson's work from theological specificity: "Though he frequently makes reference to Christian themes, his art is not sectarian or denominational. It is a secular expression of spirituality . . . his art openly courts a consideration of metaphysical and spiritual issues that might apply to almost any system of beliefs, and that especially resonate with basic tenets of Christianity."[56] While I understand the impulse to make Hawkinson's work amenable to any viewer who might be open to "spiritual issues" (whatever that might mean), this approach runs the risk of significantly evacuating the work. We do not make similar efforts to de-specify the political themes of artists like Hans Haacke or Kara Walker, for instance, such that their work "might apply to almost any system of [political] beliefs." Indeed, attempting to treat their work in this way would (rather viciously) compromise its conceptual integrity to such an extent that there would be nothing much left to work with. Interpretive thickness demands that we allow artistic intention some limited voice to prompt critical lines of questioning — which in Hawkinson's case necessitates theological questioning.

Artworks Dealing with Subjects or Concepts
That Are Theologically Significant

To stick with Hawkinson as an example, his work *Humongolous* (1995) is a careful meditation on phenomenological method and the constraints of self-understanding — and as such it addresses itself to large-scale questions of human being-in-the-world. In Hawkinson's case (and not only his), these are ultimately theological questions, inevitably begging the question of God. But if a critic were to unpack the theological significance of Hawkinson's phenomenology, then wouldn't it immediately open into dialogue with other major artists working on similar problems today? Consider Marina Abramović, Janine

---

56. Howard N. Fox, "Speaking in Tongues: The Art of Tim Hawkinson," in *Tim Hawkinson*, ed. Lawrence Rinder (New York: Whitney/LACMA, 2005), p. 31.

Antoni, Mireille Astore, Wafaa Bilal, Douglas Gordon, Terrence Koh, Bruce Nauman, Gabriel Orozco, Marc Quinn, Do-Ho Suh, and endlessly so on. Are similar theological questions alive in all of these, regardless of the presence or absence of overt theological concerns in the mind of these artists?

Theologian Kevin Vanhoozer would argue *yes*: "What is at stake both in cultural texts and in the process of their interpretation is the meaningful and the good, both of which are matters of universal human concern. All interpreters of culture work with some idea, however tacit, of what is or is not conducive to human flourishing" — and they are thus inevitably assuming and projecting some sort of "proposal about what it is to be human."[57] For Vanhoozer, any such proposal implies some kind of theological structure, which flings open the suggestion that artworks are in some way always already making tacit theological claims, whether intentionally or not. He wouldn't argue that identification of these claims would in any way exhaust the meaning of the work, or even provide the most important explanation of the work; he would argue only that "our understanding of what is happening in culture remains relatively thin to the extent that we fail to describe things at the theological level."[58] If this is indeed the case, then it seems impossible to pre-emptively close any artwork to theological questioning.

We must readily admit that the "visibility" of any axis of meaning is largely contingent upon an interpreter's commitment to the viability of particular frames of reference, and over the course of the past century the theological axis has become largely invisible and unviable in the writing of art history, theory, and criticism. And in the process theological art criticism has become and remains anemic and underdeveloped with regard to contemporary art, which makes it difficult to argue for its critical relevance. For now, we might simply allow for the modest possibility that the "human concerns" of contemporary art might also be theological concerns — and that entertaining this possibility might have some sort of beneficial thickening effect on the broader discourse. And, if we grant this, then the only responsibility that falls on non-religious critics is to be hospitable;[59] the far greater responsibility is for religious critics *to do better criticism*.

---

57. Kevin J. Vanhoozer, "What Is Everyday Theology?: How and Why Christians Should Read Culture," in *Everyday Theology: How to Read Cultural Texts and Interpret Trends*, ed. Kevin J. Vanhoozer, Charles A. Anderson, and Michael J. Sleasman (Grand Rapids: Baker Academic, 2007), pp. 40, 48.

58. Vanhoozer, "What Is Everyday Theology?," p. 47.

59. Elkins offers a striking example of this posture of hospitality. Though he does not locate himself within a particular religious tradition, he consistently engages artists and critics of faith in gracious and winsome ways — both in writing and in conversation.

Theological Art Criticism

It is at this point that we need to make some clarifications. First, I am not arguing for a theological interpretation of art *at the expense* of other interpretive levels. We must recognize that theological interpretations are extremely prone to being thin and reductive — perhaps more so than other models, and usually with more tragic results. Instead, what is being maintained here is that a properly thick understanding of art must at some level be open to theological reflection as one of its potentially significant dimensions. We want to avoid the tendency for theological commitments to pulverize artworks into an unacceptable thinness, but we also want to avoid the thinness that results from precluding those commitments altogether.

If this could be done, theological criticism would operate analogously to (and in conjunction with) the existing *October* models: it could not rightly claim an exhaustive interpretation or totalizing perspective but would instead aim at sensitively and creatively opening up what is already going on in an artwork from a theological frame of reference. And, given the scope of theological significance, this should be a truly collaborative endeavor with existing critical models that at the same time respects the integrity of these models. All the deliverances of Marxist or feminist critical methods, for instance, should be of great interest and support to the theological critic for whom the social, political, and economic power structures implicit in the production and reception of artworks are riddled with massive theological concerns. Theologies of social justice, human personhood, and so on are all at stake in contemporary art — and they are as such often in concert with (and certainly in relation to) the prevailing concerns of Marxist or feminist or deconstructive criticism. In short, working in a theological critical register should not lead one away from a common critical discourse or into soliloquys on utterly foreign or arcane topics; rather, the entire purpose of theological criticism is to deeply engage the primary issues, artifacts, and dynamics in contemporary art and art-writing but to do so out of theologically formed sensitivities and frames of reference.

Second, such criticism further compares to the *October* models in that it engages art objects with some level of suspicion. As with the workings of language or social power or the unconscious, the theological significance of an artwork is not restricted by authorial intention — in fact, the conscious intent of the artist might very well be contradicted or subverted by the theological implications of what she has made. As such, theological criticism might be interested in explanations (and critiques) that operate beneath or behind the face value of a work. This doesn't imply an unhinged "free play" of meaning

— criticism must always be derived from and accountable to evidence in the work itself — but it does imply that artworks are too densely (theologically) meaningful to be exhausted by the artist's own account.

Of course, opening the art discourse to theological methods of criticism will be an extremely noisy, untidy affair. On the one hand, there are many for whom the question of God is precisely the question that twentieth-century art did well to abandon; and on the other hand, once the question is posed, discussion immediately cascades into particular theological claims that are often divisive, abstruse, even unintelligible. And, further, because of the weakness of theological thinking about art for the past century, there are huge gaps to fill in order for such thinking to be both artistically and theologically rigorous.

Ultimately, however, such problems are intrinsic to all criticism. All art criticism is idiosyncratic, biased, and debatable — and is usually attempting to span across massive disciplinary divides (this is certainly true of the *October* models). Baudelaire believed that "to justify its existence, criticism should be partial, passionate, and political, that is to say, written from an exclusive point of view, but a point of view that opens up the widest horizons."[60] As far as I'm concerned, that well articulates the goal of theologically oriented criticism: to engage artworks within a particular frame of reference for the sake of opening up the widest and thickest interpretive horizons.

Some Notes on Method

Christian art historians and critics have begun to invest significant labor in writing about contemporary art over the past several years, and the quality of the work is getting better. But there continue to be many problems with the project of theological art criticism. One problem is the massive scale and range of interdisciplinary study necessary for such a project. To be proficient and well-informed in art history, theory, and criticism on the one hand and contemporary theology on the other is a massive task indeed, especially given the historical rift by which these disciplinary subcultures have developed their own languages, conceptual models, canonical texts, and histories quite independently from each other. Each of these fields has become increasingly specialized, and skillful interdisciplinary work between them threatens to be prohibitively demanding.

60. Charles Baudelaire, "What Good Is Criticism?" in *The Salon of 1846*, ed. David Kelly (Oxford: Oxford University Press, 1975), p. 44.

A second (perhaps more difficult) network of problems inhabits the ways we think about the nature of this interdisciplinary work. Not surprisingly, most of the writing on theology and the arts tends to prioritize the theological side of the relationship — to the extent that it really functions as theological aesthetics or theology of art more than as art criticism. Much of this work has been valuable, but the majority of it resides in worlds of academic theology and often doesn't adequately account for and make sense of contemporary art theory — and as such it rarely has much purchase in the interpretive categories of contemporary art criticism.

Dan Siedell rightly complains that Christian commentaries on the arts "rarely address modern art on its own terms, within its own framework of critical evaluation," but instead approach the work with "a rigidly stable 'Christian perspective' that is then merely applied to art."[61] This might have some virtues, but, stated bluntly, such approaches simply "do not produce art criticism,"[62] because they do not respect the integrity of the artworks or their position in the existing discourse. In some cases, this can be attributed to a deficient or outdated visual hermeneutic. (Some Christian critics default to a fairly traditional pictorial hermeneutic that is ill-equipped to read contemporary art.) But in most cases, the problem is that the interpretive agenda is so theologically overdetermined that it flattens artworks into shapes more conducive to the critical apparatus. At one extreme, we have examples of a combative critical posture that heavy-handedly reads almost the entirety of twentieth-century art as fearfully nihilistic. At the other extreme (and perhaps more common today), we see the tendency to uncritically read contemporary art as confirming (one's own) theological truths at nearly every turn. In arguing for the re-inclusion of theology to the discourse, we must be careful not to simply trade one reductionism for another.

Instead, good theological criticism starts from the rather modest claim that artworks inevitably have some sort of theological significance and can be scrutinized as such. Timothy Gorringe expresses it this way: "To read secular art theologically is to insist on questioning, on the dimension of depth, to resist premature attempts at the closure of meaning. It is to situate art within such a tradition of questioning and reflection."[63] And this questioning can't possibly be unidirectional: it can properly proceed only through a hermeneutic circling in which artworks and our interpretive frameworks mutually challenge and

61. Daniel A. Siedell, *God in the Gallery: A Christian Embrace of Modern Art* (Grand Rapids: Baker Academic, 2008), pp. 13-14.

62. Siedell, *God in the Gallery*, p. 14.

63. T. J. Gorringe, *Earthly Visions: Theology and the Challenges of Art* (New Haven: Yale University Press, 2011), p. 192.

shape one another. Theological thinking can indeed thicken our engagements with contemporary art by way of the questions, concerns, and concepts it brings to interpretive investigation, but this thickness is possible only as these are attuned to the artwork itself and to the disciplinary frameworks of contemporary art.[64] And, ultimately, the criteria for judging the success of such criticism *as criticism* is the extent to which it has weight and consequence within the existing art discourse.

So at this point we might try to make some adjustments. I want to identify "theological art criticism" as criticism that is (1) primarily concerned with providing careful, thick interpretations of contemporary artworks in ways that (2) compellingly account for and resonate within the existing contemporary art discourse, in the very act of (3) bringing theological questions, concerns, and positions to bear in its strivings to understand the work. Let me offer a few words about each component of this definition.

Careful, Receptive Prioritization of the Artwork Itself

Good criticism is rooted in the desire to genuinely encounter and more deeply understand an artwork. In proper criticism, said C. S. Lewis, "we seek an enlargement of our being."[65] And for such enlargement to be possible,

> We must not let loose our own subjectivity upon the pictures and make them its vehicles. We must begin by laying aside as completely as we can all our own preconceptions, interests, and associations. We must make room for Botticelli's Mars and Venus, or Cimabue's Crucifixion, by emptying out our own. . . . The first demand any art makes upon us is surrender. Look. Listen. Receive. Get yourself out of the way. (There is no good asking yourself first whether the work before you deserves such a surrender, for until you have surrendered you cannot possibly find out.)[66]

Such criticism demands risk, and it flourishes in open encounters in which we are committed to potentially ever-thickening meaning. "We must, and should,

---

64. Perhaps what is in view here is something analogous to the "creative mutual interaction" worked out by Robert John Russell in his interdisciplinary work in theology and science. See his *Cosmology: From Alpha to Omega* (Minneapolis: Fortress Press, 2008), pp. 1-32.

65. C. S. Lewis, *An Experiment in Criticism* (New York: Cambridge University Press, 1961; 13th printing: 2009), p. 137.

66. Lewis, *An Experiment in Criticism*, pp. 18-19.

remain uncertain," Lewis says. "Always, there may be something in it that we can't see. . . . The question could always without absurdity be re-opened."[67] The kind of theological criticism really worth doing is one thoroughly persuaded of the dense meaningfulness of human life and human art, which demand and reward sensitive and scrupulous searching.

As such, theological criticism must avoid its tendency to strong-arm artworks, "bending"[68] them toward Christian affirmations in ways that don't satisfyingly account for the works themselves. Such approaches generally have to bracket out (or simply disregard) much of the density and complexity of the works themselves, thus closing down and shrinking both the thickness of the works and our sensitivities to them.

Deeper Engagements with the Contemporary Art Discourse

If theological art criticism is going to be a live contributor to contemporary art criticism, then it must first and foremost be *contemporary art criticism*. This means that its primary discursive community is the art world, not the seminary: it must be primarily intelligible within (and structuring its arguments in) the grammar, logic, and concerns of contemporary art. To this end, we need more insightful, more rigorous understandings and critiques of twentieth-century and twenty-first-century art history, theory, and criticism. Elkins is quite right to suggest that serious thinking about art today must account for, and can be situated only in relation to, the established art narratives hammered out over the past decades. And thus, in Matthew Milliner's words, "Only serious historical and critical reflection can move us towards that possibility that Elkins tantalized us with: 'a change in the sum total of people who give us our best account of art.' "[69] In this, Milliner advises that the posture with which we

---

67. Lewis, *An Experiment in Criticism*, p. 137.

68. Siedell would be the first to decry heavy-handed "Christian art criticism" (and does so throughout *God in the Gallery*), but he also repeatedly refers to his own criticism as "bending" artworks toward Christ (e.g., p. 13). The possible virtue in thinking of criticism in this way is that it might subtly employ the Augustinian/Lutheran notion of sin as a disfiguring/curving of creatures away from God; and thus it could be argued that Siedell's bending is a "bending-back" — a re-aligning. However, that's a fairly subtle association; this muscular language more immediately connotes manipulation of artworks rather than a close reading of them. I prefer the language of reading along interpretive axes or horizons: we need not "bend" as much as more carefully attend to what is already in the work.

69. Milliner, "A Tale of Two Art Worlds," p. 17.

delve into this reflection not be defensive or combative but oriented toward genuine contribution:

> Instead of a rag-tag peasant uprising to take over the *October* Kingdom, Christians involved in the arts need to emerge from exile and become serious, independent landowners. The increasingly favorable place of religion in academia invites just such an emergence. [But] our inexhaustible aquifer of theological aesthetics means little without the up-to-date scholarly equipment that enables it to irrigate dry, barren historical land. Fruitful landowning would mean that instead of seeking the validation of *October,* we could offer them needed nourishment instead by generating what David Morgan calls the "produce of intellectual labor."[70]

Milliner, for his part, directly and helpfully engages *October,* carefully locating points of commonness as well as "the destabilizing theological touchpoints within *October,*" which are "a permanent part of the journal's history that Christians should feel willing to engage."[71] He reads *October* as laced with theological claims and norms throughout, which Christians should (winsomely and generously) unpack and critically develop. This demands wisdom, patience, and dexterity — and some attentively suspicious re-reading of the contemporary art canons.

Doing Theology in Other Registers

Serious theological art criticism will be serious interdisciplinary scholarship, seeking theological understanding within other disciplines and critical methods. And that's an awfully tall order, not least because it is theologically demanding. Navigating the possibilities and pitfalls of theological discourse simultaneously with those of contemporary art is extremely difficult, and the strain of this task often causes religious criticism to default to strategies of

70. Milliner, "A Tale of Two Art Worlds," p. 17.

71. Milliner, "A Tale of Two Art Worlds," p. 17. Milliner identifies at least four of these "touchpoints" in *October:* (1) it offers a *necessary critique* of modern art/theory, (2) it offers unforeseen *epistemological possibilities* in its "epistemology of the miraculous" (his argument here remains unclear), (3) it sometimes delivers — unknowingly and in spite of itself — *concepts consistent with Christian theological norms* (e.g., Steinberg's fully sexualized yet chaste Christ), and (4) it often implicitly relies on and overlaps with *traditional Christian sources* (e.g., Fried's quotation of Jonathan Edwards).

collating superficial similarities between points of doctrine and contemporary artworks. It is an unfortunate commonplace, for example, to see the Incarnation thinned out to the point where one might generically christen almost any artistic action "an incarnational approach which embodies the immaterial in the material" (to borrow a line from one Christian critic). Similar maneuvers routinely deflate (in order to collate) the Resurrection, the Eucharist, and so on. This strategy is understandable, given the relative lack of serious theological thinking about contemporary art, but it makes for fairly unsatisfying interpretation.

Instead, the kind of theological rigor we are after here is that which takes shape precisely within the cultural-historical particularity of what is going on in the arts today. Christian critics need to have clarity and professional seriousness about the extent to which their theological thinking must be alive in today's conversations, precisely inside the interpretive pressures and problems that frame today's art discourse. This demands theological understanding that is both deeper and also more agile and *improvisational*.

On this point, Kevin Vanhoozer has been helpful in articulating the practice of theology in terms of "creative fidelity." He believes that "the ultimate goal of theology is to foster creative understanding — the ability to improvise what to say and do as disciples of Jesus Christ in ways that are at once faithful yet fitting to their subject matter and setting."[72] In that sense, theology that is lived *in* a contemporary art museum will necessarily be "spontaneous" and highly responsive in the way that it makes sense of *this* artwork in light of *this* history/context. But this is not to imply carelessness or whim; as Vanhoozer points out, "Spontaneity instead describes the state of an actor's readiness: one's preparedness to fit in and contribute to whatever starts to happen. Such readiness, far from being a native reflex, is actually the result of years of disciplined preparation."[73] To improvise extremely well in any given discipline — consider the best examples from music, sports, debate, comedy, and so on — is possible only through deep immersion into the practices, models, and histories of that discipline.

In my estimation, the project of theological art criticism can successfully function only when it has a strong sense of its own improvisational character. It must be deeply apprenticed to the disciplines of both theology and contemporary art, but it must do so in full recognition that the real work to be done is

---

72. Kevin J. Vanhoozer, *The Drama of Doctrine: A Canonical-Linguistic Approach to Christian Theology* (Louisville: Westminster John Knox Press, 2005), p. 32.

73. Vanhoozer, *The Drama of Doctrine*, p. 338.

unscripted and will necessitate extremely creative solutions. This recognition is important, because (1) it reframes questions of method into more holistic questions of scholarly *posture* (posture determines one's "field of vision" and potential "range of motion"), and (2) it helps clarify that the preparation and apprenticeship necessary here are a matter not only of theoretical knowledge but of performative *skill* (there are pedagogical implications here). Contemporary art criticism is by definition an ongoing, ever-evolving conversation, eager for whatever future contributions that can freshly address, account for, and challenge its disciplinary traditions within our historical context. The task of Christian critics will be to more fully enter that conversation and to improvise compelling understandings of and contributions to it.

The value of an essay such as this — and a volume such as this — is to set aside time for reflection about what it is we're trying to do, and in what context. For better or worse, however, this essay limits itself to theory; what we desperately need today are excellent examples of theologically rich art criticism.

Steering a Course between Fundamentalism and Transformationalism: J. Gresham Machen's View of Christian Scholarship

Dariusz M. Brytko

Christian religion flourishes not in the darkness but in the light. Intellectual slothfulness is but a quack remedy for unbelief; the true remedy is consecration of intellectual powers to the service of the Lord Jesus Christ.[1]

J. Gresham Machen did not present his views on Christian scholarship in a systematic manner, and therefore analyzing his philosophy of education can at times be challenging — yet it is not impossible. Machen extensively addressed education, and his opinions on scholarship are spread throughout his speeches, essays, books, and book reviews. We also possess a transcript of Machen's testimony before the U.S. Congress against the act proposed to form the U.S. Department of Education.[2] In the midst of the current discussion

---

1. J. Gresham Machen, "Christian Scholarship and the Defense of Faith," in *J. Gresham Machen: Selected Shorter Writings*, ed. D. G. Hart (Phillipsburg, N.J.: P&R Publishing Co., 2004), p. 152.

2. For a complete bibliography of Machen's writings, please see *Pressing toward the Mark: Essays Commemorating Fifty Years of the Orthodox Presbyterian Church,* ed. Charles G. Dennison and Richard C. Gamble (Philadelphia: Committee for the Historian of the OPC,

The research for this essay was made possible thanks to generous support from the Center for Christian Thought at Biola University, where I spent the spring semester of 2012. The essay in a slightly different form was delivered at Biola University on 19 May 2010 and later reviewed and published (in two parts) in the *Ordained Servant Online* (November and December 2012 issues) in the form in which it appears here.

about the nature of Christian scholarship and education, and on the seventy-fifth anniversary of Machen's death, I would like to reflect on his educational writings and what I have come to call his "militant view of Christian scholarship," which may perhaps serve as a middle way between those who question the idea of Christian education and those who see a direct biblical imperative for it.[3] Further, Machen has been credited with fostering a renaissance of academic pursuits among fundamentalists and conservative evangelicals in America (both free and confessional) from his day until the advent of Dutch Neo-Kuyperianism (sometime in the 1960s), and it seems worthwhile to revisit his writings in light of the current spiritual and academic identity crisis of American Christian scholarship.[4]

George Marsden, in his book *Understanding Fundamentalism and Evangelicalism*, argues that most early opponents of liberalism who became leaders in the fundamentalist and (later) evangelical movements were in some way connected to Machen.[5] The list of familiar people and institutions that Machen directly influenced is long, so let us mention just a few, such as Harold Ockenga, the founder of Fuller and Gordon-Conwell Theological Seminaries as well as *Christianity Today* magazine, and pastor of the historic Park Street Church in downtown Boston; Carl McIntire, the popular broadcaster and founder of the Bible Presbyterian Church; Francis Schaeffer, the well-known Christian intellectual whose L'Abri community in the Swiss Alps became an intellectual refuge for European evangelicals;[6] and Samuel Sutherland, the president of the Bible Institute of Los Angeles, under whom the institute founded and accredited Talbot Seminary.[7] Further, Cedarville and Bryan Colleges both offered their presidencies to

---

1986). My appreciation goes to D. G. Hart and John Muether, who pointed me to some helpful sources.

3. I am referring here to the recent exchange in *Ordained Servant Online* between David C. Noe and Benjamin W. Miller as well as to the current debate between the Two-Kingdoms and Kuyperian camps. See also William D. Dennison, "Is Classical Christian Education Truly Christian? Cornelius Van Til and Classical Christian Education," in *Essays Commemorating Seventy-Five Years of the Orthodox Presbyterian Church*, ed. John R. Muether and Danny E. Olinger (Willow Grove, Pa.: Committee for the Historian of the OPC, 2011), pp. 101-25.

4. George M. Marsden, *Understanding Fundamentalism and Evangelicalism* (Grand Rapids: Wm. B. Eerdmans, 1991), p. 149.

5. Marsden, *Understanding Fundamentalism and Evangelicalism*, p. 149.

6. Marsden, *Understanding Fundamentalism and Evangelicalism*, p. 183.

7. Biola in its early days hired conservative Presbyterians (such as Paul Aijian, Dean Nauman, and Vernon McGee) who taught at Talbot and who in the mid-1950s were challenged by the Los Angeles Presbytery of the Presbyterian Church USA to dissolve their relationship with the school because its "spirit, doctrinal position, and program" were different from the Presbyterian

Machen, Columbia Theological Seminary and Southern Presbyterian Seminary offered him New Testament professorships, and Canada's Knox College asked him to be its principal.[8] Also, Machen was one of the main founders of Westminster Theological Seminary in Philadelphia, which came into existence not only due to his initiative but also due to his family fortune. Finally, if we add that the National Association of Evangelicals (NAE) and Moody Bible Institute asked Machen to speak at public events and zealously sought his support, it seems safe to say that the renaissance of academic pursuits among conservative evangelicals through the 1960s could, in large measure, be credited to Machen.

When it comes to the secondary literature, we have a few biographies of Machen and other helpful sources dealing with his theology. However, Machen's philosophy of education has received only minimal treatment and is a topic that deserves further attention.[9]

Perhaps the most insightful analysis of Machen's views of science can be found in D. G. Hart's book *Defending the Faith: J. Gresham Machen and the Crisis of Conservative Protestantism in Modern America,* which I will later bring into our discussion. We also will find George Marsden's earlier analysis helpful, as he offers insights on Machen's Southern influences and his use of common-sense realism. Marsden traces the decline of Machen's popular-

---

stance. In response to this, Samuel Sutherland wrote an article in which he quotes extensively from the Westminster Confession, showing how the Bible Institute of Los Angeles was more faithful to historic Presbyterianism than the mainline Presbyterians were. He writes, "Shades of John Calvin, John Knox, John Witherspoon, and a great host of other theological spiritual giants of former generations! These men held the same doctrines which were enunciated in the great Westminster Confession of Faith . . . which has stood as a mighty confession of faith through the centuries as it bred and fed spiritual giants!" See Samuel Sutherland, "Modernism and Los Angeles Presbytery," *King's Business* 45, no. 9 (September 1954): 14-17. I am thankful to Dr. Fred Sanders of Biola's Torrey Honors Institute for his assistance in finding these materials.

8. D. G. Hart, *Defending the Faith: J. Gresham Machen and the Crisis of Conservative Protestantism in Modern America* (Grand Rapids: Baker, 1994), p. 105.

9. Carl Trueman, foreword to J. Gresham Machen, *Christianity and Liberalism,* new edition (Grand Rapids: Wm. B. Eerdmans, 2009), pp. ix-xv; Stephen J. Nichols, *J. Gresham Machen: A Guided Tour of His Life and Thought* (Phillipsburg, N.J.: P&R Publishing Co., 2004); Terry Chrishope, *Toward a Sure Faith: J. Gresham Machen and the Dilemma of Biblical Criticism, 1881-1915* (Fearn Ross-shire, U.K.: Christian Focus, 2001); Coray W. Henry, *J. Gresham Machen* (Grand Rapids: Kregel, 1981); Allyn C. Russell, *Voices of Fundamentalism: Seven Biographical Studies* (Philadelphia: Westminster Press, 1976); Ned B. Stonehouse, *J. Gresham Machen: A Biographical Memoir* (Grand Rapids: Wm. B. Eerdmans, 1954); Paul Woolley, *The Significance of J. Gresham Machen Today* (Phillipsburg, N.J.: P&R Publishing Co., 1977). See also George M. Marsden, *The Outrageous Idea of Christian Scholarship* (New York: Oxford University Press, 1997), and Mark A. Noll, *The Scandal of the Evangelical Mind* (Grand Rapids: Wm. B. Eerdmans, 1994).

ity among evangelicals to two causes. The first was the early 1960s critique made by the president of Fuller Theological Seminary, Edward J. Carnell, that Machen lacked vision and greater involvement with non-Presbyterians. The second cause Marsden gives for Machen's declining popularity was the growing influence of the nineteenth-century Dutch Reformed perspective embodied in the writings of Abraham Kuyper.[10]

What Makes Scholarship Intellectual?

Machen has often been labeled a fundamentalist — and in many ways he was, as he shared the majority of his doctrinal convictions with those who, early on, represented the fundamentalist camp and expressed their views in the *Fundamentals of Faith,* a set of ninety essays that the Bible Institute of Los Angeles published in twelve volumes between 1910 and 1915.[11] Machen also was a major source of inspiration and intellectual ammunition for the fundamentalist and later neo-evangelical camp in its struggle against liberal efforts to redefine the historic Christian faith.[12]

However, there were some differences between Machen and the fundamentalists. First of all, Machen had had an elite education. A graduate of Johns

---

10. "Yet Machen remained controversial, and even many evangelical scholars repudiated his heritage. The most notorious example came in 1959 when Edward J. Carnell, president of Fuller Theological Seminary, devoted a chapter in his volume *The Case for Orthodox Theology* to the 'cultic mentality' of Machen. Repudiations of Machen's narrowness have been frequent since then. Almost all evangelical scholars who are not strictly Reformed have found his Presbyterian confessionalism too narrow, and even many of the strictly Reformed have rejected his Princetonian apologetics for Kuyperian models, or have been unhappy with his insistence on ecclesiastical separatism." See Marsden, *Understanding Fundamentalism and Evangelicalism,* p. 184. For more, see George Marsden, *Reforming Fundamentalism: Fuller Seminary and the New Evangelicalism* (Grand Rapids: Wm. B. Eerdmans, 1987), pp. 188-92.

11. See also Annette G. Aubert, "J. Gresham Machen and the Theology of Crisis," *Westminster Theological Journal* 64 (2002): 337-62. Aubert carefully argues that Machen's critical yet careful response to Barth set him apart from the anti-intellectual fundamentalist response. She writes, "The basic point for Machen was that one needs to possess knowledge about a subject in order to point to its errors. This was a general principle that Machen applied in his own approach to liberal scholarship" (p. 341).

12. Machen's *Christianity and Liberalism* became one of the main tools of defense against liberal attacks on fundamentalists. See George Marsden, *Religion and American Culture* (Belmont, Calif.: Thomson, 2001), p. 193. However, as D. G. Hart notes, Machen's book was written mostly for a Presbyterian (not fundamentalist) audience, and thus its fullest application could never be realized among non-Reformed ecclesiastical bodies (Hart, *Defending the Faith,* p. 65).

Hopkins University, the University of Chicago, and Princeton, Machen also pursued foreign studies at Marburg, Germany, under Wilhelm Herrmann, with whom Karl Barth and Rudolf Bultmann also trained.[13] Politically, Machen was a Democrat with a strong libertarian bent. He stood against the religious mainstream of his day by opposing prohibition, opposing prayer and Bible teaching in public schools, and even openly promoting the rights of non-Protestant religious minorities and sects.[14] Culturally, Machen was a Southern gentleman, coming from the upper Baltimore elites with high family connections, including the president of the United States, a close friend of the Machen family.[15]

Thus, Machen's Ivy League education, almost aristocratic background, and uncommon political views set him apart most from the fundamentalists. Beyond that, the growing anti-intellectualism and non-confessionalism of the fundamentalist camp were what kept him from fully identifying with the movement. This is well-illustrated by the fact that in 1927 Machen politely declined to become the president of the nondenominational university named for William Jennings Bryan, the prosecutor in the famous Scopes "monkey trial." In his letter declining the offer, Machen wrote,

> I never call myself a "fundamentalist." There is indeed no inherent objection to the term; and if the disjunction is between Fundamentalism and Modernism, then I am willing to call myself a fundamentalist of the most pronounced type. But after all, what I prefer to call myself is not a "fundamentalist" but a "Calvinist" — that is, an adherent of the Reformed Faith.[16]

There are numerous reasons why Machen declined this particular offer, and these are better understood in the context of the entire letter. But it is ap-

---

13. Nichols, *J. Gresham Machen*, pp. 32-33.

14. For the scope of this discussion, we will concentrate only on some of those differences; however, it is worth mentioning the following: Machen refuted the church's direct involvement in politics, did not join the Prohibition movement or the anti-evolution crusade, felt uneasy with the emotion-driven religion of the revivalists, argued against teaching Bible and prayer in public secular schools, supported the rights (free speech) of Mormons, Jews, and other religions for the full exercise of their religion, and was sympathetic to the fundamentalists in their common goal to preserve orthodox Christianity. He was a libertarian who opposed child labor legislation, national parks (but not preservation of nature), and Philadelphia's ordinance against jaywalking. See Marsden, *Understanding Fundamentalism and Evangelicalism*, p. 184.

15. See Katherine Lynn Tan Vandrunen, "The Foothills of the Matterhorn: Familial Antecedents of J. Gresham Machen," Ph.D. diss., Loyola University, 2006.

16. "Dr. Machen Declines the Presidency of Bryan University," reprinted in *Moody Bible Institute Monthly* 28 (September 1927): 16.

parent from the quoted text that, when asked to lead a nondenominational, fundamentalist university, Machen made it clear that he preferred to be identified with *a particular Protestant confession*. We should not underestimate this point when seeking to understand Machen's approach; however, for present purposes, we will not delve into Machen's ecclesiological and confessional stands, as they are less essential to his views on Christian education (which go beyond Presbyterian and Reformed identity). Here I would like to emphasize that Machen turned down a chance to preside over an institution so closely associated with the Scopes Trial.

Machen knew William Jennings Bryan, and Bryan personally asked him to testify at the trial, but Machen withheld his support from a cause that did not seem essential in the battle against liberalism. D. G. Hart argues that this act showed Machen to be committed to the university world and confirmed his stand against anyone who would separate Christianity from science, even fellow believers. For Machen, the dialogue about faith and science was essential to refuting the liberals and thus to preserving the historic Christian faith, because science has the ability to verify that the Christian faith is based on historical facts, confirming the truthfulness of Christianity. In Machen's view, the "trueness" of the Christian religion was deeply rooted in actual, historically verifiable events, and in this sense theology as a science was not different from any other scientific inquiry; after all, both theology and chemistry are concerned with the "acquisition and orderly arrangement of truth."[17] Thus, using biblical interpretation to disqualify the claims of science was, to Machen, unacceptable. That being said, I note here that Machen was not arguing that true faith in God could be acquired through and/or limited simply to an intellectual argument or assent. For Machen as for other conservative Presbyterians, faith ultimately comes only by the mysterious and creative power of the Holy Spirit enabling one to trust in Christ's atoning work and follow his commands.[18]

It was the fundamentalists' insistence on literal six-day creation that alarmed Machen the most — not because they held to this interpretation personally, but rather because they turned it into the litmus test for proving one's Christian orthodoxy. In Machen's view, this position hurt the Christian cause because it minimized the significance of the Fundamentals of Faith, which included Christ's divinity, the Second Coming, the virgin birth, the bodily

---

17. J. Gresham Machen, "What Fundamentalism Stands for Now," in *J. Gresham Machen: Selected Shorter Writings*, p. 118.

18. Machen, "Christian Scholarship and the Defense of the Faith," in *J. Gresham Machen: Selected Shorter Writings*, p. 144.

resurrection of Christ, the infallibility of the Bible, and the historical reality of miracles. Machen felt that fundamentalists had a low view of natural revelation, and left no room for academic discussion about the findings of science and how they could relate to biblical interpretation. To be sure, Machen saw the dangers of naturalistic evolutionism, but he also believed that science must have an important voice in the discussion even if it cannot be treated on an equal basis with biblical revelation.[19]

The anti-intellectualism of fundamentalists also became evident to Machen through their emphasis on a personal experience of salvation, suggesting that spiritual intimacy and subjective experience somehow carried superior value to the knowledge acquired through toilsome study of the Bible, original languages, and theology. Machen was convinced that religion without science would lead to superstition or false religion based on feelings and emotions — the very definition of religion that liberals tried to advocate. Against revivalism and pietism, Machen argued that education and knowledge were necessary for effective preaching because religion is primarily doctrine-oriented, and experience must follow — never the other way around. He wrote,

> Men are not saved by the exhibition of our glorious Christian virtues; they are not saved by the contagion of our experiences. We cannot be the instruments of God in saving them if we preach to them thus only ourselves. No, we must preach to them the Lord Jesus Christ, for it is only through the gospel which sets him forth that they can be saved.[20]

Because faith consists of trust, Machen rejected the so-called simple faith proclaimed by some revivalist preachers, for it is impossible to *trust* someone unless we first determine whether he is trustworthy. In Machen's view, we must possess knowledge to have true faith in Christ. He wrote, "What these advocates of a 'simple faith' which involves no knowledge of Christ really mean by 'simple faith' is faith, perhaps; but it is not faith in Christ. It is faith in the practitioners of the method."[21] Machen worried that many conversions that take place upon so-called simple faith are nothing more than a psychological

19. According to D. G. Hart, "Machen tried to construct a mediating position that subordinated the naturalism of liberal Protestantism to the supernaturalism of fundamentalism but still kept the two ideas together" (*Defending the Faith*, pp. 104-5).

20. Machen, "Christian Scholarship and Evangelism," in *J. Gresham Machen: Selected Shorter Writings*, p. 141.

21. Machen, "Christian Scholarship and Evangelism," in *J. Gresham Machen: Selected Shorter Writings*, p. 138.

manipulation. He contrasted these false conversions to biblical examples of true conversions, which always contain a doctrinal element. He recalled Peter's sermon at Pentecost, which included facts about Christ and not just an account of Peter's own personal experience; the conversion of the jailer in Philippi, where Paul and Silas preached to him the "word of the Lord"; and the words of Jesus when he addressed the theological inquiry of the Samaritan woman about the proper place of worship.

It is important to note here that although Machen was a proponent of highly educated clergy, he did *not* argue that all evangelists must necessarily be scholars. However, at the same time, he maintained that "evangelists who are not scholars are dependent upon scholars to help them get their message straight,"[22] and that the most powerful evangelism in the history of the church has been done by scholars.

Machen refused to overlook the anti-intellectualism of the fundamentalists with whom he shared so much in common because he was convinced that it would hurt the movement, leading to the decline of theology and the spread of populism in Christian faith and practice.[23] Moreover, as surprising as it may at first sound, anti-intellectualism was one of his main critiques of *liberalism* as well, so to tolerate it among fundamentalists would not be fair. Granted, the liberal expression of anti-intellectualism was different; nevertheless, Machen could not ignore that fact that both the fundamentalists and the liberals were guilty of it.

Machen criticized liberal theologians for abandoning the grammatical-historical method of biblical interpretation, allowing the Bible to become an ineffectual and useless book, a collection of inspirational stories describing various human emotions. For Machen, Christianity was either based on historical facts or it was philosophically bankrupt, perhaps able to sustain moral living for a while but not the gospel.[24] He once wrote that "a gospel independent of history is simply a contradiction of terms"[25] and that "the foundation of the church is either inexplicable, or else it is to be explained by the resurrection of Jesus Christ from the dead. But if the resurrection is accepted, then the lofty claims of Jesus are substantiated; Jesus was then no mere man, but God and man, God come in the flesh."[26]

---

22. Machen, "Christian Scholarship and Evangelism," in *J. Gresham Machen: Selected Shorter Writings,* p. 141.

23. Hart, *Defending the Faith,* p. 95.

24. Aubert, "J. Gresham Machen and the Theology of Crisis," p. 346.

25. Machen, "History and Faith," in *J. Gresham Machen: Selected Shorter Writings,* p. 105.

26. Machen, "History and Faith," in *J. Gresham Machen: Selected Shorter Writings,* p. 105.

Further, Machen argued that modernists degraded science by excluding from it the sphere of religion. This separation of reason from faith led to decadence in the academic community, producing a "horrible Frankenstein"[27] whose knowledge and skill hurt humanity. Machen wrote,

> I think we can say that science alone, unless something else goes with science, is bound by an inexorable logic to result just exactly in that decadence which so distresses. . . . In fact, science has served to improve enormously the technique of tyranny in our days as over against the cruder tyrannies of fire and sword which reigned in the past. It is in accordance with an inexorable logic that Hitler is practicing fiendish wickedness in Germany today in the name of science. . . . The fact ought to be perfectly clear to every thoughtful observer that humanity is standing over an abyss. When I say humanity, I include America; indeed, I am thinking particularly of America. Russia and Germany are already in the abyss. But how shall it be with our country?[28]

If we consider that Machen wrote these words before the Second World War, we have reason to stand astonished by his prophetic voice.

The anti-intellectualism of the liberals also became evident to Machen through their widespread acceptance of the modern pedagogical method. Machen observed that liberals were preoccupied with the "method of study" and emphasized practical rather than theoretical knowledge. This issue surfaced during his disputes with Charles Erdman, professor of practical theology at Princeton Seminary. Erdman, supported by the new president of Princeton, J. Ross Stevenson, advocated a curriculum that downplayed the study of biblical languages and reduced core biblical and theological courses for the sake of practical electives, with strong emphasis on pastoral care and spiritual formation. Machen strongly opposed this reform, lamenting that the seminary would not produce "specialists in the Bible" but rather congregational CEOs (if we were to use the contemporary term).[29]

For Machen, the modern pedagogical obsession with the method of acquiring knowledge instead of the knowledge itself was defeating the very

27. Machen, "The Necessity of the Christian School," in *J. Gresham Machen: Selected Shorter Writings*, p. 168.

28. Machen, "The Christian School: Hope of America," in *Education, Christianity, and the State*, ed. John W. Robbins (Jefferson, Md.: Trinity Foundation, 1994), pp. 135, 136.

29. Machen, "The Minister and His Greek Testament," in *J. Gresham Machen: Selected Shorter Writings*, p. 211.

purpose of education. He wrote, "The modern conception of the purpose of education is that education is merely intended to enable a man to live, but not to give him those things that make life worth living."[30] Also, the main role of the academic instructor was no longer the transmission of knowledge; it had been reduced to the "developing of the faculty of the mind." All of this, Machen ironically concluded, led modern educators to a great discovery: that it is "possible to think with a completely empty mind."[31] This pursuit would lead American education to complete disaster, Machen argued, where shameful superficiality and ignorance of the most basic facts about the world would become a new norm. He wrote,

> We shall never have a true revival of learning until teachers turn their attention away from the mere mental processes of the child, out into marvelous richness and variety of the universe and of human life. Not teachers who have studied the methodology of teaching but teachers who are on fire with a love of the subjects that they are going to teach are the real torchbearers of the intellectual advance.[32]

Unfortunately, this pedagogical anti-intellectualism is something Machen also observed among fundamentalists, whose Bible colleges and institutes often sought quick and practical education for the sake of evangelism and mission work or spiritual formation, rather than training reflective and critically thinking graduates. This deeper training was something he desired to achieve with the newly founded Westminster Theological Seminary in Philadelphia.

What Makes Education Christian?

Presbyterians in America were not always strong advocates of distinctly Christian education, and in many cases were comfortable supporting public and private schools that did not possess explicit Christian identity. This was not the case with the Dutch Reformed churches, which much earlier came to advocate distinctly Christian education. In large measure, the growth of

30. Machen, "The Minister and His Greek Testament," in *J. Gresham Machen: Selected Shorter Writings*, p. 211.
31. Machen, "Christian Scholarship and Evangelism," in *J. Gresham Machen: Selected Shorter Writings*, p. 135.
32. Machen, "Christian Scholarship and Evangelism," in *J. Gresham Machen: Selected Shorter Writings*, p. 137.

Christian scholarship among the Dutch is credited to Abraham Kuyper, the renowned Reformed theologian and politician who, in 1901, became prime minister of the Netherlands. Politically, Kuyper introduced a new model of society in which various religious and social groups enjoyed separate yet equal spheres of sovereignty.[33] This political system enabled the Dutch Reformed to develop a network of Christian schools, including the well-known Vrije Universitet in Amsterdam. Unfortunately, in the aftermath of the Second World War, Kuyper's political model fell out of grace, as Dutch society perceived it as highly divisive. Despite this setback, the Dutch Reformed continued to promote Christian education, supplying powerful theological justification for it. Further, many followers of Kuyper immigrated and became some of the most outspoken supporters of Christian scholarship on the American continent — something that, as George Marsden notes, competed with the classic Presbyterian model. Neo-Kuyperians also had a deep impact on the philosophy of cultural involvement held by many mainline evangelicals (such as the late Chuck Colson and others). It is important to note here that the Dutch Reformed philosophy of Christian education was partially due to the amicable political situation in the Netherlands, where churches, with the government's help, were seeking to fulfill their cultural mandate in the sphere of culture and education — something that became very important for the Dutch, especially during the Second World War, during which Dutch churches took a stand against Nazi Germany and against German Lutherans who failed to oppose (and even supported) Hitler.

Perhaps because of their initial success, Kuyper and his followers assumed a triumphalist tone in proclaiming their ideas, apparent in Kuyper's famous speech in which he said, "There is not a square inch in the world domain in our human existence over which Christ, who is sovereign over all, does not cry 'Mine!'" This triumphalism is more explicit when he writes,

> Calvinism means the completed evolution of Protestantism, resulting in both a higher and richer state of human development. Further . . . the worldview of Modernism, with its starting-point in the French Revolution, can claim no higher than that of presenting an atheistic imitation of the brilliant ideal proclaimed by Calvinism, therefore being unqualified for the honor of leading us higher on.[34]

33. Richard J. Mouw, *The Challenges of Cultural Discipleship: Essays in the Line of Abraham Kuyper* (Grand Rapids: Wm. B. Eerdmans, 2012), pp. 33-57.

34. Abraham Kuyper, *Lectures on Calvinism* (Grand Rapids: Wm. B. Eerdmans, 1961), p. 41.

Kupyer's triumphalism, which sounds so odd — if not vexing — today, was not out of the ordinary for the intellectual elites of the early twentieth century, and in many ways embodied the optimistic expectations of those who taught that the approaching era would be a "Christian century," or, as in the case of Kuyper, a Calvinist century. Kuyper's triumphalistic Calvinism and high expectations of Reformed Protestantism went beyond the church and evangelism. It became a worldview that penetrated political, social, and cultural convictions, seeking to transform the whole of human society and culture. This worldview found its stronghold in Western Michigan.

Without a doubt, Machen and Kuyper shared much in common. As Calvinists, both were committed to the historic Christian faith and adhered to creeds of Reformed and Presbyterian churches. They were also influential in their day — part of the upper class with political, religious, and cultural connections. In addition, in 1898 Kuyper delivered the famous Stone Lectures at Princeton, which continued to be discussed when Machen attended and later started teaching at Princeton. In Machen's speech titled "Christianity and Culture," delivered in 1912 at the beginning of the fall semester, we can hear echoes of Kuyper's triumphalistic transformational imperative.[35]

However, Machen later moved away from Kuyperian ideas, forming his own views on faith, culture, and Christian scholarship. It has been observed that Machen's non-military service with the YMCA in France during the First World War had a powerful impact on him. Experiencing the horrors of war far from the comforts and luxuries of American life planted doubts in Machen's mind about whether the twentieth century really would bring peace, prosperity, and the growth of the Christian faith. His optimism continued to diminish later, after he returned to America, where he carefully observed the rise and spread of Nazism, Fascism, and Marxism.[36] Further, the re-organization of Princeton Seminary and the Presbyterian Church's acceptance of the Auburn Affirmation[37] caused Machen to realize that the challenges facing the church

35. Machen, "Christianity and Culture," speech delivered at the beginning of the fall semester at Princeton Theological Seminary in 1912. It is available in Machen's *J. Gresham Machen: Selected Shorter Writings*, pp. 399-410.

36. Nichols, *J. Gresham Machen*, pp. 137, 154.

37. In May of 1924, the Presbyterian Church in the USA signed a document that pledged the church's fidelity to the ministers who no longer affirmed the Fundamentals of Faith (the inerrancy of Scripture, the virgin birth, substitutionary atonement, Christ's bodily resurrection, and the authenticity of miracles). The document was supported by moderates who, although they did not agree with modernists, saw it as necessary to preserve the unity and liberty of the church.

might have been greater inside the church than outside of it. All of this eventually brought him to believe that the church, when set on "redeeming the culture," loses its integrity and becomes very much like the surrounding culture.

In effect, Machen developed a vision that no longer directly burdened the church with the task of cultural transformation. Instead, it set before the church the spiritual goal of proclaiming the gospel though Word and sacrament. Although Machen no longer saw a direct role for the church in affecting culture, this did not mean that he withdrew from or avoided political and cultural involvement in society. Quite the contrary: Machen's activism continued when he addressed a number of political and social issues, including prohibition, prayer in school, environmental preservation, jaywalking, and the establishment of the Department of Education, against which he testified before the U.S. Congress. However, his activism here was motivated more by his libertarian and civic (rather than purely religious) sensibilities. As D. G. Hart puts it,

> Machen was not implying that Christianity is unrelated to any range of activity beyond the ministry or fellowship of the church. Instead he was raising questions about the much more difficult issue of how Christianity is related to these other areas of human activity [and how] . . . Christians, even Reformed ones, may actually give different answers to the questions about the best form of government, cultural and religious diversity in a single nation, the value of mountain climbing or the significance of advanced learning.[38]

The conviction that Christianity was *not* able to provide a sufficient basis for public life in a pluralistic American society came from Machen's deep conviction that "historic Christianity was fundamentally narrow, exclusive, and partisan."[39] Thus Christians who used the church as a vehicle for political involvement were in danger of being intolerant or of treating the Christian faith instrumentally to promote morality or American culture.

The spiritual aspects of Machen's Christianity become evident in his commencement speech, titled "Consolation in the Midst of Battle," delivered at Westminster Theological Seminary in 1931, when he said,

> Remember this, at least — the things in which the world is interested are the things that are seen; but the things that are seen are temporal, and the

38. Hart, introduction to *J. Gresham Machen: Selected Shorter Writings*, p. 14.
39. Hart, *Defending the Faith*, p. 138.

things that are not seen are eternal. You, as ministers of Christ, are called to deal with the unseen things. You are stewards of the mysteries of God. You alone can lead men, by the proclamation of God's word, out of the crash and jazz and noise and rattle and smoke of this weary age into the green pastures and beside the still water; you alone, as ministers of reconciliation, can give what the world with all its boasting and pride can never give — the infinite sweetness of the communion of the redeemed soul with the living God.[40]

Furthermore, Machen argued that the spiritual direction of the church needs to be accompanied by a strong militant approach, which, as he argued, stands in continuity with the New Testament's witness. He writes, "Every really great Christian utterance, it may almost be said, is born in controversy. It is when men have felt compelled to take a stand against error that they have risen to really great heights on the celebration of truth."[41]

The theme of the spiritual militancy of the church finds its best application in Machen's view of Christian scholarship. In "Facing the Facts before God," a speech he delivered before the League of Evangelical Students, Machen compared the situation in which the church found itself to the biblical battle of King Hezekiah, described in the book of 2 Kings. He warns believers against the danger of complete annihilation if they do not seek their refuge in the Lord, writing, "Do you think that this is a happy or blessed age? Oh no, my friends. Amid all the noise and shouting and power and machinery, there are hungry hearts. The law of God has been forgotten, and stark slavery is stalking through the earth — the decay of free institutions in the state and a deeper slavery still in the depths of the soul."[42] It is when we read words such as these that we see Machen no longer possessing the optimism and triumphalism of his earlier days of Kuyperian Calvinism. Instead, he holds to a pessimism that can be overcome only when the Christian seeks refuge in God by claiming his revealed Word, and openly challenges the world with it. Rhetorically, Machen expresses this challenge in militant terms.

Machen is not interested in negotiating with modernism (or the culture) because he ultimately sees it as anti-Christian and anti-academic in nature, seeking to destroy not only the historic Christian faith but scholarship alto-

---

40. Machen, "Consolations in the Midst of Battle," in *J. Gresham Machen: Selected Shorter Writings*, p. 205.

41. Machen, "Christian Scholarship and the Defense of Faith," in *J. Gresham Machen: Selected Shorter Writings*, p. 149.

42. Machen, "Facing the Facts before God," in *J. Gresham Machen: Selected Shorter Writings*, pp. 199-201.

gether. Thus he calls for battle, and for conservative Protestant theologians who are committed to biblical truths and serious intellectual engagement to aid the evangelistic work of the church:

> Evangelists, if they are real evangelists, real proclaimers of the unpopular message that the Bible contains, are coming more and more to see that they cannot do without those despised theological professors at all. It is useless to proclaim a gospel that people cannot hold to be true; no amount of emotional appeal can do anything against truth. The question of fact cannot permanently be evaded. Did Christ or did he not rise from the dead; is the Bible trustworthy or is it false?[43]

However, theologians are not the only ones who can be involved in truly Christian scholarship. For Machen, all academics, to some extent, are to participate in it — that is, if they continue to take Christian revelation into consideration in their academic work. He explains,

> A Christian boy or girl can learn mathematics, for example, from a teacher who is not a Christian; and truth is truth however learned. But while truth is truth however learned, the bearings of truth, the meaning of truth, the purpose of truth, even in the sphere of mathematics, seem entirely different to the Christian from that which they seem to the non-Christian; and that is why a truly Christian education is possible only when Christian convictions underlie not a part, but all of the curriculum of the school. True learning and true piety go hand in hand, and Christianity embraces the whole of life — those are great central convictions that underlie the Christian School.[44]

So then, Machen believed that non-Christians could practice the non-theological sciences (or disciplines) because "all truth is God's truth"; but he also believed that modernity's anti-religious bias had rendered this impossible. Therefore, Christian academics need to take a stand to defend not only Christianity but also the integrity of faith and science. *This* is where Machen's philosophy of Christian education takes root, rather than in a biblical imperative to make Christian education binding or compulsory, as was the case with the

---

43. Machen, "Christian Scholarship and the Defense of Faith," in *J. Gresham Machen: Selected Shorter Writings*, p. 146.

44. Machen, "The Necessity of the Christian School," in *J. Gresham Machen: Selected Shorter Writings*, p. 172.

Dutch Reformed. For Machen, defending the integrity of a discipline itself is in the Christian's interest, as both theology and philosophy (or the truths found in every discipline) are true and cannot contradict one another.

On the margin, it could be argued that this approach has a long trajectory in the Protestant approach to education, and can be traced back to the Calvinist theologian, philosopher, and pedagogue Bartholomäus Keckermann (ca. 1572-1609), who, during his tenure at the Academic Gymnasium in the Polish city of Gdańsk (Danzig), implemented a curriculum reflecting this conviction. Since Keckermann's work influenced Reformed academics in Europe and the New World, we can suspect that it also impacted the way some at Princeton viewed the relation between theology and science.[45]

On a practical level, Machen argued that Christian education must be all-encompassing and in clear contrast to secular science, which does not take divine revelation into consideration. This comprehensive approach to Christian education must originate with *doctrine* and not with a general Christian ethos in the schools. In other words, Christian education is so not because it is done by Christians, but rather because of its content. An institution whose primary goal is to promote Christian culture, civic society, gender equality, or social justice is not what Machen had in mind. Instead, he saw Christian scholarship as based on a set of non-negotiable principles expressed in Scripture and the historic confessions, and anyone departing from these in the name of academic freedom was no longer practicing scholarship that could call itself "Christian."

Machen set forth as a positive example the classic Roman Catholic system of education, which roots the whole academic curriculum in the context of established doctrine and with consideration for natural law. Scripture and the creeds guide students in the discovery of the natural world, and that forms the dialogue with the non-Catholic and secular culture. Further, studying ancient languages and authors, logic, and metaphysics is an essential prerequisite

---

45. Keckermann writes, "True philosophy in no way disputes sacred theology," and elsewhere, "In sum, the natural knowledge of God is not contrary to the supernatural, knowledge gained from nature is not repugnant to knowledge gained by grace, the book of nature does not overturn the book of scripture: therefore neither does philosophy conflict with theology." For these quotations and a discussion, see Richard Muller, *After Calvin* (Oxford: Oxford University Press, 2003), pp. 122-36, 127-28. See also *Gdańskie Gimnazjum Akademickie. Szkice z dziejów*, vols. 1-4, ed. Edmund Kotarski, Lech Mokrzecki, and Zofia Głobiowska (Gdańsk: Wydawnictwo Uniwersytetu Gdańskiego, 2008); William T. Costello, *The Scholastic Curriculum at Seventeenth-Century Cambridge* (Cambridge: Harvard University Press, 1958); and Joseph Freedman, "The Career and Writings of Bartholomew Keckermann (d. 1609)," *Proceedings of the American Philosophical Society* 141, no. 3 (1997): 305-28.

for any fruitful academic labor.[46] This model of Christian education sees the world as *already* integrated where sciences are consecrated to the person and work of Christ and his church; and where the students who are broad in their interests, cultured, and well-rounded are always ready to defend the hope they have in Christ.[47]

In the face of the modern hostility toward historic Christianity among secularized academics and liberal theologians, Machen argued for the necessity of *narrowly defined* Christian scholarship. For Machen, Christian scholarship becomes essential for the proper functioning not only of the church but also of science itself. Just as the church desperately needs well-educated scholars who will defend the historic Christian faith and its truth claims, so also science needs to be practiced in an unsecularized form. Machen held that faith and science must relate to each other; otherwise, neither would be able to find truth — or, worse, science without religion would fall into decadence, while religion without science would become superstitious.

The reactionary nature of Machen's philosophy of Christian education caused him to adopt a militant tone, helpful in communicating great urgency as well as the antithetical relationship between the church and the world. Further, Machen's definition of Christian scholarship is narrow, pointing to doctrinal orthodoxy and ecclesiastical commitment rather than to the general religious ethos of the school or its honorable heritage. Community-oriented goals — such as the preservation of liberty, civic society, or culture — are not the direct tasks of Christian scholarship (or of the church), just as they are not the goal of even nonreligious academic work, but rather are by-products (or desirable side effects) of education. Chasing after the *results* of education — no matter how noble — instead of honoring its *principles* is a dangerous exercise in utilitarianism, defeating the purpose of scholarship and rendering it inherently unreliable. At the same time, liberty, civil society, tolerance, and open dialogue are naturally and organically preserved when good scholarship is practiced, and most effectively when Christian scholarship is practiced. Therefore, while it is not the direct task of Christian education to promote these values, they are indeed promoted when Christian scholarship is practiced faithfully.

---

46. Machen, "The Minister and His Greek Testament," in *J. Gresham Machen: Selected Shorter Writings*, p. 210.

47. Machen, "Consolations in the Midst of Battle," in *J. Gresham Machen: Selected Shorter Writings*, p. 204.

Structuring the Scholarly Imagination: Strategies for Christian Engagement with the Disciplines

M. Elizabeth Lewis Hall

From our vantage point at the beginning of the twenty-first century, the future appears promising for Christian scholarship. While the larger academy continues largely antagonistic to or disinterested in Christian contributions to scholarship, there are some disciplines, such as philosophy, where Christian perspectives are increasingly being taken seriously. In addition, Christian higher education is flourishing. In 2009 the National Center for Education Statistics listed 888 religiously affiliated institutions of higher education; 69 percent were affiliated with Protestant Christian groups, many of them evangelical.[1] Mark Noll's "scandal of the evangelical mind" appears to be becoming less scandalous.[2] However, there remain a number of challenges to Christian scholarship, including historical, sociological, ideological, and economic factors, many of which have been discussed by other authors. I would like to focus on yet another challenge, a much more pragmatic one: the lack of scaffolding or structure for Christian scholarship.

1. U.S. Department of Education, 2010. Fall enrollment and number of degree-granting institutions, by control and affiliation of institution: Selected years, 1980 through 2009. Retrieved June 5, 2012: http://nces.ed.gov/programs/digest/d10/tables/dt10_205.asp?referrer=list.
2. Mark A. Noll, *The Scandal of the Evangelical Mind* (Grand Rapids: Wm. B. Eerdmans, 1995).

I'd like to thank Brent Ridley and the rest of the 2011 Coalition of the Willing faculty integration group for the original concept for this paper, Rick Langer for stimulating discussion that resulted in the basic categories employed, my Center for Christian Thought co-fellows and directors for their stimulating interactions around the ideas in this paper, and the Spring 2013 Colloquium of the Willing participants for valuable feedback.

In my various roles as an academic, I regularly encounter thoughtful Christians who desire to engage their discipline with their faith, and yet have very little concept of how to actually go about doing so. Christians in the academy have largely not been educated and socialized to produce Christian scholarship. In my discipline, psychology, the largely abstract and theoretical discussions about the integration of faith and psychology produce the illusion that education is happening, but may actually inhibit scholarly efforts by making the task seem excessively complicated and controversial. In psychology and in Christian academia more broadly, there seems to be an abundance of books talking in the abstract about Christian scholarship: its foundations, goals, commitments, history, and so on. But many fewer resources exist that come alongside faculty in the daily labor of making connections between their disciplines and their faith.

I am not the first to note this gap. Other Christian scholars have likewise reflected on the vagueness of the task of Christian scholarship. Nicholas Wolterstorff, in a paper written in the 1980s, commented,

> I began to be discontent with the ways in which I had been taught to describe the relation between faith and learning. For one thing, I began to think that the words used did not have much content; they remained too abstract. It was said that Christians approach scholarship with a different perspective, and that it shapes their scholarship into something different. Perhaps so; but just how does that take place? It was said that Christians approach scholarship with different presuppositions and that those shape their scholarship into something different. Perhaps so, but how does this shaping by presuppositions work? I wanted more clarity, and more concreteness of insight, on the connection.[3]

Similarly, psychologist Darryl Stevenson, in reviewing fifty years of Christian scholarship in the field of psychology, wrote, "Perhaps more elusive than the what of integration (that is, the task) is the how (the method). Scholars have wrestled with the how, perhaps more frequently than the what, because it appears that is where we need to roll up our sleeves and get to work."[4]

---

3. Nicholas Wolterstorff, "Autobiography: The Story of Two Decades of Thinking about Christian Higher Education," in Nicholas Wolterstorff, *Educating for Shalom*, ed. Clarence W. Joldersma and Gloria Goris Stronks (Grand Rapids: Wm. B. Eerdmans, 2004), p. 158.

4. Darryl H. Stevenson, "Introduction: The Nature of Integration and Its Historical Context," in *Psychology and Christianity Integration: Seminal Works That Shaped the Movement*, ed. D. H. Stevenson, B. E. Eck, and P. C. Hill (Batavia, Ill.: Christian Association for Psychological Studies, 2007), p. 6.

Lev Vygotsky, the Russian developmental psychologist, suggested that optimal learning occurs in children when assistance is given within the "zone of proximal development." This zone is the distance between what the child can do by himself or herself, and what the child can do with guidance. So the teacher's role is to produce a type of "scaffolding" in which the teacher stays one step ahead of the student, providing guidance until the child can accomplish the task alone, while the teacher then encourages the next step.[5] I think you will find that this makes sense intuitively; if you have ever taught someone to do research in your discipline, you will know the kind of progressive learning that occurs from, say, the first statistics course that an undergraduate in psychology takes, to the complex tasks required of an empirical doctoral dissertation. It would be pointless to ask a sophomore to write a doctoral dissertation. Yet we often assume that scholars who have spent most of their education mastering the skills and content of their own disciplines should be fully equipped to do Christian scholarship well. This ignores the fact that Christian scholarship involves, at a minimum, an additional set of theological skills and content, and probably requires yet a third set of skills (e.g., disciplinary translational skills, epistemological bilingualism) to bring the theological piece together with the disciplinary piece.

So I am proposing here to provide a sort of scaffolding or structure for Christian scholarship, in the form of a kind of typology, or menu of options, of ways in which Christians have brought together their faith and their scholarship. The intent is not to be formulaic or prescriptive. Rather, it's my hope that this will provide some guidance and will spur the imagination of those wanting to more intentionally pursue Christian scholarship. To supplement my own experiences as a Christian scholar, get beyond my disciplinary boundaries, and avoid re-inventing the wheel, I have attempted to identify the major works addressing Christian scholarship in the last twenty years or so, and have looked through them for implicit or explicit modes of engagement recommended by the authors. In what follows, I will first present a broad definition of Christian scholarship, then present my typology of modes of engagement, and finally suggest some factors that regulate the selection of the specific modes of engagement.

5. L. S. Vygotsky, *Thought and Language* (Cambridge, Mass.: MIT Press, 1934/1986).

What Is Christian Scholarship?

Scholars writing on Christian scholarship appear reluctant to be prescriptive in their definitions of Christian scholarship, preferring instead very broad descriptions that focus on intent rather than product. For example, George Marsden calls it "scholarship by persons who are Christian and who consciously relate their faith to what they say or write" or "pretty simply scholarship that is shaped in part by Christian perspectives."[6] Wolterstorff says, "Christian learning is faithful learning; learning faithful to faith in the triune God, learning faithful to the Christian community and its tradition, learning faithful to the Christian scriptures."[7] Drawing on this literature, and with similar intent to describe rather than prescribe, I propose to use the phrase "Christian scholarship" to refer to a variety of ways in which Christians strive to bring together their character, convictions, and practices, as shaped by their faith, and their academic disciplines. I note that, in common with the descriptions provided above, the emphasis is on the process or striving, which may or may not result in overt, detectable markers in the resulting product. My intent in defining Christian scholarship this way is not to provide a set of defining criteria by which one might examine a piece of scholarship and decide whether or not it is, in fact, Christian scholarship. Rather, my intent is to provide the broadest possible umbrella for Christian scholarship, one that will accommodate the work of Christian scholars in a variety of disciplines and work settings, in order to move on to what I think is the more interesting question: What are the modes of engagement that Christians might utilize in order to meaningfully engage their faith and their discipline?

Although most references to Christian scholarship focus on how Christian *beliefs* or *convictions* influence scholarship, I also want to briefly acknowledge the role that Christian *practices* and *value commitments* play in scholarship. To do Christian scholarship, we have a responsibility to know our Bibles well, but we also have a responsibility to properly form our moral intuitions, as these play a role in some of the modes I will describe, and also affect the practices we will adopt in the process of doing scholarship.

Although I describe my own work as integration, I avoid the use of the phrase "the integration of faith and learning" here. This is not because of per-

---

6. George M. Marsden, "Beyond Progressive Scientific Humanism," in *The Future of Religious Colleges*, ed. P. J. Dovre (Grand Rapids: Wm. B. Eerdmans, 2002), pp. 44-45.

7. Nicholas Wolterstorff, "Christian Learning In and For a Pluralist Society," in *Educating for Shalom*, p. 256.

sonal discomfort with a term that essentially means to bring together things that have been separated, but because I've discovered that people have a variety of notions in mind when they use that phrase, and consequently it is often used as a sort of "straw man" against which to contrast some alternative perspective on Christian scholarship.[8] I actually think that in contemporary usages of "integration," what people have in mind is much broader than the vision that was articulated most clearly by Arthur Holmes and by Nicholas Wolterstorff in his earlier writings on integration.[9] Perhaps the emphasis in "integration" is on those modes of Christian scholarship that are more explicit, in which case "Christian scholarship" is the broader umbrella term under which "integration" falls.

Which Christian beliefs or convictions shape scholarship? A number of authors have provided lists of Christian beliefs they see as foundational to the task of Christian scholarship.[10] Theologian and poet Harry Lee Poe sees the underlying unity of the doctrine of creation as being central, with subcategories of this doctrine (i.e., humanity, the physical world) providing unifying themes to clusters of disciplines.[11] Of particular note are recent books that are moving away from more comprehensive lists to focus in on belief in the person and work of Jesus Christ as the most foundational of these. Mark Noll in *Jesus Christ and the Life of the Mind* argues extensively for this position, affirming that "For 'Christian scholarship' to mean anything, it must mean intellectual labor rooted in Christ, with both the rooting and the laboring essential," and "For rationale, means, methods, paradigms, and telos, the tasks of Christian scholarship depend pervasively on the work of

8. For example, D. Jacobsen and R. H. Jacobsen, *Scholarship and Christian Faith: Enlarging the Conversation* (New York: Oxford University Press, 2004).

9. See Arthur Holmes, ed., *The Making of a Christian Mind: A Christian World View and the Academic Enterprise* (Downers Grove, Ill.: InterVarsity Press, 1985); Arthur Holmes, *The Idea of a Christian College*, 2nd ed. (Grand Rapids: Wm. B. Eerdmans, 1987); Nicholas Wolterstorff, "The Integration of Faith and Learning — The Very Idea," in *Educating for Shalom*, pp. 36-45.

10. See C. S. Evans, "The Calling of the Christian Scholar-Teacher," in *Faithful Learning and the Christian Scholarly Vocation*, ed. Douglas V. Henry and Bob R. Agee (Grand Rapids: Wm. B. Eerdmans, 2003), pp. 26-49; Arthur Holmes, *The Making of a Christian Mind;* Duane Litfin, *Conceiving the Christian College* (Grand Rapids: Wm. B. Eerdmans, 2004); George M. Marsden, *The Outrageous Idea of Christian Scholarship* (Oxford: Oxford University Press, 1998); Stephen Monsma, "Christian Worldview in Academia," *Faculty Dialogue* 21 (1994); Michael L. Peterson, *With All Your Mind: A Christian Philosophy of Education* (Notre Dame: University of Notre Dame Press, 2001); and Nicholas Wolterstorff, *Reason within the Bounds of Religion* (Grand Rapids: Wm. B. Eerdmans, 1976).

11. Harry Lee Poe, *Christianity in the Academy: Teaching at the Intersection of Faith and Learning* (Grand Rapids: Baker Academic, 2004).

God in Christ."[12] Similarly, Duane Litfin says, "Distinctively Christian think-ing involves an exploration of the full Trinitarian implications of what we study, and its Christ-centeredness in particular, for as Karl Barth says, 'The doctrine of the Trinity is what basically distinguishes the Christian doctrine of God as Christian . . . in contrast to all other possible doctrines of God.'"[13]

A Typology of Modes of Engagement

Most scholars who have written about the task of Christian scholarship are in agreement that Christian scholarship is marked by ways in which faith-based convictions shape that scholarship. What is more ambiguous is how that shaping occurs. A variety of strategies are offered, sometimes in detail,[14] and sometimes only in passing. Some offer brief lists of strategies.[15] These strategies might be thought of as addressing the spectrum of activities involved in scholarship, including *motivation* for scholarship, *epistemology* (primarily in the form of critique of prevailing epistemological assumptions and meth-ods), diverse ways in which Christian commitments influence the *content* of the scholarship, the *process* of scholarship, and application or *outcomes* of the scholarship. The identified strategies will be described according to these five categories. (See the table on p. 118 for an overview.)

Motivation for Scholarship

Several authors speak to the motivational function of the Christian faith in enriching scholarship. While all seem eager to avoid accusations of triumphal-ism, they nonetheless speak of faith as providing a multitude of benefits to the task of scholarship. William Dyrness, for example, speaks of the hope provided by faith: "It is hard to understand how some can insist the Christian faith puts people in a box. The opposite is in fact true — the faith is not a box but a win-dow. Christian convictions about creation and redemption make the world

12. Mark A. Noll, *Jesus Christ and the Life of the Mind* (Grand Rapids: Wm. B. Eerdmans, 2011), pp. 147-48.

13. Litfin, *Conceiving the Christian College*, p. 62.

14. E. L. Johnson, "A Place for the Bible within Psychological Science," *Journal of Psychol-ogy and Theology* 20, no. 4 (1992): 346-55; Wolterstorff, *Reason within the Bounds of Religion*.

15. See, for example, Marsden, "Beyond Progressive Scientific Humanism," pp. 45-46, and Peterson, *With All Your Mind*, p. 134.

open to its transcendent purpose and to the future that God has planned for it. Through his Spirit, God has revealed to us 'what no eye has seen, nor ear heard, nor the heart of man conceived . . .' (1 Cor. 2:9)."[16] Dorothy Chappell concurs, arguing that our theological commitments give faculty "the *stamina, hope, and confidence* to maximize their scholarly efforts for the Kingdom of God."[17]

Anthropologist Jenell Williams Paris proposes that love is the motivation that underlies Christian scholarship. Coming from a pietist perspective, she points to the limitations of reason because of its detachment from virtue. Love, in contrast, merges knowledge and practice. Love can, of course, be apparent in attempts to use the results of scholarship to strengthen ministry efforts and church life, and to aid those in need. Perhaps less obviously, love can be demonstrated in basic research, as scholars work in research on religious subjects or in areas that affect oppressed and marginalized populations.[18]

Duane Litfin sees all Christian scholarship as having a common end: "a unified, Christ-centered understanding of the world."[19] However, in his view the motivation involves knowing not only the creation, but also the creator:

> This tethering of the temporal to the eternal provides meaning and significance and beauty to what [Christian scholars] do and generates the highest motivation for excellence. . . . They work not merely to understand the created order, as worthwhile as that goal is within itself; they also study the created order to deepen their understanding and appreciation of, and ultimately their relationship with, the One who fashioned it and who occupies its center, its Creative orderer, the Lord Jesus Christ.[20]

Mark Noll also ties motivation for Christian scholarship to knowledge of Christ: "Since the reality of Jesus Christ sustains the world and all that is in it, so too should the reality of Jesus Christ sustain the most wholehearted,

16. William A. Dyrness, "The Contribution of Theological Studies to the Christian Liberal Arts," in *Making Higher Education Christian: The History and Mission of Evangelical Colleges in America*, ed. Joel A. Carpenter and Kenneth W. Shipps (Grand Rapids: Christian University Press, 1987), p. 182.

17. See M. Hamilton, J. A. Carpenter, D. E. Chappell, and D. W. King, "Reflection and Response: The Elusive Idea of Christian Scholarship," *Christian Scholar's Review* 31, no. 1 (2001): 24.

18. Jenell Williams Paris, "A Pietist Perspective on Love and Learning in Cultural Anthropology, and Response to Todd M. Vanden Berg's 'A Reflection on Jenell Williams Paris's "A Pietist Perspective on Love and Learning in Cultural Anthropology,"' " *Christian Scholar's Review* 36, no. 3 (2006): 371-98.

19. Litfin, *Conceiving the Christian College*, p. 147.

20. Litfin, *Conceiving the Christian College*, p. 75.

unabashed, and unembarrassed efforts to understand the world and all that is in it."[21] In an inspiring statement that is worth repeating in full, he points to the Christological hymn in the first chapter of Colossians:

> The apostle says, in effect, that if we study anything in the realms of nature or the realms of the spirit, we study what came into existence through Jesus Christ. Likewise, if we study human interactions or spiritual-human interactions (thrones, dominions, rulers, powers), we are studying realms brought into existence by Jesus Christ. If our study concerns predictability, uniformity, regularity, we are working in the domains of the one who "is before all things, and [in whom] all things hold together." If our study concerns beauty, power, or agency, it is the same, "for God was pleased to have all his fullness dwell in him." And if we succeed to any degree, we are only following after Jesus Christ, "in whom are hidden all the treasures of wisdom and knowledge."[22]

Paul Gould draws on the concept of the Lordship of Jesus Christ as motivation for Christian scholarship: "Christ as Lord means that he is Lord of all aspects of our lives — including the research projects we engage in and even the very questions that we ask. . . . Lordship unto Jesus demands that all aspects of our being, including our thought life and academic work, lead to and result in love and worship of God."[23]

Motivational factors are more personal for Jean Bethke Elshtain, who ties Christian scholarship not to ideology or calling or relationship, but to identity. She draws the comparison with runner and missionary Eric Liddell, about whom a member of the British Olympic Committee said, "He would surely lose if he ran on a Sunday, don't you see. His faith makes him fast." Elshtain then goes on to say, "The religious convictions reflected in scholarly and pedagogical work are a bit like that. Without them, some of us wouldn't have energy for the race and wouldn't be able to run half so fast. In fact, we wouldn't even know what the race was all about."[24] Nicholas Wolterstorff also envisions the

21. Noll, *Jesus Christ and the Life of the Mind*, p. 22.

22. Noll, *Jesus Christ and the Life of the Mind*, p. 28.

23. Paul M. Gould, "The Two Tasks Introduced: The Fully Integrated Life of the Christian Scholar," in *The Two Tasks of the Christian Scholar: Redeeming the Soul, Redeeming the Mind*, ed. W. L. Craig and Paul M. Gould (Wheaton, Ill.: Crossway Books, 2007), pp. 46-47.

24. Jean Bethke Elshtain, "Does, or Should, Teaching Reflect the Religious Perspective of the Teacher?," in *Religion, Scholarship, and Higher Education: Perspectives, Models, and Future Prospects*, ed. A. Sterk (Notre Dame: University of Notre Dame Press, 2002), p. 201.

motivation for scholarship in deeply personal (or interpersonal) terms, as an act of gratitude:

> *To be human is to be that place in creation where God's goodness finds its answer in gratitude.* I see Christian learning as fundamentally an act of gratitude to God. The Greek word for gratitude, or thanksgiving, is *eucharistia.* Christian learning is a Eucharistic act. "O the depth of the riches and wisdom and knowledge of God!" exclaims St. Paul. "To God be the glory forever" (Rom. 11:33, 36). One of the Eucharistic acts of the Christian community — by no means its only such act, and then not of each and every member of the community but of the community as a whole — one of the Eucharistic acts of the Christian community is the scholarly exploration of that richness. Out of a spirit of deep gratitude to engage in philosophy, literary criticism, sociology, or whatever, doing so *as* Christians, that is, as someone formed by Christian culture — while also allowing what one learns to correct one's Christian culture where that proves necessary.[25]

So Christian scholarship may be fueled by hope, confidence, love, and gratitude, and may be aimed at knowing God and his world better and at submitting to Christ's lordship over all areas of life. These motivational factors suggest the importance of scholarship nourished by spiritual practices, not only to know more deeply the content of our faith, but to manifest more the fruit of the Spirit in hope, love, and gratitude, to have our moral sensibilities sharpened, and to be energized and strengthened by the Spirit (e.g., 1 Cor. 12:6; Col. 1:29; Acts 3:15).

Epistemological Assumptions and Methods

Every discipline has a set of epistemological assumptions and methodological practices that govern the practice of the discipline. Some of these are explicitly taught in courses on methodology. In addition, in almost every discipline at least some scholars recognize that certain pre-theoretical and largely implicit assumptions and commitments, or "first principles," shape the way the discipline is practiced. In spite of this recognition, these assumptions and commitments continue to mold the disciplines as they are embedded in their methods, theories, and discourses, into which each successive generation of scholars is

25. Wolterstorff, "Christian Learning In and For a Pluralist Society," p. 258.

socialized. Furthermore, in some disciplines, many scholars seem to operate in continued unawareness of these assumptions. For example, in my own field, logical positivism has had enduring influence on what counts as good scholarship, even though it was discredited long ago in philosophical circles. Positivist beliefs are widely held by psychologists, appearing as an "unspoken grammar" and privileging reductionistic, mechanistic theories and quantitative, experimental methodologies.[26] In describing her own graduate school experience, political scientist Jean Bethke Elshtain noted, "The by-far most common form of indoctrination or inculcation was neither political nor religious but, instead, methodological and epistemological."[27] She went on to note that there was little or no room for challenge, interpretation, or critique of these ideas.

Many of these assumptions and commitments are in conflict with Christian beliefs about ontology, epistemology, and ethics. Consequently, in some disciplines, Christian scholars have challenged the very rules by which the disciplinary game is played, noting the presence of these pre-theoretical commitments and suggesting alternatives consistent with Christian commitments. For example, Mark Noll has written about epistemology in the field of history, J. P. Moreland and William Lane Craig, Del Ratzsch, and D. W. Aiken have written about epistemological issues in the sciences, Christian Smith has critically evaluated methods in sociology, and Peter Hill has examined epistemological issues in psychology.[28]

Some scholars have attempted to move beyond criticism to proposing distinctively Christian methodologies in their disciplines. One example is Alan Jacobs, who suggests a "theology of reading" in studying literature, in which

---

26. B. D. Slife and M. Whoolery, "Are Psychology's Main Theories and Methods Biased against Its Main Consumers?," *Journal of Psychology and Theology* 34, no. 3 (2006): 217-31; C. W. Tolman, ed., *Positivism in Psychology: Historical and Contemporary Problems* (New York: Springer-Verlag, 1992).

27. Elshtain, "Does, or Should, Teaching Reflect the Religious Perspective of the Teacher?," p. 193.

28. See Noll, *Jesus Christ and the Life of the Mind*; J. P. Moreland and W. L. Craig, *Philosophical Foundations for a Christian Worldview* (Downers Grove, Ill.: InterVarsity Press, 2003); Del Ratzsch, "Design in Nature: What Is Science Properly Permitted to Think?," in *Faithful Imagination in the Academy: Explorations in Religious Belief and Scholarship*, ed. J. M. Curry and R. A. Wells (Lanham, Md.: Lexington Books, 2008), pp. 57-58; D. W. Aiken, "Bernard Lonergan's Critique of Reductionism: A Call to Intellectual Conversion," *Christian Scholar's Review* 16, no. 3 (2012): 233-52; Christian Smith, *What Is a Person?: Rethinking Humanity, Social Life, and the Moral Good from the Person Up* (Chicago: University of Chicago Press, 2010); and Peter C. Hill, "Implications for Integration from a New Philosophy of Psychology as Science," *Journal of Psychology and Christianity* 8, no. 1 (1989): 61-74.

a hermeneutic of love is employed in order to balance out the prevailing hermeneutic of suspicion. Drawing on Augustine's counsel that the reading of Scripture be motivated by love, he suggests that we read charitably, striving to grow in the love of God and of our neighbor.[29]

The Content of Scholarship

A variety of ways in which Christian beliefs, values, and practices influence the content of the scholarly process have been proposed. This variety is perhaps explained by the fact that academic disciplines vary considerably in the focus of scholarship and in their methodological approaches. Consequently, not all strategies will be relevant to all disciplines, and a variety of strategies are necessary in order to make the concept of Christian scholarship relevant to all disciplines. Given my disciplinary background, I will largely draw on the research with which I am most familiar. In particular, when drawing on examples from my own work, I want to clarify that I use these not because I see my work as in any way representing an exemplar of these processes, but simply because I know it well!

Providing Direction

The broadest way in which Christian commitments make a difference in scholarship is in the scholarly agendas they influence. Not only beliefs but also values and even affections influenced by Christian commitments are relevant here. Christian *values* determine what are legitimate projects of study; moral sensibilities shaped by Christian practices might render some projects ethically unacceptable, while highlighting others that are important and consistent with broad Christian callings. Aesthetic *affections* may also provide some direction. It is noteworthy that both Duane Litfin and Mark Noll, in quotations provided earlier, mention beauty as aspects of Christian scholarship.[30] Swiss theologian Hans Urs von Balthasar speaks of beauty as having a Trinitarian grounding: if God is truth, goodness, and beauty, it makes sense that his creation would draw us to himself. For von Balthasar, experiencing nature as beautiful is a consequence of faith in Christ. Given this divine influence on our aesthetic

29. Alan Jacobs, *A Theology of Reading: The Hermeneutics of Love* (Boulder, Colo.: Westview Press, 2001).

30. Litfin, *Conceiving the Christian College*; Noll, *Jesus Christ and the Life of the Mind*.

affections, it is possible that they also draw us towards certain projects in our scholarship.[31]

Christian beliefs are also, of course, important in providing direction. George Marsden highlights the role of *beliefs* as follows: "Serious religious beliefs help shape not only our overt ways of valuing things, but also our priorities. What do we see as important to study? What is it about that subject that makes it interesting? What are the questions we ask that will organize our interpretations of this topic?"[32] These same commitments may direct us to assent to certain premises relevant to our scholarship and to reject others.

Sometimes Christian beliefs do not merely direct toward some topics and away from others; instead, they have heuristic value in suggesting hypotheses or new ways of approaching the interpretation of data. This is perhaps the mode that French philosopher Étienne Gilson had in mind in his Gifford Lectures early in the twentieth century, when he proposed that the Christian faith suggests various perspectives, which are then worked out by the use of reason. He quoted Gotthold Lessing as saying, "The great religious truths were not rational when they were revealed, but they were revealed so that they might become so."[33] In more contemporary mode, writing about the role of religious beliefs in psychology, Stan Jones noted that religious belief "contributes positively to the progress of science by suggesting new modes of thought that transform an area of study by shaping new perceptions of the data and new theories."[34] A recent example of this in the field of psychology has been the scientific study of forgiveness. Christian scholar Everett Worthington has played a large role in bringing this neglected topic to the attention of psychologists; there is now an extensive body of literature exploring multiple facets of this profoundly Christian virtue.

It is possible that the heuristic value of Christianity is not limited to its beliefs, but is also mediated by the emotions it shapes. In addition to directing us toward certain topics, our religiously influenced affections might provide us with insights into our subject matter. Goethe is widely quoted as having said "a man doesn't learn to understand anything unless he loves it." The following quotation, while not alluding directly to emotions, certainly appears to be

31. Hans Urs von Balthasar, *The Glory of the Lord: A Theological Aesthetics,* ed. J. Fessio and J. Riches (San Francisco: Ignatius Press, 1962/2003).

32. Marsden, *The Outrageous Idea of Christian Scholarship,* pp. 62-63.

33. Lessing, quoted in Étienne Gilson, *The Spirit of Mediaeval Philosophy: Gifford Lectures, 1931-1932,* trans. A. H. C. Downes (New York: Charles Scribner's Sons, 1940), p. 19.

34. S. L. Jones, "A Constructive Relationship of Religion with the Science and Profession of Psychology: Perhaps the Boldest Model Yet," *American Psychologist* 49 (1994): 194.

commenting on more than simply cognitive beliefs. Engineer Walter Bradley quotes C. S. Lewis — "I believe in Christianity as I believe that the Sun has risen, not only because I see it, but because by it I see everything else" — and goes on to explain, "Christianity provides a different kind of light that will give us insights that we will not find by just 'poking' around, much like black light (ultraviolet wavelengths) will cause a display that is sensitive to ultraviolet light to radiate, allowing one to see things that simply are not visible within the normal visible spectrum of radiation."[35] Speaking directly of this function within the natural sciences, Alister McGrath writes,

> Christian theology is the elixir, the philosopher's stone, which turns the mundane into the epiphanic, the world of nature into the realm of God's creation. Like a lens bringing a vast landscape into sharp focus or a map helping us grasp the features of the terrain around us, Christian doctrine offers a new way of understanding, imagining, and behaving. It invites us to see the natural order, and ourselves within it, in a special way — a way that might be hinted at but cannot be confirmed by the natural order itself.[36]

Confirming

Confirmation is perhaps the most basic of the strategies for Christian scholarship that have been described, and consists simply in lining up insights from the disciplines with the corresponding Christian conviction.[37] For example, the emphasis on love and respect in Paul's instructions to married couples (Eph. 5) is echoed in the words of marital researcher John Gottman: "I [have learned] that . . . most couples I've worked with over the years really wanted just two things from their marriage — love and respect."[38]

---

35. W. L. Bradley, "On Being a Christian Professor in the Secular Academy," in *The Two Tasks of the Christian Scholar: Redeeming the Soul, Redeeming the Mind*, ed. W. L. Craig and P. M. Gould (Wheaton, Ill.: Crossway Books, 2007), p. 122.

36. Alister McGrath, *The Passionate Intellect: Christian Faith and the Discipleship of the Mind* (Downers Grove, Ill.: InterVarsity Press, 2010), pp. 78-79.

37. My thanks to Bruce Narramore, who many years ago introduced me to the idea of "components of integration," including the concepts of confirming, evaluating, clarifying, and complementing.

38. John M. Gottman, *Why Marriages Succeed or Fail . . . And How You Can Make Yours Last* (New York: Simon & Schuster, 1994), p. 18.

Evaluating

One of the most frequently cited strategies in the literature on Christian scholarship is Nicholas Wolterstorff's use of religious beliefs as *control beliefs*. The scholar "ought to reject certain theories on the ground that they conflict or do not comport well with the belief-content" of his or her faith. In addition, the scholar "ought to devise theories which comport as well as possible with, or are at least consistent with, the belief-content" of his or her faith. Using control beliefs to set the boundaries on what is or is not acceptable illustrates how Christian convictions can be used as standards against which to evaluate the content of the disciplines — a function that Wolterstorff sees as "absolutely central to the work of the Christian scholar."[39]

Often, the critiquing function of the control beliefs will be directed at the pre-theoretical assumptions and commitments of problematic theories, which form part of the initial knowledge base in disciplines that rely primarily on reason, and which influence the interpretive process in disciplines that rely on reason to make sense of empirical data. Some of these assumptions may have to do with views regarding what constitutes reality. George Marsden and Alvin Plantinga, for example, have critiqued the widespread influence of scientific naturalism.[40] Other assumptions have to do with epistemology, as has been noted in an earlier section. Yet other assumptions have to do more narrowly with the field of study, such as the influence of mechanistic determinism in the sciences,[41] secular humanism in the humanities and social sciences, anti-realism in the humanities,[42] or with ethics and basic values in the applied disciplines.

---

39. Wolterstorff, *Reason within the Bounds of Religion*, p. 72, p. 66.

40. Marsden, *The Outrageous Idea of Christian Scholarship*; Alvin Plantinga, "On Christian Scholarship," in *The Challenge and Promise of a Catholic University*, ed. T. M. Hesburgh (Notre Dame: University of Notre Dame Press, 1994), pp. 267-95; Alvin Plantinga, "The Twin Pillars of Christian Scholarship," in *Seeking Understanding: The Stob Lectures, 1986-1998* (Grand Rapids: Wm. B. Eerdmans, 2001), pp. 117-62.

41. David A. Van Baak, "Can Scientific Laws Teach Us the Nature of the World?" in *Faithful Imagination in the Academy: Explorations in Religious Belief and Scholarship*, ed. J. M. Curry and R. A. Wells (Lanham, Md.: Lexington Books, 2008), pp. 45-56.

42. For example, George Marsden, *The Outrageous Idea of Christian Scholarship* and "Beyond Progressive Scientific Humanism"; E. H. Meneses, "No Other Foundation: Establishing a Christian Anthropology," *Christian Scholar's Review* 29, no. 3 (2000): 531-49; Alvin Plantinga, "On Christian Scholarship" and "The Twin Pillars of Christian Scholarship"; and Mary Stewart Van Leeuwen, "Psychology's 'Two Cultures': A Christian Analysis," *Christian Scholar's Review* 17 (1988): 406-24.

The opposite may also occur in the process of conducting Christian scholarship. Sometimes the data or theories of the discipline appear incompatible with certain Christian convictions, and lead to re-evaluation of those Christian convictions. If careful study of the issue suggests that the conviction is faulty — based, perhaps, on inadequate interpretation of the relevant biblical texts — then it may occur that the conviction is changed. Alternatively, Christian belief may allow for more than one legitimate interpretation of relevant biblical texts; the content of the disciplines may lead the scholar to conclude that one of those biblical interpretations is to be preferred over the other, as it is more consistent with disciplinary content.

Clarifying

A Christian scholar can utilize the data or theories of a discipline to clarify the meaning or significance of a biblical passage or principle. For example, in a paper I co-wrote a few years ago,[43] I drew on two psychological theories of suffering to clarify how God's response to Job in the final chapters of the account effected the dramatic changes in Job's stance toward God and his circumstances that are seen in the narrative.

Elaborating

A Christian scholar can utilize the data or theories of a discipline to extend the understanding or specific application of a biblical passage or principle. For example, the Bible instructs parents to discipline their children (e.g., Prov. 13:24), but the details provided about how to do so are sparse. Psychological research on the effects of different disciplinary styles can assist in applying these instructions.

Complementing

A more comprehensive view of any aspect of reality is possible when we bring together insights from our discipline with relevant faith-based convictions and allow them to engage with each other. Out of the reflective discourse that occurs at the conjunction of the two kinds of knowledge, there can emerge

---

43. M. E. L. Hall and E. Johnson, "Theodicy and Therapy: Theological/Philosophical Contributions to the Problem of Suffering," *Journal of Psychology and Christianity* 20, no. 1 (2001): 5-17.

a fuller, more complete picture of that part of reality. In recent years my research has focused on issues of embodiment. In attempting to understand the embodied aspect of our experience, I have drawn both on theological insights and on literature from the social sciences.[44] Theology and the social sciences complement each other: theology provides answers to the intended functioning or purpose of the creation of humans (and of their bodies) by telling us what they were created for, while the social sciences focus on description, documenting in detail the actual functioning of the body. Bringing both of these answers together can provide us with a more complete understanding of what the body is for.

Reflecting

Mark Noll suggested that in the creative arts, an important task of the Christian scholar is to accurately reflect reality. By this, he does not mean that Christians should engage in naïve realism. Rather,

> if atonement theology suggests that narrative is basic to human expression, including artistic expression, the question of narrative shape is also important. Since atonement involves tremendous complexity and great mystery, the best narratives will not be simplistic . . . , Manichean (where the good guys are all good and the bad guys are all bad) . . . , heroic (where protagonists triumph over obstacles through reliance on their own inner resources), or simply nihilistic (where the point is to enact the futility of human existence . . .). Rather, the best narratives will be morally complex. . . . Such morally complex narratives are most satisfying because, in terms of atonement theology, they are most true to life.[45]

It could be argued that all of the disciplines are about reflecting reality to some extent. If this is accurate, then an interesting question to ponder is whether any discipline can ultimately do its job well and still avoid the spiritual or nonmaterial dimension of reality. If our Christian ontology is accurate, and there are aspects of reality that are not captured well by materialistic methodologies, these deficits should become increasingly evident over time. For example, in the field of psychology, C. Brugger notes that "the problems of

44. M. E. L. Hall, "What Are Bodies For?: An Integrative Examination of Embodiment," *Christian Scholar's Review* 39, no. 2 (2010): 159-76.
45. Noll, *Jesus Christ and the Life of the Mind*, p. 71.

human origin and human destiny, transcendent questions like the existence of God, the soul and life after death, and moral and existential questions like the problems of good and evil and human suffering are relevant to clinical psychology and often relevant for success in psychotherapy"; he further notes that these questions cannot be answered through the methods of psychology.[46]

Providing a Moral Compass

While the sciences purport to be morally neutral, self-consciously assuming a descriptive stance, many aspects of science (particularly the human sciences) do involve moral values. Eric Johnson notes that faith-based convictions provide moral guidance in areas where the sciences are ill-prepared to do so — what he calls the "axiological role" of the Bible:

> Ultimately, research on humans can only tell us how humans are, not how they should be. However, it is necessary in science (especially in human science) to make many value judgments. Are there some things we should not investigate? How should we treat the subjects of our research? Is authority essentially good or evil? What constitutes human abnormality? . . . On the basis of scriptural revelation (as well as other considerations), we are better equipped to make wise choices regarding what human phenomena to investigate, how to investigate them, and how to interpret the results of our investigation.[47]

Outside of the natural and human sciences, morality also infuses scholarship. George Marsden writes, "Scholars, like all people, are moralists. Nothing is more common, at least in scholarship having to do with human behavior, than moral judgments, whether explicit or, more often, implicit. Moral judgments, like other commitments, help determine what subjects people study, what questions they ask about their subjects, and what answers they will give to those questions." In his own field, history, he notes the influence of moral judgments in two ways: "How do I, implicitly or explicitly, evaluate various developments as positive, negative, or something in between? . . . How do these evaluations shape my narrative?"[48]

---

46. C. Brugger, "Anthropological Foundation for Clinical Psychology: A Proposal," *Journal of Psychology and Theology* 36, no. 1 (2008): 3-15.

47. Johnson, "A Place for the Bible within Psychological Science," p. 351.

48. Marsden, *The Outrageous Idea of Christian Scholarship*, p. 80, p. 48.

Contextualizing

Contextualizing consists of placing the data or theories of the discipline into a biblical framework so that its meaning and significance become apparent. Psychologist Mary Stewart Van Leeuwen notes that all scholarly endeavors have "two faces": a logical face, which follows the methodological rules of each discipline, and an interpretive face. With respect to the latter, she states that "scholars attach meanings to what they study and perceive structures in it on the basis of highly personal intuitions and belief structures."[49] When these personal intuitions and belief structures are formed by the Christian faith, they will shape interpretations in Christian ways. All scholars have interpretive frameworks. For example, a Marxist scholar will interpret facts across many disciplines in light of power structures. A Christian might see the thread of God's interactions with humanity in the data. Alternatively, situating the data in the particular place which we occupy in the larger story — the already and the not-yet — may lead to insights about the meaning of our data.

George Marsden offers the analogy of a gestalt picture for understanding how our Christian commitments influence our interpretation:

> We organize experience according to available patterns that the mind has at its disposal. . . . To the extent that we deal with many aspects of individual "facts," our scholarship will be identical [to that of non-Christians]. . . . At higher levels of interpretation, however, we might differ radically on the overall meaning or relative importance of the facts . . . background beliefs will have a vast influence on which pattern we see when we look at "the facts."[50]

In addition to Christian background beliefs that focus on a specific area of study that is being addressed, our Christian beliefs also include a grand story, a metanarrative with several important acts: creation, fall, redemption, sanctification, and glorification. Stephen Evans notes that this narrative "needs to become the 'frame' or context in terms of which everything else is understood." He calls it the "basic or foundational narrative in terms of which we under-

---

49. Mary Stewart Van Leeuwen, "Bringing Christian Criteria to Bear on Academic Work," in *Making Higher Education Christian: The History and Mission of Evangelical Colleges in America,* ed. Joel A. Carpenter and Kenneth W. Shipps (Grand Rapids: Christian University Press, 1987), p. 198.

50. Marsden, *The Outrageous Idea of Christian Scholarship,* p. 61.

stand the world."[51] William Dyrness likewise notes "God's great pattern of redemption," and states that "any study, therefore, of human life and community must be approached in the light of this pattern of thinking, and alternative patterns must be confronted and evaluated in relation to this fundamental conception."[52] Psychologist Eric Johnson states, "Through the Scriptures, we are told about the meaning and purpose for creation and ourselves. . . . At the very least, then, modern psychological truth must be re-contextualized and brought into the Christian framework so that it is seen in the light of God. . . . This re-contextualization may or may not change the conception we have of something."[53] The picture these authors present is of the story of history as the outline of a puzzle or the overall plot of a story; individual puzzle pieces, small portions of narrative, take on full meaning only when placed within their context.

Reclaiming

This last mode is perhaps not properly situated in the section on content, as it does not always directly address the subject matter of our disciplines. Instead, it steps back to look at the disciplines themselves. Arthur Holmes notes the creative and redemptive influence that Christianity has had on the development of Western culture, including the development of science, and encourages Christian scholars to recover and claim this history as a model of Christian scholarship.[54] Mark Noll, for example, provides a brief history of Christianity and science that challenges popular conceptions of the relationship as being characterized by tension and antagonism.[55] In many disciplines there are important ways in which key historical figures have brought their faith to bear on their discipline in ways that are now overlooked or ignored; the proper source of these insights deserves reclaiming.

---

51. Evans, "The Calling of the Christian Scholar-Teacher," p. 37; see also M. W. Goheen and C. G. Bartholomew, *Living at the Crossroads: An Introduction to Christian Worldview* (Grand Rapids: Baker Academic, 2008); and Gould, "The Two Tasks Introduced."

52. Dyrness, "The Contribution of Theological Studies to the Christian Liberal Arts," p. 180.

53. Johnson, "A Place for the Bible within Psychological Science," p. 351.

54. Holmes, *The Idea of a Christian College.*

55. Noll, *Jesus Christ and the Life of the Mind.*

The Process of Scholarship

As noted above, it is not just our Christian beliefs but also our Christian practices and values that influence our scholarship. This is true not just of the content of scholarship but also of the process of scholarship. For example, awareness of our finitude may lead us to approach our subject matter with epistemological humility. Love of God and neighbor may lead us to work on certain projects and not others. Hospitality may lead us to interact with criticism of our work in nondefensive and engaging ways. Generosity may lead us to give freely of our time and of our ideas to our colleagues and students. Many of these values and practices seem at odds with the common values and practices of the academy, in which competitiveness, autonomy, and silo-building are common.

There is yet another dimension of the process of Christian scholarship that may set it apart from mere scholarship: the context in which it is practiced. Whether or not the Christian scholar in question is employed at a Christian institution of higher education, he or she forms part of the church universal. All of our callings take place within this context. If we consider our work Christologically, then the context of the body of Christ has the potential to influence our work through support, participation in common goals to benefit the body and to extend the kingdom of God, and distribution of labor in light of the giftedness of each body part. Many of the "one anothers" used to describe the relationships of the body of Christ seem relevant to the practice of scholarship, and in this area they serve the additional purpose of helping us to see beyond the limitations of our own unique (and perhaps un-Christian) perspectives on truth. The individualism prevalent in most sectors of the academy is at odds with the picture of interdependence presented in Scripture. Our work together in community may be one of the most profound ways our scholarship could be marked as Christian, and suggests the need for intentional development of practices of collaboration.

Outcomes of Scholarship

Three types of outcomes or applications of scholarly work are widely endorsed by proponents of Christian scholarship: service, enhancing our knowledge of reality, and worship. Philosopher Stephen Evans's definition of Christian scholarship includes the notion that it is "scholarship that is done to further the kingdom of God [and is] carried out as part of a *calling* by citizens of that kingdom. . . ."[56] According to Nicholas Wolterstorff, the desire to benefit others may lead the scholar to propose distinctively Christian applications of the results of scholarship to the problems of human life. Wolterstorff proposes that our vision of the kingdom of God be that of shalom, and that our scholarly efforts specifically address issues of injustice around the world in pursuit of that shalom.[57]

Similarly, theologian William Dyrness notes that Christian faith requires *response* to nature as well as understanding it. By this he means that becoming aware of problems in the natural world or of human suffering through our scholarship should result in a sense of responsibility to do something about them. Furthermore, once we see how the piece of reality we are studying fits in with God's larger story, "this discovery demands an active response, a *mission*: we must make God's task our task; we too must be involved with God's purpose to redeem the world and thus glorify him."[58]

Joel Carpenter likewise offers a vision for Christian scholarship: to be "agents of cultural discipleship." By this he means that we have a missionary calling to "bring the gospel to bear on every realm of nature and human experience," giving witness in our intellectual work to God's vision of shalom.[59]

Philosopher William Hasker notes a second outcome of Christian scholarship, which he calls "world-view contribution." In this mode of Christian scholarship, the question to be asked is this: "What specific contribution does this discipline make to the Christian vision of reality? How does it enable us to understand God, and his world, and our fellow human beings differently than if the insights of the discipline were not available? What insights, projects, and activities does the discipline make possible? In short, what difference does the discipline make for Christians who are not its students and practitioners?"[60] The task of the Christian scholar, as Hasker sees it, is not merely to work Christianly within each separate discipline, but to contribute to an overall vision of reality in the light of Christ for the benefit of the Christian community.

Scholarship is also conceptualized as a call to worship. As an example,

---

56. Evans, "The Calling of the Christian Scholar-Teacher," p. 34.

57. See Wolterstorff, *Reason within the Bounds of Religion* and *Educating for Shalom*.

58. Dyrness, "The Contribution of Theological Studies to the Christian Liberal Arts," p. 179.

59. Joel A. Carpenter, "The Mission of Christian Scholarship in the New Millennium," in *Faithful Learning and the Christian Scholarly Vocation*, ed. Douglas V. Henry and Bob R. Agee (Grand Rapids: Wm. B. Eerdmans, 2003), p. 68, p. 72.

60. William Hasker, "Faith-learning Integration: An Overview," *Christian Scholar's Review* 21, no. 3 (1992): 245.

Duane Litfin presents his vision for scholarship in chemistry: "I want them [students] not only to be fascinated and delighted by the intricacies of chemical behavior but also to realize that what they're exploring is the handiwork of the Lord Jesus Christ. . . . I also want them to see at every moment what these things are telling them about the One they know as their Savior so that in the end they are lifted up to him, even in a chemistry course."[61]

A Typology of Modes of Christian Engagement with the Disciplines

Category	Mode or Strategy
Motivation	Hope
	Love
	Understanding
	Knowing Christ
	Submitting to Christ's lordship
	Gratitude
Epistemology	Challenging assumptions in ontology, epistemology, methodology, ethics
Content	Providing direction
	Confirming
	Evaluating
	Clarifying
	Elaborating
	Complementing
	Reflecting
	Providing a moral compass
	Contextualizing
	Reclaiming
Process	Examplifying Christian values and practices
	Recognizing the body of Christ
Outcome or Application	Service
	Enhanced knowledge of reality
	Worship

61. Litfin, *Conceiving the Christian College*, pp. 76-77.

Factors Influencing the Selection of Modes of Engagement

There appear to be a number of factors that influence which modes of engagement are chosen by any given scholar. Among these, I focus on three: the scholar's discipline, the level of specificity of the scholarship, and the audience for which the scholar is writing. Depending on these factors (and likely others), scholars may vary in the degree to which their scholarship is overtly Christian. Stephen Evans distinguishes between three kinds of Christian scholarship. Academics in disciplines that do not have much overlap in content with Scripture, or who do scholarship for secular audiences, may be satisfied with doing scholarship that is Christian only in that they work with excellence, contributing to the general good, and living as Christians in their setting. Evans calls this *purely vocational Christian scholarship*. Sometimes Christian scholars' work is influenced in its content by their Christian faith, but this connection is implicit rather than explicit — what Evans calls *implicit Christian scholarship*. Christians in fields with a greater degree of overlap with content from the Christian faith may choose to pull in Christian content in much more overt ways, producing *explicit Christian scholarship*. This kind of scholarship may play an apologetic role in the discipline, or it may be intended for Christian audiences.[62]

What this means is that much Christian scholarship may not, on the surface, seem radically different from scholarship produced by those who are not Christians. Perhaps this should not surprise us, given the notion of the unity of truth in a world created by God. In any case, several Christian scholars have commented on the issue of the "distinctiveness" of Christian scholarship.[63] Wolterstorff summarizes the sentiment of these views as follows: "I have suggested that Christian scholarship is faithful scholarship. By this I mean that it is to be defined not by its difference but by its fidelity."[64] And faithfulness may take different forms, depending on the specific calling of the scholar.

Disciplinary Differences in Content

Academic disciplines vary in the degree to which the content of their disciplines overlaps with content addressed by faith. George Marsden distinguishes

---

62. Evans, "The Calling of the Christian Scholar-Teacher."
63. Richard T. Hughes, *How Christian Faith Can Sustain the Life of the Mind* (Grand Rapids: Wm. B. Eerdmans, 2001); Marsden, *The Outrageous Idea of Christian Scholarship*.
64. Wolterstorff, *Educating for Shalom*, p. 79.

between fields that primarily focus on empirical investigation and those that touch on issues of wider significance or meaning:

> So on topics that have the most to do with interpretation and with the larger significance and meaning of humans in relation to each other and the universe, faith-related perspectives will have the most bearing. Such implications are more often apparent in the humanities and social sciences than in the hard sciences. Philosophers are likely more often to be able to identify the pertinence of religious perspectives for their work than will historians or social scientists, who in turn will be able to point to religious influences more often than will chemists or physicists.[65]

Marsden also notes that religious commitments will have more of an influence in disciplines where religion is explicitly an issue and where moral judgments are made.[66]

Similarly, Stephen Evans proposes what he calls a "relevance continuum," according to the frequency with which Christianity might bear in a substantive manner on any given academic discipline. He puts mathematics, natural sciences, human sciences, history, literature and the arts, and philosophy and theology on a continuum ranging from "least frequent" to "most frequent." Of course, even within disciplines, there will be variability from subfield to subfield.[67]

Put another way, this continuum can be described as one across which the noetic effects of sin vary. Emil Brunner noted this many years ago, stating, "The nearer anything lies to that center of existence where we are concerned with the whole, that is, with man's relation to God and the being of the person, the greater is the disturbance of rational knowledge by sin; the farther away anything lies from this center, the less is the disturbance felt, and the less difference is there between knowing as a believer or as an unbeliever."[68]

William Hasker makes a distinction between theoretical and applied disciplines. He argues that the epistemological and metaphysical issues in Christian scholarship are more relevant for the former than for the latter. In contrast, issues around application in service are most relevant to the applied disciplines. He notes that applying theory brings up a distinct set of questions that must be addressed: "What are the implications and results when this theory

---

65. Marsden, *The Outrageous Idea of Christian Scholarship*, p. 63.

66. Marsden, *Beyond Progressive Scientific Humanism*.

67. Evans, "The Calling of the Christian Scholar-Teacher"; see also Holmes, *The Idea of a Christian College*.

68. Emil Brunner, *Revelation and Reason* (Philadelphia: Westminster Press, 1946), p. 383.

is put into practice?" In making this distinction, he provides the example of Skinnerian behaviorism. The theoretical questions about behaviorism might include questions about the foundational assumptions of this approach, its mechanistic anthropology, determinism, materialism, and denial of free will and dignity. On the applied side, however, the question is "What are the effects in practice of using behavior modification, for example, as one's primary method of discipline in the elementary classroom? And how do those effects coincide or conflict with one's ultimate objectives as a Christian educator?"[69] He also sees questions of ethics and values as becoming more prominent in the applied disciplines than in the theoretical disciplines.

Level of Specificity

Scholars in all disciplines do scholarship that varies in its level of abstraction. When scholarship is being done at very specific levels, such as conducting tightly controlled empirical observation in the sciences, Christian commitments may make very little difference. But as the scope of the scholarship becomes broader, involving interpretation, it is likely that questions of significance or meaning will be more influenced by matters of faith. David Naugle's distinction between disciplines is based on the influence of epistemic worldview issues. Like the authors reviewed above, he divides the disciplines according to their reliance on epistemic worldview issues, but then adds, "This seems intuitive, unless one is talking about the philosophy of chemistry or mathematics, for then one has slipped away from the practice of these disciplines into a discussion of their first principles. When this occurs, worldview factors become quite significant."[70] In other words, while a continuum of intersection with Christian beliefs can be described among the disciplines, at certain levels of abstraction, Christian beliefs become relevant in all the disciplines.

Audience

Some of the modes of engagement I have described are consistent with the practices of the secular academy (although I note here that what is acceptable

---

69. Hasker, "Faith-learning Integration: An Overview," p. 247.

70. David Naugle, *Worldview: The History of a Concept* (Grand Rapids: Wm. B. Eerdmans, 2002), p. 328.

in the secular academy seems to vary greatly by discipline); other approaches are intended to challenge the practices of the secular academy; still others seem most suited for audiences that share similar Christian commitments. Psychologist Eric Johnson, in describing Christian scholarship in psychology and using the language of integration, distinguishes between *strategic integration* and *maximal integration*.[71] Strategic forms of Christian scholarship use the rules of discourse of the secular discipline, but find ways to advance a Christian agenda to the extent that it is allowed or tolerated by the discipline. This may take the form of addressing Christian topics through the lens of the discipline or bringing topics suggested by Christian commitments into the field as objects of study. It may even involve challenging the discipline by pointing out weaknesses of some of the rules of the discipline in the rules' ability to help the discipline achieve its aims, or noting times when disciplinary practices fall short of the discipline's own ideals. This type of integration is challenging and important, and requires Christian scholars to develop tools of translation and bridge-building.

In contrast, maximal Christian scholarship is practiced "by, within, and for the Christian community" and is not constrained by disciplinary rules.[72] Since the goal in maximal scholarship is the unification of knowledge about disciplinary content (e.g., the unification of knowledge about human beings in psychology), it involves all sources of knowledge relevant to the content area. These sources include Scripture and the Christian tradition, as well as content coming from the disciplines. Johnson acknowledges that it is an ideal, a teleological concept, in that it is an attempt to approximate God's understanding of that area — a goal we will always fall short of. Whether any given scholar practices strategic or maximal Christian integration will be influenced in part by the intended audience of the specific project.

The Is and the Ought of Christian Scholarship

To this point, I have attempted to be primarily descriptive in my comments on Christian scholarship. Before concluding, however, I would like to briefly offer some prescriptive comments. For a variety of reasons, which I suspect are primarily undergirded by socialization pressures to conform to disciplinary

71. Eric L. Johnson, "The Three Faces of Integration," *Journal of Psychology and Christianity* 30, no. 4 (2011): 339-55.

72. Johnson, "The Three Faces of Integration," p. 349.

norms, many Christians in the academy intentionally keep their Christianity out of their scholarship. At an interdisciplinary Christian academic conference I attended some years ago, a presenter was asked how his Christian faith came to bear on his discipline. In response, he stated that he engaged in the practices of his religious tradition regularly, then sought to be the best scholar he could be. Further interaction with his comments made it clear that from his perspective there was no connection between his religious practices and his scholarly work. While one might wonder if his Christian commitments had managed to sneak into his scholarship in spite of his best efforts to keep them out, his response still puzzles me. With the wealth of motivational and intellectual resources offered by our faith, it would seem to me that wise engagement in scholarship by Christians would mean, at a minimum, that the scholarship be motivated by one's Christian values and commitments on the basis that Jesus is Lord of all aspects of life. Furthermore, thoughtful awareness of potential conflicts between the methods and predominant paradigms of the discipline and one's Christian values and commitments would seem necessary for responsible engagement in Christian scholarship, even if the individual did not himself or herself engage in scholarship that critiqued those methods and paradigms. In other words, Christian commitments might seem necessary to the process of scholarship by a Christian, even if they are not evident in the product.

In terms of the areas of content and application, the concepts of vocation and of community seem relevant. Christian values and moral sensibilities should influence the content of scholarship, even if only in indirect ways, in the Christian scholar who has been formed by the Holy Spirit. It would also seem to be the path of wisdom to know the ways in which Scripture/theology addresses our area of scholarly inquiry, if there is some sort of meaningful overlap. So, all other factors being equal, I would argue that maximal Christian scholarship should be preferred, given its potential to more fully understand reality and God's agenda for human flourishing. But whether or not scriptural/theological insights are explicitly brought into the scholarship, and whether or not the outcome of the scholarship is the known good of others, may depend on the discipline, the specific area within the discipline, and the specific audience to which any given scholar is called. So an individual's vocation or calling is important to consider with respect to content and outcomes of Christian scholarship.

My prescriptive comments with respect to content and application are, I think, fairly modest. Others who have written on Christian scholarship offer much stronger prescriptions in this area. Paul Moser, for example, argues that Jesus' love commands are relevant and binding to those who recognize Jesus as Lord. According to Moser, Jesus' commands to love God and neighbor imply that "our projects are acceptable only to the extent that they contribute . . . to satisfying the love commands."[73] So in his view, scholarly projects should be prioritized according to whether they allow us to be obedient to Jesus' love commands. Moser explicitly disallows vocation or calling to provide scholars with exemptions to fulfilling the command to love others through their scholarship — although love may be expressed differently, depending on a particular calling or gifting. An important caveat to Moser's statement is that the history of scholarship demonstrates that scholars often make discoveries without any specific generative applications in mind. Yet they often prove to actually make a great deal of difference in people's lives. For example, exploration of the properties of prime numbers may seem like an extraordinarily abstract area of study to many of us, yet these properties have been applied to cryptography, which allows us to keep our personal information secure during Internet transactions.

In addition to vocation, the concept of community is important. As mentioned earlier, Christian scholars are part of the body of Christ. Scholars are part of a group of Christians working in their area of study; the full spectrum of Christian scholarship should be seen as the task of the community rather than that of the individual scholar, so that some do the basic research, others critique disciplinary assumptions, and yet others develop practical applications of the work. Perhaps this observation carries with it a prescriptive encouragement to actively engage with other Christians in the discipline. The notion of community also suggests the possibility of collaborative scholarship. In our age of specialization and the expansion of knowledge, one individual may not be equipped to do maximal Christian scholarship well. Collaborations between scholars in theology and the disciplines may be the way forward. In either case, Christian scholars can be encouraged in their work knowing that they are part of a larger body of believers who are working together to enlarge human understanding and contribute to human flourishing.

In this chapter I have outlined a number of strategies for engaging the disciplines Christianly. This survey of ways in which Christian scholars have interfaced with their disciplines demonstrates that the task of Christian scholarship is multilayered and complex. But with this challenge and complexity come the possibility of engaging in our disciplines in ways that richly reflect the world created for, through, and by Jesus Christ. It is my hope that this brief attempt to provide a scaffold for Christian scholarship will also encourage believers to delve into this rewarding task.

---

73. Paul K. Moser, "Jesus and Philosophy: On the Questions We Ask," *Faith and Philosophy* 22, no. 3 (2005): 264.

The Cross and Christian Scholarship

Craig J. Slane

When Jesus Came to College

On a spring morning in 1981, I and other undergraduate students were leaving chapel in the usual manner — chattering about the speaker and hustling to get to class — when a gaunt man around thirty years of age met us on the steps outside. Long-haired and with a life-sized cross on his back, he wore a first-century-style tunic and was heard imploring the college community to repent. He was full of prophetic conviction, animated, and earnest. Students dodged him. Staff and administrators mobilized against him.

To this young Christian student, it was an occurrence most strange. Over and again I heard chapel speakers praise us for being among the "best and brightest." I considered it a shining example of divine providence to have landed with such fortune in the citadel of evangelical higher education where faithful servants of God took to their callings with such sobriety. For all I knew then, I was at the epicenter of true Christianity. So when an anguished Jesus look-alike tried to jolt me from the naïve security of my religious world, I was dumbfounded. I had few categories for assimilating what I had seen. As I remember it, the intruder was escorted off the campus as quickly as possible, his rapid removal restoring order once again to our tranquil suburban grounds. Consensus among those who witnessed this interruption was that the young man was freakish, misguided, choosing poorly the setting for a message that belonged elsewhere, perhaps at the local mission. From the perspective of those responsible for student welfare, the whole episode was an unfortunate disturbance. However, for a few of us, a crack had appeared, through which a small ray of light began to shine on our religious landscape. I wondered: Did those responsible for the intruder's removal ask themselves, perhaps that evening as the day's doings came up for review, just how their actions might have helped or hindered the purposes of God?

Something like this scenario involving the removal of Jesus was played out in the life of the apostle Paul. As a distinguished rabbi at the epicenter of Judaism, having earned expertise in its history and traditions, and having devoted himself splendidly to its protection against those who were preaching falsely, Paul suddenly discovered by an experience with the risen Jesus that for all his orthodoxy and good intentions he had astonishingly become party to God's removal. In an unexpected reversal of perspective, he had discovered his complicity in the deep structure of human sin. He had discovered himself in opposition to God, who, by raising Jesus from the dead, had justified Jesus and his followers. When we discover that what we do in the best interests of the god we think we know runs precisely contrary to the actual will of God, it sends us reeling. If we allow ourselves to be undone by this discovery, it can become our conversion. It's not that Paul had made a small miscalculation about God that could be corrected with greater learning. Rather, his discovery meant that he now had to wrestle with the terrible truth that his learning had formed him in ways that conditioned him to misrecognize God. Something had prevented him from interpreting rightly those things that had recently taken place in his corner of the Roman Empire. By lending assistance to the persecution of Christians under the aegis of Yahweh, Paul had demonstrated the truth of Jesus' words: "an hour is coming when those who kill you will think that by doing so they are offering worship to God" (John 16:2, NRSV). Thus Paul's theology had to be stripped to the foundation and rebuilt to account for the irony that he, a Jewish scholar and teacher devoted to Yahweh, had himself become an enemy of God.

Unlike Paul, I returned to my daily college routine without a discernible conversion and without a rebuilt theology. I had precious little to rebuild. But the event lodged itself in my memory and slowly became an important tool in my growing theological understanding. I can't delete the memory of that day when Jesus and his cross were chased from the campus of my alma mater. As I understand it now, the bearer of the cross on that morning was attempting to deconstruct an established institution — indeed, an established *people* who, despite their noblest sacrifices to create the best Christian education on offer, had somehow not taken full account of Jesus. He had prepared for us established people a theatre in which we could discover our roles in Jesus' expulsion. I do not know this man, but he offered me the gift of a lifetime.

So then, these questions: Might the institution of Christian scholarship be vulnerable to the removal of Jesus? If so, how can Christian scholars learn to detect when and where Jesus is cast out? And, assuming we can make such detection, what would it mean to undergo a Pauline-style conversion, placing the crucified Christ at the center of our identity as Christian scholars?

Framing Christian Scholarship

Let me be clear about what I have been trying to communicate so far: our ability to think and act faithfully under the label "Christian" depends on the discovery that we — from those nearest to religious discourse to those farthest away — are susceptible to the misrecognition of God. Further, our ability to see rightly and correct course depends on whether we are willing to see Jesus as an expelled messenger of Yahweh and assess honestly the role we Christian scholars might unwittingly play in his removal. The failure to discern Jesus as a victim of habits and powers in which we participate is, I submit, part of the blindness of Christendom and the malaise plaguing so much of what has been promoted under the adjective "Christian."

When the term "Christian" is used as an adjective, we can be sure we are reproducing the habits of Christendom, says Stanley Hauerwas in his collection of essays called *The State of the University*.[1] Wishing not to reproduce the bad habits of Christendom, some would prefer to abandon the term "*Christian* scholarship" and speak rather of "*scholarship* by Christians," weighting the noun "scholarship" and deleting the adjective "Christian." Maybe that's the best we can do. Certainly it respects the other in our pluralistic space, and we could shift emphasis as needed between the common task of scholarship and the particularities deemed relevant to the one who performs it as a Christian. There is much to commend this suggestion. Fine scholarship is being done by professing Christians who minimize the impact of Christian convictions on their methodologies, evidence, sources, argumentation, and so on. Yet two observations are in order: first, the audacious title of this volume invites serious reflection on the adjective, and second, the bad habits of our Christian forbears should be distinguished from Christ himself. Indeed, it is to be hoped that Christ corrects them.

Thus, the problem with the term "Christian scholarship" is not the adjec-

---

1. Stanley Hauerwas, "Introduction," *The State of the University: Academic Knowledges and the Knowledge of God* (Malden, Mass.: Blackwell, 2007), p. 7.

tive per se, *but the fact that in the opinion of many this adjective is conditioned so thoroughly by past deployments of imperial power that the "way of Jesus" is no longer conjured by the term "Christian."* We live in a time of awakening to and reckoning with the triumphal tendencies of our Christian past, a time when practically every scholar is acutely conscious of the supporting role played by Christian thinkers in the colonial project. Willie James Jennings in his award-winning book *The Christian Imagination* has shown how Christian thinkers adapted the traditional theology of creation and providence in service of Portuguese and Iberian conquests of the Americas in such a way as to justify the displacement of peoples on the basis of a racial hierarchy.[2] Closer to home, racial hierarchy was played out in the displacement of both Native Americans and Africans, the latter stolen from their land and held in slavery for 246 years, often with the aid of arguments based on the Bible. After emancipation there followed a stretch of history wherein lynching became a white supremacist mechanism of terror designed to "keep blacks *in their place*" — that "place" being the bottom of the hierarchy. The parallels between the crucifixion of a Jewish body and the lynching of the black body are striking. Indeed, as James Cone shows in *The Cross and the Lynching Tree,* lynchers were blind to the fact that they were reproducing the mob who cried out against Jesus, "Crucify him!"[3]

Of course, most of us would be quick to point out that none of these injustices related to Christian empire represent authentic Christianity. We might easily conclude that those self-professing Christians caught up in them clearly moved against the grain of the very God to whom they gave their worship and adoration. When, as in our time, people widely succumb to the false impression that such injustices are actually undergirded by Christian belief — an assumption that spans wide swaths of contemporary intellectual life — we sense that something must be done to boost belief's credibility or at least to assess whether and how what is alleged to be supported by Christianity relates to Christianity's founding revelation. Both overtly and subtly Christian scholars may find themselves motivated to rescue Christian belief and practice from various misperceptions and distortions. Certainly it is both good and useful to distinguish true Christianity from its bastard forms. As long as sin damages epistemic functioning, Christian existence will require it, not

2. Willie James Jennings, *The Christian Imagination: Theology and the Origins of Race* (New Haven: Yale University Press, 2011). Among other cases, Jennings follows carefully the career of José de Acosta, a star of the young Jesuit order with the finest scholastic training, as he renders theologically his engagement with the Indians of Peru.

3. James H. Cone, *The Cross and the Lynching Tree* (Maryknoll, N.Y.: Orbis Books, 2011).

just in the domain of theologians, but across a broad spectrum of disciplines in which Christian scholars are working. However, there is a danger in such work. By it we may all too easily miss our complicity in such injustices and instead scapegoat our forebears on the assumption that we, now enlightened, have been liberated from such practices.

Since scholarship is deeply connected to the university and conducted in close proximity to it, and since the university has been a powerful engine of emancipation from all sorts of past hegemonies, scholars may be prone to imagine themselves by proxy to be categorically on the side of justice, standing for victims past and present over and against their victimizers and their atrocities. This is a vital work of scholarship in the humanities today. Yet if we ignore the possibility that the entire apparatus of Christian scholarship *itself* can operate in ways that exclude others and drive them out, then we have in biblical terms tried to remove the speck from our brother's eye while impeded by the log in our own. It may be more useful to acknowledge with Paul that we have unwittingly been accomplices in expulsion and seek therewith to reorient ourselves to Jesus.

It is not the purpose of this essay to dwell in detail on the exclusionary practices undertaken by Christian universities and Christian scholars. But I think I can convey the practices and habits I have in mind by asking how scholars and their supporting institutions deal with *difference*. Differences abound: ideological, religious, political, racial, sexual, and so forth. Though key to dynamic social structures, differences are also the occasion for rivalry and conflict. They create obstacles and in the course of time threaten unity and thus survival, at which point differences must be somehow overcome. *How* they are overcome determines whether we have been conditioned more by the logic of God or by the ancient logic of human social belonging. For difference can be overcome either by love, which goes to extraordinary lengths to discover unity in difference (or differentiated unity), or by violence, which, exasperated by difference, seeks to destroy it.

Imagine a professor advising and supervising student research. As happens frequently, a student will gather a set of sources she would like to read to produce a term paper, some of which are likely to be outdated, outside scholarly consensus, originating in a school of thought or perspective unsuitable to the professor, produced by substandard publishing houses, and so forth. The professor's training has conditioned her to include some sources and exclude others. So how does she respond to the student's bibliography? Which *persons* are permitted to have influence on developing minds? Or imagine the scholar asked to review a new book from a colleague whose research he considers inferior to his own, or perhaps a well-known rival in the discipline. How does the reviewer deal with the differences between himself and the author in question? And what are we to make of the fact that the academy is akin to a competitive arena wherein procuring grants, getting tenure, advancing to promotion, and publishing are often obtained over and against one's colleagues and fellow practitioners? How do academic administrators react when faculty members publish research that seems to stretch existing doctrinal or political boundaries, or to faculty who outspokenly challenge institutional practices?

In each of these examples a sectarian or tribal spirit may appear wherein one party, person, or institution is considered superior to another, closer to the truth than another, or wherein incessant comparisons with others are deployed to "brand" or achieve distinct identity. Here the logic of expulsion is close at hand. The issue is not so much whether differences exist. They will be present in any social order. The issue is whether we construct our identity and strive for unity by means of those differences. If the gospel is one of reconciliation, then we are offered the opportunity to achieve identity from the gracious love of God and avoid building a social order over against anyone at all. To be a Christian, I take it, is to be in the often painful process of acquiring a new identity rooted in the Trinitarian love of God. Though ultimately a gift of God, the acquisition of identity in this way requires relinquishing some habits of the academy, since the traditions surrounding human knowledge and its dissemination are often locked into identities achieved "over against."

My hope is that Christian scholarship — so long as we agree to use the term — would become more attentive to the scandal of the cross.[4] For therein we have a symbol that is both quintessentially Christian and, rightly understood, potentially corrective of those illegitimate deployments of power that tarnish Christian identity. The cross carries the advantage of a double revelation: at the same time that it reveals something decisive about God, it reveals something about the human condition that perhaps could be dredged up in no other way: the deep structure of human sin. This, then, brings me to the thesis I want to argue for the remainder of this essay.

By exploring what the cross means anthropologically, Christian scholars may reduce their susceptibility to justify practices of exclusion and expulsion.

---

4. In his Abraham Kuyper lectures, Mark Noll proposed "adding cross to crown" in Christian political discourse. I call attention to his work as a significant attempt to recover the cross as correction to past abuses of power. See Mark A. Noll, *Adding Cross to Crown: The Political Significance of Christ's Passion* (Grand Rapids: Baker, 1996).

Christian thinkers have been duly attentive to what *God* was doing in the cross. But we have not contemplated deeply enough what *humanity* was doing in the cross. If we could see more clearly the mechanisms by which Jesus was crucified, the old habits of human culture and religion on display in the passion narrative, we might recognize the subtle ways our work as scholars can sometimes move contrary to the gospel. To argue this thesis, I will offer a reading of Justin Martyr and the role he plays in the "imaginary" (to use Charles Taylor's term) of Christian scholarship. Justin's readers often render him an early Christian scholar in whose thinking human and divine wisdom harmonize. I will try to offer an alternative to this reading, one which puts him along the trajectory of what has typically been called a *theologia crucis* — the trajectory I am recommending for faithful Christian scholarship. I will also argue that Justin's failure to distinguish clearly the two kinds of logic on display in the event of Jesus' death left him vulnerable to just the sort of error that Christian scholars are prone to make — which, in Justin's case, took the form of anti-Semitism. As for many of us, Justin's life work is a combination of splendid success and dismal failure.

Reconsidering Justin Martyr: Seven Theses

T1 *The standard interpretation of Justin Martyr (d. 165) posits deep continuity between the best thinking of the ancient Greek philosophers and the Logos of John's Gospel.*

What I am here calling the standard interpretation of Justin can be found in the renowned scholar of early Christianity, Henry Chadwick, whose comments gathered below provide apt illustration:

> Of all the early Christian theologians Justin is the most optimistic about the harmony of Christianity and Greek philosophy. For him the gospel and the best elements in Plato and the Stoics are almost identical ways of apprehending the same truth.

> Justin's second ground for affirming the positive value of philosophy is that all rational beings share in the universal Logos or Reason who is Christ. So both Abraham and Socrates were "Christians before Christ." So also the noble morality of the Stoics comes from their share in the "seminal Logos," the divine Reason who has sown the seeds of truth in all men as beings created

in God's image. Accordingly the philosophers have been able to read God both in the book of nature and in the inner deliverances of their reason.

Justin does not merely make Socrates a Christian. His Christ is a philosopher, "no sophist," but a genuine teacher of the way to "happiness" *(eudaimonia)*, in himself the personification of the "right reason" *(orthos logos)* teaching "divine virtue." His teaching in the Sermon on the Mount is wholly in line with natural law; it is a universal morality, valid for all races and stripped of the national particularism of Judaism.[5]

Reading through the three works of Justin available to us — the *First Apology*, the *Second Apology*, and the *Dialogue with Trypho* — one has the impression that Chadwick's interpretation must be right, or at least reasonably close to what this second-century Christian was trying to say. Yet I wonder whether that impression originates in part from the fact that the winning proposals for understanding Christ in relation to classical philosophy were worked out on the premise of continuity. Perhaps I can best express my concern with a set of questions. Did the powerful articulations given later by Augustine and Aquinas create the plausibility structure within which the standard interpretation of Justin now seems obvious? Or, was it Justin's early articulation that helped to frame the future projects of Augustine and Aquinas? Whatever the sequence, do these articulations now resonate together in sufficient force and volume so as to shape definitively our engagement with ancient wisdom? Can we imagine that Socrates or Plato would have been any less scandalized by Jesus than Peter, John, or Judas? How would the ancient philosophers have fared in the nexus of forces playing themselves out in the passion of Christ? To ask my question another way, how does the cross as *skandalon* inform our thinking about human wisdom? Clearly it would be unwise to sever completely the relation between ancient wisdom and Christ, yet *how* they connect is no settled matter.

Since my questions quickly broaden beyond Justin, one may fairly ask why I wish to converse with Justin at all. Here's why:

T2 *Writing before the age of Constantine, Justin's thinking about continuity is situated in the context of cultural opposition to Christianity, when the scandal of the cross was close at hand in the daily experience of believers.*

---

5. Citations are from Henry Chadwick, *Early Christian Thought and the Classical Tradition* (New York: Oxford University Press, 1966), pp. 10-17.

Justin himself is in danger as he writes, "expecting to be plotted against and fixed to a rack."[6] Indeed, the most likely motivation for his Apology was the recent martyrdom of Polycarp, who was sought and found as a result of a mob agitating for his execution.[7] Any theory of "continuity" advanced for Christian faith and Greek philosophy on the basis of Justin's writing must be nuanced enough to account for widespread opposition in the cultural establishment. Chadwick located the ground of continuity in the fact that "all rational beings share in the universal Logos or Reason who is Christ." True enough, but Justin says *more* than this in his account.

T3 *Justin's confidence in continuity between the logos embedded in creation and the Logos of God revealed in Jesus Christ is a corollary of his insight that within the created order there exists a stubborn resistance to Reason.*

The Stoics, Socrates, Heraclitus, and Jesus — and apparently Justin means to include Christians of his own generation in this list — all met with opposition and hatred for their teaching. Consider this passage from the *Second Apology:*

> And those of the Stoic school, since they were honorable at least in their ethical teaching, as were also the poets in some particulars, on account of a seed of the logos implanted in every race of men and women, were, we know, hated and put to death, as for instance Heraclitus mentioned before and, among those of our own time, Musonius and others. For, as we have intimated, *the demons have always* effected that all those who ever so little strived to live by logos and to shun vice be *hated.* And it is not astonishing that the demons are proved to cause those to be *much worse hated* who lived not by a *part* only from the logos, the Sower, but by the knowledge and contemplation of the *whole* logos, who is Christ.[8]

I have added emphasis to Justin's words "part" and "whole" to highlight the symmetrical structure underlying the traditional interpretation: what Socrates had in part, Christ has in whole. I have also highlighted two additional phrases that point in the direction of my claim. In this passage, at least, the link from

---

6. Justin Martyr, *Second Apology* 3. Justin was flogged and beheaded in Rome in 165 C.E.

7. See Robert M. Grant, *Greek Apologists of the Second Century* (Philadelphia: Westminster Press, 1988), p. 53.

8. Justin Martyr, *Second Apology* 8. The "Musonius" of whom Justin speaks is the Stoic philosopher Gaius Musonius Rufus, who was banished from Rome under Nero's reign in 65 C.E. Other philosophers were banished by Vespasian in 71 C.E.

ancient thinkers to Christ is forged by a common hatred of those who live by logos. Such hatred reaches its dramatic climax in Christ, who, by implication, is hated wholly. Several parties are on exhibit here: (1) the human race as such, each member of which possesses in some manner a "seed of the logos" by virtue of the Sower; (2) a subset of humans striving to live in accord with what is in them by nature; (3) the climactic figure of Christ, who personifies logos; and (4) an incrementally organized resistance to the logos as it is distributed among the first three parties. It is not clear from this citation how the opposition — "the demons" — is constituted, so let's augment it with another citation taken from the *First Apology*:

> For the truth shall be told; since of old these evil demons manifested themselves, both defiled women and corrupted boys, and showed terrifying sights to people, that those who did not use their reason in judging the acts that were done, were filled with terror; and being taken captive by fear, and not knowing that these were demons, *they called them gods,* and gave to each the name which each of the demons had chosen for himself. And when *Socrates tried, by true reasoning and definite evidence, to bring these things to light,* and deliver people from the demons, then the demons themselves, by means of people who rejoiced in wickedness, compassed his death, as an atheist and impious person, on the charge of introducing new divinities; and in our case they show a similar activity.[9]

Throughout Justin's writings, demons are held responsible as agents of evil. They are the source of idolatry, fomenters of violence, deceivers of Adam and Eve, the impetus behind the schemes of heretics, the origin of Christ's sufferings, developers of mythology, and more — in short, they explain everything that opposes logos.

T4   *Myth obscures logos.*

Without getting tangled up in the question of demons as discrete personal forces, let's draw focus once again to the emphasized phrases. When Justin says "they called them gods" he means to suggest that demons have by fear and deception succeeded in their quest to be recognized as deities. I suggest we have in this phrase a clear allusion to mythology. Interestingly, the root of the Greek word *muthos* is *mu,* meaning "to close" or "keep secret." *Mu* is the stem

9. Justin Martyr, *First Apology* 5.

of a word like "mute," as in "to mute the voice," as well as words like "music" and "muses," each of which possesses strong aesthetic-cultural connotations. In Greek tragedy, the Muses remember the past fondly and heroically not because they are interested in truth, but because they are the agents of mythological remembrance, for myth is the foundation of culture itself.[10] By their repetitive remembrance of myth, they surround truth in a fog at the same time they reinforce Greek culture. When the demons passed themselves off as gods, they pulled off the mother of all illusions, conscripting *religion* as an ally in their attempt to obfuscate logos. Under this arrangement, "devout" and "pious" persons become also the best patriots. They are convinced that they are friends of the good, but all the while they are helping the demons keep their secret. Conversely, those who seek logos appear to be non-religious, deniers of the good, even atheists.

T5 *Those who align with logos over and against myth are likely to meet with violence and expulsion.*

By camouflaging myth in religion, the demons concocted the perfect antidote to logos. But then along came Socrates, who "tried, by true reasoning and definite evidence, to bring these things to light." Like early Christian martyrs, the victim Socrates was accused of atheism because he questioned the absoluteness of myth. Unable to bear the exposure of their secret, the demons colluded against him, reasserted their gods, and preserved the order of Athens. The majority report will surely construe the removal of Socrates as a divine deliverance. But the minority report says that these powers are in error, set against truth. The demons of mythology resist the light of Reason. It will be instructive also to recall Justin's report about Socrates having rejected the explanations of Homer and the poets. After making this point, he then adduces the words attributed to Socrates in Plato's *Timaeus,* "that it is neither easy to find the Father and Maker of all, nor, having found Him, is it safe to declare Him to all."[11] Here the conflict is put in the sharpest of terms: *muthos versus logos.*

On this reading, then, what Justin labors to unveil is a massive scheme of deception and resistance. Justin personifies this operation when he calls it "demons." We needn't follow him at this point. Remembering Jesus' words from the cross, it is better perhaps to say that demons represent cultural pow-

---

10. Gil Bailie, *Violence Unveiled: Humanity at the Crossroads* (New York: Crossroad, 1995), p. 33.

11. Justin Martyr, *Second Apology* 10.

ers, habits, and explanations unaware of what drives them. They support the current arrangement of the world by a logic that rivals the logos: the logic of social order. Justin does not notice the rationality implied by the operation of demons, an omission we must say more about soon. But he notices clearly the nature of the conflict in which the world is caught.

T6 *Precisely as the rejected and expelled Logos does Christ connect meaningfully with certain of those who came before.*

Once we work expulsion into our thinking about Logos, our reading of the first chapter of John's Gospel goes in a slightly different direction. Instead of landing on those opening verses which read very much like creation cosmology, our attention moves along to sayings like the following:

> The light shines in the darkness, and the darkness did not overcome it. (John 1:5, NRSV)

Or again,

> He was in the world, and the world came into being through him; yet the world did not know him. He came to what was his own, and his own people did not accept him. (John 1:10-11, NRSV)

John's Gospel explores the historical expulsion of the Logos in the story of the man born blind (John 9), who is driven out by Jewish leaders because he has told the truth about Jesus in the heated dispute between Jesus and those who claim to be children of Abraham at the same moment they are plotting to kill him (John 8), and ultimately in the passion narrative itself. By focusing on resistance, Justin helps us see what many readers of John's prologue miss: the Johannine Logos is an *expelled* Logos, and as such brings to light a serious problem, a defect, in the order of human reason.

Whereas most interpreters of Justin move straightaway to his statements of continuity between Greek philosophers and Christ, I want to underscore that we are dealing not with a continuity of thought pure and simple but rather with *continuity forged in resistance to Logos*. To Justin, might the evidence that compels him to align a segment of ancient Greek philosophy with Christ lie in the consistently hostile treatment of those who try to unmask deception? As Logos incarnate, Christ may embody in full that rationality which Socrates had in part, as the standard interpretation asserts. But is *that* the best way to describe Justin's vision of continuity? By stressing continuity of *Logos* over continuity of *resistance,* the traditional interpretation overloads Justin's part-whole dialectic with more rationality than it can bear. What if the truth of the part-whole paradigm lies in a partial-versus-complete unmasking of mythology?

I imagine Justin to be saying something like this: History has always had its truth-seekers, a hated minority of the persecuted, standing in *discontinuity* with the prevailing opinion of culture, vulnerable to prevailing powers, and subject to unjust expulsion and death. Plato, Socrates, and Jesus stand together in this lineage of persecution in such a way that Jesus' ordeal — *only* Jesus' ordeal — reveals definitively what was going on before. Jesus is like the midday sun blazing directly overhead that leaves no shadows. The scheme by which the demons held creation in bondage is now fully revealed. The line of resistance has progressed to its logical end, which is nothing other than the cross, the hidden rationality of logos.

If I am correct, then Justin is giving a philosophical version of the speech that Stephen gave before being stoned. Sifting Jewish history, Stephen showed how Jesus' death fitted together with the persecution of the Jewish prophets that came before him: "You stiff-necked people . . . you are forever opposing the Holy Spirit, just as your ancestors used to do" (Acts 7:51, NRSV). Unfortunately, not being Jewish, Justin could not critique the Jewish response to Christ from within. He overlooked the excruciating labor done by Jews to bring to light the true God vis-à-vis the resistance of their Gentile neighbors — the same sort of work for which Justin lauds Heraclitus, Plato, and Socrates! — and saw *only* a Jewish rejection of Jesus. Instead of lamenting this development, Justin resorted to the language of "curse"[12] and attributed Jesus' death solely to "the Jews." According to the inner logic of Justin's account of Socrates, it would have been possible for him to attribute the death of Jesus to mythological powers at work in a vast array of cultural institutions. Justin himself seems to have fallen out of touch with reason at this point. Thereby he became an accomplice in Christian anti-Semitism when he had within reach an argument that might have avoided it! That brings me to my final premise, one that exposes, I think, a flaw in Justin's otherwise helpful narrative of resistance.

T7 *Justin seems not to appreciate that expulsion participates in a formidable rationality — a logos that conserves (violently, if need be) the structure of human institutions by fending off the Logos that deconstructs that order.*

12. Justin Martyr, *Dialogue with Trypho* 133.

Justin sees rightly that the fraternity of resistance is at bottom a fomenter of *violence,* but for him this can only be opposition to Reason itself. If Justin had noticed that what happens in the case of Jesus only repeats what happens in human cultures universally — that they preserve themselves in times of crisis by locating a victim, a scapegoat — he could have been rescued from his anti-Semitism. When a society encounters differences that threaten to destabilize it, and thus throw it into catastrophic episodes of violence, it responds akin to the logic of vaccination, meting out a smaller dose of the disease in order to prevent a calamitous outbreak. Admittedly, such rationality possesses little creativity. It does not innovate or suggest a truly novel state of affairs. There is nothing praiseworthy here, nothing like the optimal functioning of creation. Indeed, faced with God's desire for a new creation, such rationality must eventually break down. This logic, deeply rooted in human sinfulness, plays yet today a vital role in sustaining human culture and its institutions.

It has long been recognized that on the surface Jesus' death is more or less identical to the dying and rising gods of mythology, who give cultural unity and vitality to their worshippers by means of sacrificial violence. Heraclitus saw this connection when he said, "*Polemos* [war] was the father and king of all things" and "Opposition is good . . . everything originates in strife. . . ."[13] There exists a cultural logic — not to be confused with divine logic — by which the stable structures of human life are created. Violence is generative and necessary, or so it would seem. To victims, violence may appear as chaos, injustice, pain, an end of life. But to those who survive, violence transmutes into a new experience of unity, identity, and salvation. On the way to war at Troy, Agamemnon's troops cannot sail because the god Artemis has stopped the wind. So, as Euripides has it in *Iphigenia,* by the revelation of an oracle Agamemnon must appease Artemis with the bloody sacrifice of his own daughter. Differences threaten — Greeks versus Trojans. Heroically, Iphigenia agrees to her own sacrificial death in order to allow her father's men to sail and save Greece. Here we see the "good" that violent sacrifice achieves in mythology.

Compare the story of Iphigenia to the events surrounding Jesus' death. Jerusalem is crowded with Passover pilgrims. Jewish passions for messianic deliverance are rising to fever pitch. Roman authorities are on high alert, ready to crush any impulse that looks like insurrection. Jerusalem is in trouble because of the crowds' aspiration for Jesus, who just might be the expected Mes-

13. The citations are from fragments 44 and 46. See Milton Nahm, *Selections from Early Greek Philosophy* (New York: Appleton, 1964), p. 71.

siah. He has recently raised Lazarus, providing material evidence for liberating possibilities that lie ahead. Differences threaten — Romans versus Jews. The high priest Caiaphas suggests that it would be better "to have one man die for the people than to have the whole nation destroyed" (John 11:50, NRSV) and therewith trips the mechanism of expulsion whereby Jesus becomes a sacrificial victim, offered up to solve a regional crisis. So far, Iphigenia and Jesus are caught in a similar plight. Except that unlike the victims of pagan mythology, Jesus can't be swept away successfully. A resurrection follows his death, giving rise to a new community which forms rapidly around him as a witness. This victim community gains momentum, and eventually the point of view belonging to the victim — that Jesus was *innocent*, wrongfully accused, and unjustly killed — becomes encoded in the New Testament literature. From a Roman perspective, the sacrifice goes completely wrong. A secret wisdom was at work here, comments Paul: "None of the rulers of this age understood this; for if they had, they would not have crucified the Lord of glory" (1 Cor. 2:8, NRSV). So what appears to be another instance of violence fitting the old mythological pattern mutates radically into a thorough criticism of the pattern itself. The Spirit of God is responsible for this revelation, adds Paul. Thus Jesus was an altogether different sort of victim even if his martyrdom was carried out by a very old, universal logic.[14] One cannot blame Justin for missing the rationality implied by the work of the demons in resisting logos. But if he had grasped this, he would have been able to organize somewhat more clearly a conflict in the order of reason.

To complete the argument of this section, then, the expulsion of the Johannine Logos fits a pattern of human behavior structured by sin. As an expelled Logos, Christ locates Socrates and others along a trajectory of progressive revelation, but that does not constitute harmony between Christianity and Greek philosophy. What it reveals most clearly is how entrenched opposition to the divine Logos can be. Justin was not as clear on this point as he could have been because he failed to explore Christ's death as a collision between

---

14. In *The Will to Power*, Nietzsche saw the similarity between the death of Dionysus and that of Christ, saying, "It is *not* a difference in regard to their martyrdom — it is a difference in the meaning of it" (section no. 1052). By calling attention to Jesus' victimization and suffering, Christianity thus ruined the heroic sense of culture creation implied by Dionysus, the dying god of whom Nietzsche said, "[He] is an ecstatic affirmation of the total character of life . . . the feeling of the necessary unity of creation and destruction" (section no. 1051). The distinction between "Dionysus" and "the Crucified" stands as one of Nietzsche's great insights into the uniqueness of Christian faith, even if by it he was making an accusation against it. See Friedrich Nietzsche, *The Will to Power*, ed. Walter Kaufmann (New York: Random House, 1967).

two kinds of logos. Nevertheless, he kept in play the scandal of the cross more than his interpreters have recognized.

Distinguishing Two Logics as a Vital Part of Christian Scholarship

Throughout this essay I have been striving to show how the cross delineates two kinds of logos, one illumined by the other. No thinker has perceived this more clearly than René Girard, whose *Things Hidden Since the Foundation of the World* contains this provocative text:

> The Johannine Logos is foreign to any kind of violence; it is therefore forever expelled, an absent Logos that never has had any direct, determining influence over human cultures. These cultures are based on the Heraclitean Logos, the Logos of expulsion, the Logos of violence, which, if it is not recognized, can provide the foundation of a culture. The Johannine Logos discloses the truth of violence by having itself expelled. First and foremost, John's Prologue undoubtedly refers to the Passion. But in a more general way, the misrecognition of the Logos and mankind's expulsion of it disclose one of the fundamental principles of human society.[15]

The final sentence in the citation above is pivotal — "the misrecognition of the Logos and mankind's expulsion of it disclose one of the fundamental principles of human society" — because the misrecognition of the Logos underway in the set of activities resulting in Jesus' passion is an extraordinary bit of good fortune for Christian scholarship. Wherever the pattern of expulsion repeats itself — that is to say, wherever victims are made — the old logic of sacrificial violence becomes distinguishable *in principle* from the alternative logic rooted in the divine love. It is a gift of the gospel texts that we can recognize the difference between two types of Logos — a gift indeed, for these texts and the witness they generate constitute a counter-narrative shorn of sacrificial violence, adorned instead with the semiology of nonviolent love. The same events that reveal the Heraclitean Logos contain the possibility of its being overcome.

But that possibility has gone unrealized. According to Girard, historical Christianity has not fully assimilated the structure of its own texts:

15. René Girard, *Things Hidden Since the Foundation of the World* (Stanford: Stanford University Press, 1987), p. 271.

Historical Christianity covers the texts with a veil of sacrifice. Or, to change the metaphor, it immolates them in the (albeit splendid) tomb of Western culture. By this reading, the Christian text is able to found something that in principle it ought never to have founded: a culture.[16]

From Girard's point of view, the "veil of sacrifice" put in front of the gospel texts was inevitable. It was the only way the gospel could be heard in a Gentile world fully immersed in sacrificial understandings of religion. Since Gentile reception of the gospel was not governed by the reading of the Hebrew Scriptures — the only texts in the ancient world that begin to deconstruct the notion of sacrifice — the sacrificial reading acquired normative status, a "protective envelope" beneath which is concealed a "living principle."[17] As Christian culture developed, it gave an honored place to the Johannine Logos. Yet because this Logos was recognized through a veil, Christian attempts to draw out its proper relation to antiquity were subject to just the kind of confusion I tried to show in the standard interpretation of Justin — namely, that there must be only one Logos, and that differences must then be plotted along a spectrum from dim to bright, or from part to whole.

So what shall we say, finally, about the role of Christian scholarship with respect to these two rationalities?

When the Jewish scholar Paul had his life turned upside down by the crucified and risen Jesus, he realized something about God that, though hinted at throughout the Hebrew Scriptures, had been obscured by the human tendency to construct identity in sectarian fashion. He realized that, in Christ, God was recreating human identity precisely along nonsectarian lines. It is a mistake, I think, to render Paul as a man with a special "call" to the Gentiles, as if there were other calls a follower of Jesus might receive that allowed one to bypass Gentiles and Paul just so happened to be earmarked for this unique task. No. The new creation cannot come to pass without a profound renovation of the way humans achieve their identity. That is, to immerse oneself in the logic of the cross is to be carried *away* from something and *toward* something else. In Antioch, Paul opposed Peter (Galatians 2) because Peter's early commitment to table fellowship with Gentiles had retrenched to a stubborn sectarianism by which he and others "were not acting consistently with the truth of the gospel." The gospel Paul preaches, he insists, is not of human origin. It did not come to him through the traditions of his ancestors. That is to say, it did not come

---

16. Girard, *Things Hidden Since the Foundation of the World*, p. 249.
17. Girard, *Things Hidden Since the Foundation of the World*, p. 254.

CRAIG J. SLANE

from a source inside the system of human identity forged over and against others. This gospel appeared to him in a revelation that reversed his course and helped him discover his own violently sectarian construal of identity as *de facto* opposition to Yahweh. Paul's "mission to the Gentiles" was simply the content of this reversal, the content of the gospel itself.

Notice what this means: in a single protracted event, the sectarian logic that drives the expulsion of Christ without knowing itself or its own actions is graciously subverted by the good news that a divine logic is in the process of recreating the world. *The new creation, in other words, dawns with the clarion revelation of the difference between human and divine logic together with the wonder that love has overcome it.* If Girard is correct that historical Christianity hangs a veil over this fundamental difference — described theologically as the difference between God and sinful creatures — then it would seem that one vital role of Christian scholarship is to help lift rather than lower the veil. In the strictest sense, only God can lift the veil. At best the Christian scholar's work is a preparation, occasionally overt, often subtle, appearing in a variety of forms across diverse worlds of discourse, modulated to the tonal requirements of each discipline, and free of all partisan resentment. In my experience this is a difficult task. Failure is commonplace. Strong is the temptation either to downplay the deconstructive power of the cross and accommodate uncritically to "the guild" or to resent the guild with a putatively pure love of truth. Neither of these alternatives liberates us from sectarian identity, which now only cleverly mutates into oppositions like church and academy, Christian and secular, faith and learning, and so on.

Finally, I want to state that the only real failure is that which fails to identify failure. For scholars to perceive hypocrisy when and where it exists is by no means an un-Christian thing to do, but ranks among the most Christian activities in which we can become engaged. It demonstrates that the cross is no artifact of history but is present, dynamic, and paradigmatic, continuing to break down the structures of an old order and plunge us into something we can neither fully imagine nor control.

Dauntless Spirits: Towards a Theological Aesthetics of Collaborative Dissent

Natasha Duquette

Christian scholarship has always been a collaborative, pedagogically focused, outward-reaching, and restorative activity in tension with corrupt social structures. The early disciples went out two by two into societies within which they were perceived as dissenters and even jailed. One could argue that Christ himself taught as an individual, but he did so within the system of communal worship and historic texts of the Judaic culture into which he was born. Those texts themselves present what literary theorist Mikhail Bakhtin refers to as "heteroglossia," in an open unity comprised of multiple voices, including those of Moses, Deborah, Jeremiah, David, Habakkuk, and many others. When Jesus spoke, he was aware that he was speaking into a dynamic textual conversation. Furthermore, he spoke and acted as part of a community of three within the paradoxical unity of the Trinity. Scripture depicts Christ praying from a position of vulnerability, consulting the Father and working in dependent collaboration with him, not in absolute Kantian autonomy.

After Christ's death, resurrection, and ascension, the disciples continued to follow his pattern of collaboration. The book of Acts also presents a sublimely awe-inspiring picture of heteroglossia in the many languages of Pentecost. After Pentecost, working prayerfully in pairs, the early disciples attended to physical and spiritual suffering in the world, juxtaposed with manifestations of God's immanent beauty. They responded to the contingent details of their particular context with words and actions that triggered sublime regeneration,

---

Unless otherwise noted, all Scripture quotations are taken from the King James Version of the Bible.

wonder, and openness to learning. Their teaching challenged the powerful offi-
cials of their day, who could not ignore the force of their words and the beauty
of their loving action. How can we continue this biblical pattern of aesthetically
delightful and ethically convicting collaborative dissent as we seek to be salt
and light in a hurting world?

In envisioning an aesthetic of collaborative dissent today, I will begin by
outlining Edmund Burke's division between the sublime and the beautiful and
its theological implications; then I will consider a scriptural model of aesthetically delightful collaborative pedagogy. Next, I will trace a similar pattern running through the dissenting discourses of the eighteenth and early nineteenth
century, my own area of research, and finally I will conclude with two examples
of theologically charged, aesthetically arresting, and socially conscious collaborative dissent from our own context: twenty-first-century North America.

Gesa Thiessen has recently defined "theological aesthetics" as scholarship
that thinks about God "in the light of and perceived through sense knowledge
(sensation, feeling, imagination), through beauty, and the arts."[1] Theological
aesthetics raises important questions. How do we think about the beauty of
God? How do we picture a transcendent God as the ultimate source of earthly
beauty? How can we honor God by creating beautiful poetry, works of visual art, or architecture? How does the Incarnation relate to our ideas about
concrete manifestations of beauty in this world? And, as Reinhold Niebuhr's
work asks, is there a Yeatsian "terrible beauty" in the cross?[2] Recent work in
theological aesthetics has focused on figures such as the African Augustine of
Hippo,[3] the American Jonathan Edwards,[4] the German Immanuel Kant,[5] and

---

1. Gesa Thiessen, "General Introduction," *Theological Aesthetics: A Reader* (Grand Rapids:
Wm. B. Eerdmans, 2004), p. 1.

2. Reinhold Niebuhr, "The Terrible Beauty of the Cross," *The Christian Century* 46 (1929):
386.

3. Diane Capitani, "Augustinian Aesthetics in Jane Austen's World: God as Artist," in
Jane Austen and the Arts: Elegance, Harmony, Propriety, ed. Natasha Duquette and Elisabeth
Lenckos (Bethlehem, Pa.: Lehigh University Press, 2014), pp. 193-204; Thiessen, "General Introduction," *Theological Aesthetics,* pp. 1-7; Robin Jensen, *The Substance of Things Seen: Art, Faith,
and Christian Community* (Grand Rapids: Wm. B. Eerdmans, 2004).

4. Janice Knight, "Learning the Language of God: Jonathan Edwards and the Typology
of Nature," *The William and Mary Quarterly,* third series, vol. 48, no. 4 (October 1991): 531-51;
Kip Yin Louie, *The Beauty of the Triune God: The Theological Aesthetics of Jonathan Edwards*
(Eugene, Ore.: Wipf & Stock, 2013); Edward Farley, *Faith and Beauty: A Theological Aesthetic*
(Aldershot: Ashgate, 2001); William Dyrness, *Reformed Theology and Visual Culture: The Prot-
estant Imagination from Calvin to Edwards* (Cambridge: Cambridge University Press, 2004).

5. Richard Lane, "Kant's 'Safe Place': Security and the Sacred in the Sublime Experience," in

the Swiss Hans Urs von Balthasar,[6] but my own introduction to this field came via the Irish expatriate Edmund Burke.

In 1757 Burke published his *Philosophical Enquiry into the Origin of Our Ideas of the Sublime and Beautiful,* within which he uses extreme binary divisions to define the sublime, in very broad strokes, against its foil, the beautiful. And, in 1759, prompted by reviews asking why he did not mention God, Burke added a section titled "Power" in which he quotes from the book of Job and the Psalms in order to inflect his aesthetic system with theological meaning. In doing so, Burke draws a hard line between the Old Testament and the New, as his system does not allow for any areas of overlap. Burke is able to acknowledge that finer degrees of difference do exist, but he dismisses such subtleties as elusive and immeasurable:

> In things whose excess is not judged by greater and smaller, as smoothness and roughness, darkness and light . . . all these are very easily distinguished when the difference is in any way considerable, but not when it is minute, for want of some common measures which perhaps may never come to be discovered.[7]

According to Burke, the absolute difference between the sublime and the beautiful should be obvious. However, he acknowledges that men of "cold and phlegmatic" tempers, or those engaged in "the low drudgery of avarice," may not properly discern these aesthetic types.[8] To disagree with his strict categories is to risk moral, or at least medical, judgment. Burke is interested only in perceptions generated by men of plain reason and healthy physique. He holds up his own perceptions as the basis for universal judgments and as a result excludes aesthetic observers with infirm, phlegmatic, female, or otherwise different bodies. Essentially, Burke is excluding such individuals from his own definition of the Christian scholar.

Burke's refusal to allow for multiple perspectives is expressed when he

---

Sublimer Aspects: Interfaces between Literature, Aesthetics, and Theology, ed. Natasha Duquette (Newcastle upon Tyne: Cambridge Scholars Publishing, 2007), pp. 51-61; Ben Quash, Keynote Address at Biola University Arts Symposium, 2012.

6. Ben Quash, *Theology and the Drama of History* (Cambridge: Cambridge University Press, 2008).

7. Edmund Burke, *A Philosophical Enquiry into the Origin of Our Ideas of the Sublime and Beautiful* (1757; London: Routledge, 1958), p. 22.

8. Burke, *A Philosophical Enquiry into the Origin of Our Ideas of the Sublime and Beautiful,* p. 24.

writes, defensively, "To multiply principles for every different appearance is useless, and unphilosophical,"[9] and so shuts down any possibility of exploring categories that may exist somewhere in between his aesthetic binaries. This has theological consequences, as Burke draws an absolute divide between the sublime as powerful and terrifying, manifested in Old Testament "justice," and the beautiful as weak and comforting, displayed in New Testament love. He thus creates a seemingly unbridgeable gap between Judaism and Christianity, between justice and love. He writes, "Before the Christian religion had, as it were, humanized the idea of the Divinity, and brought it somewhere nearer us, there was very little said of the love of God."[10] Burke associates the beautiful with the closeness of loving friendship in contrast to the sublime sternness of a distant and punishing father. Due to Burke's insistence on the "wide difference"[11] between the sublime and the beautiful, there is no room for paradox, no room for what Nicholas Wolterstorff has recently termed *Justice in Love* (2011).

This is largely due to Burke's scriptural blind spots. He ignores the multiple references to God's "lovingkindness" in the Psalms and Jeremiah, for example. In attempting to restrict Christianity to the beautiful, he occludes powerful moments of sublimity in the New Testament, from which he does not quote even once in his *Enquiry*. The book of Revelation, for example, presents Christ as terrifyingly just: "And out of his mouth goeth a sharp sword, that with it he should smite the nations: and he shall rule them with a rod of iron: and he treadeth the winepress of the fierceness and wrath of Almighty God" (19:15). British scholar Ben Quash, in a recent address at Biola University, critiqued the sublime but then presented the Transfiguration (Matt. 17:1-9; Mark 9:2-8; Luke 9:28-36) as one possible example of Christian sublimity.[12] The crucifixion, resurrection, ascension, and second coming of Christ are also sublime events — both terrifying and awe-inspiring. In Matthew 28, after the resurrection, the women run from the empty tomb with "fear and great joy" (28:8), a paradoxical mixture of emotions that resists Burke's neat polarities.

In searching for a scriptural starting point from which to address the prospects and perils of Christian scholarship today, I found myself drawn to the book of Acts. Attending to the early disciples' theological aesthetic of

---

9. Burke, *A Philosophical Enquiry into the Origin of Our Ideas of the Sublime and Beautiful*, p. 27.

10. Burke, *A Philosophical Enquiry into the Origin of Our Ideas of the Sublime and Beautiful*, p. 111, p. 70.

11. Burke, *A Philosophical Enquiry into the Origin of Our Ideas of the Sublime and Beautiful*, p. 111, p. 113.

12. Quash, Keynote Address at Biola University Arts Symposium, 2012.

collaborative dissent, in the wake of the resurrection and ascension, further unsettles Burke's dichotomy. Certainly these first believers — aware of what happened to Christ, and themselves facing the possibility of imprisonment or execution — must have been keenly conscious of both the exciting, paradigm-shifting *prospects* of Christian thought as well as the hostile, life-threatening *perils* of openly Christian teaching. Acts 3, in particular, presents a striking picture of collaborative Christian pedagogy, framed by static beauty and enabled by dynamic sublimity. In his book *Hearing God,* Dallas Willard celebrates "the possibilities of a life of free-hearted collaboration with Jesus and his friends in the kingdom of the heavens,"[13] and we catch a glimpse of such dauntless, constructive friendship in the unity between Peter and John. The chapter begins, "Now Peter and John went up *together* into the temple at the hour of prayer" (3:1, my italics), suggesting that Christian thought, action, and teaching arise from communal entry into prayerful spaces.

The two men are stopped in their tracks, however, by an instance of great suffering juxtaposed with the temple's stately architectural beauty. A man "above forty years old" (4:22) and paralyzed from birth lies at the temple gate "which is called Beautiful" (3:2). Most commentators agree that this is the Nicanor Gate. "Beautiful" is not the proper name of the gate; biblical scholar Ben Witherington points out that Luke uses "Beautiful" here as a "descriptive term."[14] The Greek word is *horaios,* which signifies "seasonable, in prime, blooming"; it is a feminine adjective used only four times in the New Testament. When Jewish historian Josephus describes a seventy-five-foot gate whose beauty "greatly excelled" that of the others,[15] he is most likely referring to this beautiful gate. Made of Corinthian brass, its surface brightly reflected the rays of the sun,[16] and it is here, beside this gate's brilliant splendor, that Peter and John encounter the paralytic. He asks them for money, but instead Peter heals him in the name of Jesus, and the man leaps and praises God, astonishing a transfixed crowd.

The sublime creates opportunities for effective Christian pedagogy because it generates a state of humility, fear, and wonder: an awareness of humanity's finitude in contrast to divine omnipotence. God's power to restoratively

---

13. Dallas Willard, *Hearing God: Developing a Conversational Relationship with God* (Downers Grove, Ill.: InterVarsity Press, 1999), p. 12.

14. Ben Witherington, *The Acts of the Apostles: A Socio-Rhetorical Commentary* (Grand Rapids: Wm. B. Eerdmans, 1997), p. 174.

15. Cited in John Stott, *The Message of Acts: The Spirit, the Church, and the World* (Downers Grove, Ill.: InterVarsity Press, 1994), p. 90.

16. See Gareth Reese, *New Testament History: A Critical and Exegetical Commentary on the Book of Acts* (Joplin, Mo.: College Press Publishing Company, 1976).

heal causes the crowd in Acts 3:10 to be "filled with wonder and amazement" — in Greek, "*thaumazo* and *ekstasis*," words that denote sublimity. According to Strong's Concordance, *thaumazo* means "amazed (at), in wonder, astonished, surprised." The sublime is something that catches us off guard; it is unexpected and takes our breath away, whereas the beautiful is static and expected, like the beautiful gate of the temple. Burke recognizes astonishment as key to sublimity, arguing, "Several languages . . . frequently use the same word to signify indifferently the modes of astonishment and those of terror. Qamboß [Thambos] is, in Greek, either fear or wonder."[17] The fearful wonder of the crowd at the temple arises as they realize the limitations of their own preconceptions, thus becoming more open and teachable. Into the crowd's silent awe, Peter and John speak the truth of the gospel, and as a result, five thousand people come to believe in Jesus as Messiah.

Ekstasis, the second biblical term for the crowd's response to the healing, has historically been associated with sublime transport by writers from the first-century rhetorical philosopher Pseudo-Longinus to seventeenth-century metaphysical poet John Donne. Strong's Concordance defines *ekstasis* as a "bewilderment, amazement," and Thayer's *Greek-English Lexicon of the New Testament* adds,

> [It is an] alienation of mind, whether such as makes a lunatic (διανοίαφς, Deuteronomy 28:28; τῶν λογισμῶν, Plutarch, Sol. 8), or that of the man who by some sudden emotion is transported as it were out of himself, so that in this rapt condition, although he is awake, his mind is . . . drawn off from all surrounding objects and wholly fixed on things divine.[18]

In Acts 3 this is the state of the crowd gathered at the temple after they observe a previously paralyzed man leaping and praising God. The observers are not merely pleased, but terrified, astonished, on the edge of madness, and in this moment of *ek-stasis*, movement out of stasis, Peter and John teach them about "the Prince of Life, whom God hath raised from the dead; whereof we are witnesses" (3:15). After this instance of dynamic Christian pedagogy, the position of Peter and John as collaborative dissenters emerges starkly. The Sadducees, "grieved that they taught the people" (4:2) without official sanction, swoop

17. Burke, *A Philosophical Enquiry into the Origin of Our Ideas of the Sublime and Beautiful*, p. 111, p. 58.

18. Joseph Henry Thayer, *Thayer's Greek-English Lexicon of the New Testament* (Grand Rapids: Associated Publishers and Authors Inc., n.d.), p. 199.

down on the two men, lay hands on them, and place them "in hold unto the next day" (4:3), literally imprisoning them for their Christian thought and teaching.

Similar patterns of open teaching and resulting imprisonment are imbedded in the history of British dissent. The Quakers call this dynamic "Speaking Truth to Power." At the beginning of the eighteenth century, John Chamberlayne divided religious "Dissenters" into "four classes, Presbyterians, Independents, . . . Baptists, and Quakers."[19] The cultural products arising from such dissenting denominations can be traced back to what Mark Noll has now recognized as a uniquely dissenting theological aesthetic. In *The Scandal of the Evangelical Mind,* Noll writes, "Over its first centuries, Protestantism . . . provided an ethos in which artistic expression of unusually high quality flourished. It gave one musical genius — J. S. Bach — many of the themes for his noblest work."[20] Noll moves on to note that dissenting Protestant culture also "developed a poetics" and argues that in writers such as "John Milton and John Bunyan . . . we can observe an identifiably *Puritan aesthetic.*"[21] Like Peter and John in Acts 3 and 4, the writers of *Paradise Lost* and *Pilgrim's Progress* were themselves imprisoned for their Christian thought, John Milton for publishing *A Treatise for Civil Power* (1659), and John Bunyan for preaching and evangelizing outside of the structures of the state church.

My own research studies the women scholars of eighteenth- and early nineteenth-century Protestant Dissent who, largely inspired by Milton, generated poetry and aesthetic theory from within Presbyterian, Quaker, and Moravian networks. Though it was rare for Dissenters to be imprisoned in the eighteenth century, they could still not sit in Parliament or matriculate from Oxford. So, the British Dissenters set up their own colleges in order to equip Presbyterian, Moravian, and Quaker men to serve. Eighteenth-century British institutions such as the Presbyterian Warrington Academy did not enroll women, however. Dissenting British women were doubly marginalized, both by their commitments to non-conformist church communities and by the limits imposed on them by those very communities. In my monograph *Veiled Intent: Dissenting Women's Aesthetic Approach to Biblical Hermeneutics and Social Action,* I examine the tactics such women deployed to ensure their biblical hermeneutics and theological views were preserved for posterity; I argue that dissenting women writers published poetry and aesthetic theory

19. John Chamberlayne, *The Present State of Great Britain* (London: D. Midwinter et al., 1737), p. 148.

20. Mark Noll, *The Scandal of the Evangelical Mind* (Grand Rapids: Wm. B. Eerdmans, 1994), p. 20.

21. Noll, *The Scandal of the Evangelical Mind,* p. 40; p. 42, my italics.

as a means of tactically veiling their original biblical exegesis and trenchant social commentary.[22]

The marginalized possess unique viewpoints that can generate subtle, effective tactics appropriate and helpful to Christian scholarship in the twenty-first century. I wonder if such tactics could be compared to Peter and John's veiling their Christian thought, action, and teaching in the aesthetic forms and historic practices of Judaic worship, or to Christian scholars *today* choosing to be "shrewd as serpents and innocent as doves" (Matt. 10:16, NASB) by couching critical thought in aesthetically delightful, even sublime, forms of discourse disarming to a potentially resistant audience.

In adopting previous aesthetic forms and modes of discourse to express theological or cultural dissent, one inevitably shapes, alters, or even extends older conceptual structures, making them more flexible, in order to express new or fresh perspectives. Peter and John do this when they adopt the structures and spaces of Judaic worship to express their dynamic teaching about Jesus as Messiah. Christian scholars today face questions regarding the balance of honoring cultural traditions while at the same time remaining winsome and adaptable to the cross-cultural currents of the present. For the dissenting women theorists and poets who were engaging with earlier definitions of beauty and sublimity, it was key both to acknowledge the influence of Anglicans, such as Edmund Burke, and fellow Dissenters, such as John Milton, as well as to adjust and modify earlier aesthetic forms to new ends, such as their voicing of a female perspective and their attainment of social reforms, including the abolition of slavery. How can Christian scholars today honor their own cultural foundations *and* deploy a theological aesthetics of collaborative dissent that encourages more inclusive, socially conscious practices? Perhaps listening to the voices of dissenting Protestant women from the past can help us.

One of the perils inherent in academic pursuits from which Christian scholars are not exempt is the danger of solipsistic isolation, and dissenting women writers were keenly aware of this problem. This is also one of the dangers of the sublime as defined by Edmund Burke, who associated "entire solitude" with sublimity and "lively conversation, and the endearments of friendship" with beauty.[23] Burke's connection between solitude and the sublime led to cultural idealizations of the solitary figure, visible in paintings such as

22. Natasha Duquette, *Veiled Intent: Dissenting Women's Aesthetic Approach to Biblical Hermeneutics and Social Action* (Eugene, Ore.: Pickwick Publications, forthcoming).

23. Burke, *A Philosophical Enquiry into the Origin of Our Ideas of the Sublime and Beautiful*, p. 43.

Caspar David Friedrich's *Monk by the Sea* (first shown as part of the Berlin Academy exhibition in 1810). However, warnings regarding the dangers of excessive solitude were voiced almost immediately upon the publication of Burke's *Enquiry*. Burke's friend Samuel Johnson wrote a cautionary parable about a brilliant astronomer who studies the vast heavens without any significant human contact for forty years until he comes to believe he can control the weather with his mind. It is the discussion of astronomical concepts with two intelligent and educated women that gradually draws this scientist out of his delusion. Johnson's parable of the mad astronomer suggests that his own intellectual friendships with women were reciprocal, edifying, and mutually beneficial, perhaps even necessary to his mental health. Christian scholarship in the twenty-first century likewise needs to include both male and female perspectives.

My own research on dissenting women writers asks whether there is a difference between male and female perspectives on the sublime, and thus my work intersects with the field of feminist standpoint epistemology. What if, instead of a brooding German monk, we think about a contemplative Canadian woman by the sea? For Burke, a position on a cliff overlooking the sea is sublime because it is perilous: the depths of the sea connote the threat of drowning, and the sharp edge of a cliff suggests the danger of falling — but the open horizon also provides a sense of freedom and possibility. Joseph Addison argued that "a spacious horizon is an image of liberty, where the eye has room to range abroad,"[24] and Immanuel Kant would later connect sublimity to freedom in his *Critique of Judgment*. Throughout the eighteenth century, the sweeping perspective from a geographical height was referred to as a "prospect view." With its combined precariousness and freedom, it symbolized both the perils and the prospects of intellectual or artistic activity. Romanticist Jacqueline Labbe suggests that "the prospect view, allied as it was with . . . cultural power . . . and breadth of vision" was appealing to individual women who desired to "claim the prospect" for themselves.[25] Simply replacing a solitary male figure with a solitary female one, however, does not solve the problem of isolation and solipsism that haunts the eighteenth-century discourse of the sublime *and* the twenty-first-century pursuit of Christian scholarship. The biblical picture of Christian scholarship is neither a man nor a woman standing

24. Joseph Addison, "*The Spectator,* No. 412, Monday, June 23, 1712," in *The Sublime: A Reader in Eighteenth-Century Aesthetics,* ed. Andrew Ashfield and Peter de Bolla (Cambridge: Cambridge University Press, 1996), pp. 62-63.

25. Jacqueline Labbe, *Romantic Visualities: Landscape, Gender, and Romanticism* (Basingstoke, Hampshire: Palgrave Macmillan Press, 1998), p. 143.

alone but rather a dissenting community of brothers and sisters collaborating together. Biblical theologian Kristina Lacelle-Peterson notes that in Genesis 1:28, "the woman, along with the man, is commissioned jointly with him to carry out God's work in this world. Here we see God's original intention . . . a *collaborative* model of mutual dominion, or caretaking."[26] If such collaboration were attempted today from a prayerful space of shared vulnerability, it could result in intellectually engaging and aesthetically delightful Christian outreach towards a world in need.

In her sublime poem simply titled "A Hymn for the Scotch Kirk," Presbyterian poet Joanna Baillie paints a portrait of a diverse community brought together through obedient worship of God. She declares,

> O God! who madest earth, sea, and air,
> And living creatures, free and fair,
> Thy hallowed praise is everywhere,
>   Halleluja!
>
> All blended in the swelling song,
> Are wise and simple, weak and strong,
> Sweet woman's voice and infant's tongue,
>   Halleluja!
>
> Yea, woods, and winds, and waves convey
> To the rapt ear a hymn, and say,
> "He who hath made us we obey,
>   Halleluja!"[27]

Through her image of a "rapt ear" listening to the sounds of creation, Baillie suggests that close attention to the collaborative pedagogy of nature can trigger a state of *ek-stasis*, of sublime fear and wonder, akin to that of the crowd in Acts 3. In her alliterative grouping of "woods, and winds, and waves" (line 9), Baillie creates a gradually amplifying phonetic parallelism that echoes the rhythmic sounds of nature. By depicting diverse natural elements joining their voices with human beings — wise and simple, weak and strong, women and infants

---

26. Kristina Lacelle-Peterson, *Liberating Tradition: Women's Identity and Vocation in Christian Perspective* (Grand Rapids: Baker Academic, 2008), p. 31, my italics.

27. Joanna Baillie, "A Hymn for the Scotch Kirk," in *Fugitive Verses* (London: Edward Moxon, 1840), p. 386.

— Baillie clearly alludes to Psalm 148, where ocean "deeps" (148:7), the "stormy wind" (148:8), "mountains," and "cedars" (148:9) unite with "young men and maidens; old men, and children" (148:12) to together exclaim "Hallelujah!"

The eighteenth- and early nineteenth-century dissenting women writers who both influenced and were influenced by Joanna Baillie also actively situate their discussion of theological aesthetics within the context of communal worship. In doing so, they move against an increasingly hyper-rationalist grain within the intellectual groups and institutions established by their dissenting communities. In her essay "Thoughts on Devotional Taste" (1775), Anna Barbauld reflects on the Presbyterian Warrington Academy, where her father taught theology, worrying that the intellectual discourse at Warrington had become overly abstract and contentious, cut off from the heartfelt faith of everyday Christians, and creating too wide a distance between reverence for God's sublimity and love of incarnational beauty.[28] Unlike Edmund Burke, dissenting women writers did not divorce the beautiful from the sublime but strongly desired to bring these two aesthetic categories into reciprocal, mutually supportive, and harmonious relationship.

The voices of Joanna Baillie, Anna Barbauld, and Mary Anne Schimmelpenninck emphasize the importance of shared devotional practices to dissenting theological aesthetics. Like the women who converse with the astronomer in Samuel Johnson's parable, Baillie, Barbauld, and Schimmelpenninck sought to ground speculative thought in collaborative activities and shared experiences. Barbauld does so by noting how Hebraic scripture mixes abstract, sublime ideas about God with concrete, poetic metaphors that reflect "all that is delightful in the beauty of holiness."[29] Mary Anne Schimmelpenninck does so in her *Theory on the Classification of Beauty and Deformity* (1815) by creating a system in which the Burkean sublime of terror is one of four "species" of beauty: Schimmelpenninck's other three species are the contemplative sublime, the sentimental, and the sprightly. She uses music to explain her scale of aesthetic types, arguing that "deep tones," such as those produced by a bass drum, are sublime; "medium pitch" sounds, such as produced by a flute, are sentimental; and "high pitch" tones, such as produced by pan pipes, are sprightly.[30] She further differentiates between terrible and contemplative sublimity by arguing

---

28. Anna Barbauld, "Thoughts on Devotional Taste," in *Anna Letitia Barbauld: Selected Poetry and Prose*, ed. Elizabeth Kraft and William McCarthy (Peterborough: Broadview, 2002), pp. 209-34.

29. Barbauld, "Thoughts on Devotional Taste," p. 234.

30. Mary Anne Schimmelpenninck, *Theory on the Classification of Beauty and Deformity* (London: John and Arthur Arch, 1815), p. 363.

that, in the terrible sublime, abrupt, irregular pauses fix the attention, whereas in the contemplative sublime, "one regular, grand, sonorous swell" strengthens and stabilizes the listener.[31] Examples from poetry further elucidate her categories: according to Schimmelpenninck, Homer's classical epic form typifies the terrible sublime, Milton's Christian modification of the epic in *Paradise Lost* the contemplative sublime, William Cowper's hymns the sentimental, and Alexander Pope's satire the sprightly.

As well as expanding Burke's aesthetic dichotomy into four categories, Schimmelpenninck challenges him directly regarding the necessity of solitude to the sublime. She writes,

> Solitude is generally considered as an integral part of the sublime. That it is not essentially connected with it will appear from the following reason. It does not always produce that effect, but only under certain circumstances. Were we transported to Cheddar Cliffs, or any other sublime prospect, with all the company of a race-ball, for example, the sublime would be destroyed; but were a first-rate man-of-war . . . sinking, and the whole crew prostrate in prayer, whilst destruction was engulfing them; or had we seen the venerable assembly of Conscript fathers waiting their death by Gaul, the very circumstance of the multitude would have added to the sublime.[32]

Schimmelpenninck's examples of communal prayer at sea and calm acceptance of mortality may be loosely based on John Wesley's observation of Moravian Brethren while traveling aboard a ship bound for Georgia in 1735. When the ship was caught in a storm at sea, the English passengers, including Wesley, panicked, but the Moravians kept their eyes fixed on Christ and peacefully praised him amid their experience of physical danger. Observing the Moravians' communal dauntlessness triggered Wesley's conversion. He recognized that they were not afraid of death because they had a strong faith he did not yet share. Schimmelpenninck's own move from the Quaker beliefs of her family to Methodism and finally Moravianism suggests a similarly dynamic spiritual journey. Just as Wesley's conversion out of a cultural Christianity into a saving faith in Christ spurred him to write tracts against the British slave trade, Schimmelpenninck found herself actively involved in abolitionism after her Methodist baptism in 1808.

Schimmelpenninck's theological aesthetics were directly tied to her in-

---

31. Schimmelpenninck, *Theory on the Classification of Beauty and Deformity*, p. 370, p. 373.

32. Schimmelpenninck, *Theory on the Classification of Beauty and Deformity*, pp. 28-29.

volvement in the collaborative dissent of the anti-slavery movement, an involvement that grew as she turned more intensely to the field of biblical studies, which ultimately caused her to conclude that the ultimate beauty is in Christ, who unites love and justice within himself. In the early nineteenth century, ideas about theology, aesthetics, and justice were thoroughly integrated, as also evidenced by J. M. W. Turner's painting *The Slave Ship* (1840) or *Slavers Throwing Overboard the Dead and Dying — Typhoon Coming On.*

After the abolition of slavery in the British West Indies, and amid debates about slavery in America, Turner engaged the sublime image of a ship engulfed at sea to remind the British of their own past. In 1781 a British slave trader named Captain Collingwood cast men, women, and children into the sea in order to claim insurance money for lost "cargo." If one looks carefully at the bottom of the painting, one will see human arms and legs reaching up out of the churning waters. It is a horrific image. However, cultural historian Simon Schama also reads this image redemptively by emphasizing the light at the top of the painting and "the deep trough Turner has cut in the ocean, which at the center of the painting makes the blackly heaving swells stand still, as though the wrathful hand of Jehovah has suddenly passed over the boiling waters. For this is a day of martyrdom, . . . but also a scene, Turner must have optimistically thought, of vindication. It would be a sin redeemed. Slavery would be defeated."[33]

The cultural aftermath of slavery still reverberates through American culture today, however, and it is edifying for us to be honest about this fact within any discussion of twenty-first-century Christian thought. In *The Cross and the Lynching Tree*, James Cone critiques what he terms the "bankruptcy of any theology in America that [does] not engage the religious meaning of the African-American struggle for justice."[34] Reinhold Niebuhr reminded twentieth-century readers of the connection between justice and the sublime, writing, "Much of our contemporary moral idealism lacks the sublime faith of Jesus,"[35] and years later asserting,

> Justice cannot be approximated if the hope of its perfect realization does not generate a sublime madness in the soul. Nothing but such madness will do battle with malignant power and "spiritual wickedness in high places." [This] is dangerous because it encourages terrible fanaticisms. It must there-

---

33. Simon Schama, *Turner,* Episode 5 of *The Power of Art* (BBC Series, 2006).

34. James Cone, *The Cross and the Lynching Tree* (Maryknoll, N.Y.: Orbis Books, 2011), p. xvi.

35. Niebuhr, "The Terrible Beauty of the Cross," p. 387.

fore be brought under the control of reason. One can only hope that reason will not destroy it before its work is done.[36]

Through his research into the African-American struggle for justice and its intersection with the Christian gospel, James Cone discerns expressions of a sublime faith within African-American poetry and music. He concludes that "an imminent presence of a transcendent revelation, confirming for blacks that they were more than what whites said about them, gave them the inner spiritual strength to cope with anything that came their way."[37]

This inner spiritual strength is evident in Countee Cullen's long narrative poem *The Black Christ* (1929), within which the speaker, a young boy, describes his brother's sublime dignity and calm in the face of death at the hands of an angry white mob:

> He seemed one I had never known.
> Never such tragic beauty shone
> As this on any face before.
> It pared the heart straight to the core.
> It is the lustre dying lends,
> I thought, to make some brief amends
> To life so wantonly cut down.[38]

Like Turner's painting, Cullen's narrative poem combines deep suffering, theological aesthetics, and social ethics. Literary critic Scott Slovic has recently referred to the "urgent aesthetic" of environmentally conscious writers today,[39] and perhaps this phrase could be applied to any socially conscious writer or artist seeking justice in love.

One such artist is Lorna Simpson, an African-American photographer and filmmaker based in Brooklyn whose early work mourns the history of lynching, but whose more recent work engages the empowering effect of music within African-American community. This engagement is clear in two short film pieces she exhibited at the Los Angeles Museum of Contemporary Art in 2006. The first has a very sublime title: "Cloudscape" (2004).

36. Reinhold Niebuhr, *Moral Man and Immoral Society: A Study in Ethics and Politics* (London: Continuum, 2005), p. 181.

37. Cone, *The Cross and the Lynching Tree*, p. xviii.

38. Countee Cullen, *The Black Christ* (New York: Harper & Brothers, 1929), lines 541-47.

39. Scott Slovic, *Going Away to Think: Engagement, Retreat, and Ecocritical Responsibility* (Reno: University of Nevada Press, 2008).

Cultural theorist Trinh Minh-ha, in reference to her own film-making in Senegal, points out that "speaking nearby or together with certainly differs from speaking for and about."[40] I would like to speak in solidarity with, nearby and alongside Lorna Simpson's pieces, which truly speak for themselves. Her piece "Cloudscape" resulted from a collaboration between Simpson and her friend Terry Atkins, an African-American musician. She asked him to whistle a hymn from the turn of the twentieth century, which she filmed and then played backwards in a loop for her gallery installation. Obscurity or mystery can contribute to a sublime effect, and Simpson creates visual obscurity through the use of dry ice, and auditory mystery through the whistled hymn played backwards. In a lecture delivered at Minneapolis's Walker Art Center in 2010, Simpson explained that she intentionally chose an obscure hymn that people would not recognize. The result is sublime, and the piece has a lonely feeling due to the solitary figure and the title's connotation of a prospect view above the earth, within the clouds.

Another twenty-first-century piece by Lorna Simpson, "15 Mouths" (2001), is much more obviously collaborative. This piece was first shown just after 9/11; the viewer may be reminded of a gospel choir, but what these perform-ers are humming is a piece from John Coltrane's album *Ballads* (1963); it is a re-setting of a 1930 Rodgers and Hart show tune titled "It's Easy to Remem-ber." Simpson chose the tune for what she terms its "melodic" and "Romantic" qualities. But her friends in New York who saw her piece first exhibited just four days after 9/11 found it tragic. Regardless of the viewer's interpretation of tone, the piece definitely conveys the "open unity" of Bakhtinian hetero-glossia. Simpson gave her hummers freedom to express their individuality as each chose his or her own octave from Coltrane's multilayered improvisational jazz piece. The result is, in Simpson's words, "beautiful," *because* of the huge range of octaves — baritone, soprano, alto — expressed in male and female voices. The piece is also witty and "sprightly," to borrow Schimmelpenninck's word, because of the playful visual and audio variations, and the one mouth that occasionally smiles. In fact, "15 Mouths" contains all four categories of Schimmelpenninckian beauty. Nigerian American art critic Okwui Enwezor argues for a reading of Simpson's early photography in terms of an "American sublime"[41] of violence, and perhaps we could read her twenty-first-century

40. Trinh Minh-ha, *Woman, Native, Other: Writing, Postcoloniality, and Feminism* (Bloomington: Indiana University Press, 1989), p. 101.

41. Okwui Enwezor, "The American Sublime and the Racial Self," in *The Sublime: Docu-ments of Contemporary Art,* ed. Simon Morley (London: Whitechapel Art Gallery, 2010), p. 193.

work in light of what scholars as diverse as philosopher Nicholas Wolterstorff and literary historian Harriet Guest have called "the religious sublime," with its life-affirming dynamic movement.

A theological aesthetics of collaborative dissent, whether modeled on the diverse unity of Peter and John, Joanna Baillie and Mary Anne Schimmel-penninck, or Lorna Simpson and her cast of musicians both past and present, could serve as a response to terrible suffering that moves communities forward towards the wonder of contemplative sublimity, the affection of the sentimental, and perhaps even the uplifting wit of the sprightly. As Christian scholars in the twenty-first century, we must attend to a hurting world through collaborative writing, speaking, and teaching that both acknowledges the horrors of the past and provides hope for life-affirming, restorative movement into the future.

What could that future look like? Would prominent, established Christian thinkers of the American past, such as eighteenth-century theologian Jonathan Edwards, even recognize it? Some recent patterns in Christian scholarship give reason for hope that faith-based collaborative dissent will continue to find niches within international academia. But how will aesthetically engaging collaborative dissent be embodied in the cultural practices of future generations? Current demographics suggest that new communities of Christian thought, art, and action will arise with increasing momentum from the developing world, where there is the fastest expansion of evangelical Christianity today. Though the Americas still contain a large number of self-reported Christians, the percentage of the population identifying as Christian is significantly higher in South American countries such as Peru (97 percent) than in the United States (80 percent) or in Canada (71 percent). The fact that the newest pope of the Roman Catholic Church is an Argentinean reflects this reality. In Western European countries, the traditionally Protestant population is rapidly shrinking, and gorgeous, towering Church of England cathedrals feel cavernous and lonely when they hold only a congregation of eight on a Sunday morning.

By engaging worldwide communities in irenic, cross-cultural dialogue in the name of Christ, we can approach cultural difference with the humble expectation of learning from the other, thus adopting an intellectual position of teachable receptivity and open wonder rather than didactic judgment. Listening to Christians from other nations can help us see how, despite variations in cultural practices, Christ remains at the center. As missiologist Allen Yeh argues,

> Culture is not moral (good) nor immoral (bad); it is amoral (neutral) — and it all depends what you do with it. It is like a vessel carrying water. The

gospel is like the water; it must be carried in something, but it takes the shape of the vessel it's carried in. Still, that does not change the nature of the water, merely its shape. Unlike Islam, which is untranslatable (the Koran is always in Arabic, Sharia law is imposed wherever the religion goes, and the structure is top-down), Christianity is eminently translatable (the Bible is translated into the vernacular, worship songs are sung in the local cultural style, [and] it is bottom-up); in fact, Christianity thrives best when it is translated.[42]

If Christian scholarship is to flourish — indeed, if it is to survive — it needs to reflect the shifting and dynamic cultural shapes the gospel takes on today, which means inviting those who have been marginalized to the table, inviting them to move "from margin to center," as African-American thinker bell hooks advocates in her book of that title.[43] To avoid widening the gap between academic communities of Christian thought and the body of Christ worldwide, we need to hear the voices of those who have been historically marginalized in disciplines such as the philosophy of religion, church history, and biblical studies.

As communities of men and women generating Christian scholarship together, how can we engage in modes of collaborative writing, speaking, and teaching that empower the powerless, inspired by the patterns of reciprocal influence shared between Joanna Baillie and the male and female writers with whom she connected? One answer may lie in publishing collaborative work that serves a greater cause, rather than focusing exclusively on monographs that further our own individual career advancement within a specific or narrow field. Community in shared vulnerability can involve joint academic service, such as reviewing and editing each other's work, meeting together to discuss ideas, informally or at conferences, and editing collaborative projects.

Joanna Baillie engaged in such a project in the early 1820s, when she gathered poetry, from a wide variety of writers, men and women, members of dissenting churches and the Church of England, in order to raise money for an impoverished friend. The result was her *Collection of Poems, Chiefly Manuscript, and from Living Authors, edited for the benefit of a friend* (1823). As editor, Baillie included Anna Barbauld's compassionate elegy "On the King's Illness,"

---

42. Allen Yeh, "The Road Ahead," in *Routes and Radishes and Other Things to Talk about at the Evangelical Crossroads*, ed. Mark Russell, Allen Yeh, et al. (Grand Rapids: Zondervan, 2010), p. 47.

43. bell hooks, *From Margin to Center*, 2nd ed. (Cambridge, Mass.: South End Press, 2000).

William Wordsworth's sonnet in praise of lowliness, "Not love, nor war, nor the tumultuous swell," Felicia Hemans's exegetical poem in Spenserian stanzas, "Belshazzar's Feast," and William Smyth's "The Reformer of Newgate," a tribute to the prison activism of Elizabeth Fry. Poems by famous writers, such as the abolitionist Thomas Campbell and novelist Sir Walter Scott, appear alongside poems by relatively unknown poets, such as a "Miss Benger." As editor, Baillie carefully mixed younger, somewhat marginalized poets with the most respected poets of her nation.[44] As men and women engaging in Christian scholarship within twenty-first-century contexts, perhaps we too, whether editing collections of poems or academic essays, should seek to include relatively unknown, burgeoning writers alongside more established writers, in collections that serve larger, socially conscious causes in aid of the vulnerable.

As Christian writers, we could also generate textual projects in support of the vulnerable by cooperating with local church communities. This moves us towards the idea of developing an aesthetic of collaborative speaking. The dissenting women thinkers of the past — such as Joanna Baillie, Anna Barbauld, and Mary Anne Schimmelpenninck — had varying levels of access to public speaking within the Presbyterian, Quaker, and Moravian churches they attended. Schimmelpenninck, for example, was raised in a Quaker culture where women regularly spoke at meetings, and she did attend a Methodist church for a time after John Wesley had moved from cautioning against women's preaching to allowing it. On the other hand, women did not ever preach in the Presbyterian circles within which Joanna Baillie and Anna Barbauld moved, though women could teach children. What is true of all three women is that they did meet in salon-style gatherings within private homes to discuss science and theology, and to recite poetry and drama in patterns of mentorship. How could the church replicate this mentorship today in ways that would encourage young women (as well as men) to become the next generation of Christian scholars for the twenty-first century?

This idea of bringing young voices from the margins to the center of our public discourse and textual practices connects to the final form of collaborative dissent key for generating aesthetically engaging Christian scholarship in the twenty-first century: the mentorship of future generations, or teaching. Dissenting women poets provide unique models of such mentorship, especially Anna Barbauld, who intellectually and spiritually mentored the younger poets Helen Maria Williams and Joanna Baillie by meeting with them in church as

---

44. Joanna Baillie, *Collection of Poems, Chiefly Manuscript, and from Living Authors, edited for the benefit of a friend* (Paternoster Row: Longman, Hurst, Rees, Orme, and Brown, 1823).

well as in other public spaces, and with whom Mary Anne Schimmelpenninck stayed for a month as a young woman. It is important to encourage developing writers who are speaking from the margins and also to challenge them to be socially responsible critical thinkers whose varied and fresh voices will shape the tone of future scholarship and social practice. Sound Christian scholarship will always be God-honoring and doxological. And, as the Psalmist reminds us in Psalm 148, communities of polyphonic doxology include young men and young women, old men and children, the flora and fauna of creation, in a harmony of diverse expression unified by its shared Godward direction.

Christian scholarship in the twenty-first century, like the poetry and aesthetic theory penned by dissenting women of the past, needs to reflect the polyphonic praise of the culminating Psalms, with their pictures of communal expression. Psalm 149 begins,

> Praise ye the LORD. Sing unto the LORD a new song, and his praise in the
> congregation of saints.
> Let Israel rejoice in him that made him: let the children of Zion be joyful
> in their King.
> Let them praise his name in the dance: let them sing praises unto him
> with the timbrel and harp.
> For the LORD taketh pleasure in his people: he will beautify the meek
> with salvation. (vv. 1-4)

If we follow this psalm, as men and women engaged in Christian scholarship we are called to honor God with joyful and poetic words spoken not in solitude but "in the congregation of the saints," in a community of brothers and sisters in Christ. By doing so with the sprightly energy and artistic care of a dancer engaged with others in a collaborative production (v. 3), we can bring pleasure not only to ourselves and to our human audiences but, most importantly, to God himself (v. 4). God is our final collaborator, and through the immanence of the Holy Spirit, he can take our sincere offerings of scholarship and beautify them, and us, with restorative salvation.

By crafting inclusive, polyphonic, and joyful offerings of scholarship from liminal but dynamic spaces of communal Christian thought today, we can continue to extend the Christ-formed patterns of restoration and teaching found in the Bible. By banding together as believers on the margins and encouraging one another towards tactful and aesthetically delightful creative expression, we can also follow in the footsteps of eighteenth- and nineteenth-century dissenting women scholars, such as Joanna Baillie and Mary Anne Schimmelpenninck. Each of these women sought cross-cultural dialogue by including the practices of diverse cultures — such as Ceylon/Sri Lanka (the setting of Baillie's play *The Bride*) and Peru (Schimmelpenninck discusses Machu Picchu in her *Theory*) — in their textual representations. We too, as Christian scholars today, will benefit greatly by lifting our eyes from exclusively Anglo-American contexts to contemplate the increasingly rich and varied expressions of Christian thought around the globe. Such contemplation could ultimately draw us closer to Christ and give us a glimpse of the eternal reality when, with "every nation and kindred and tongue" (Rev. 14:6), we will stand together in awe of the Lamb.

The Holy Spirit and the Christian University: The Renewal of Evangelical Higher Education

Amos Yong

Another essay on Christian higher education?[1] Truth be told, there is by now an industry of such writings that would take any researcher more than a year-long sabbatical to digest. To be sure, part of the reason for the especially recent explosion of works in this domain has to do with criticisms of the university as it has developed in the modern West on the one hand, and with the growth of specifically Christian institutions of higher education on the other hand. With regard to the former, many have lamented that the processes of secularization have eviscerated the fundamental spiritual and moral impulses at the foundation of the Western higher educational experiment, in effect undermining its capacity to contribute to the formation of a free society and to enable the flourishing of human life.[2] Perhaps in reaction to such trends in

---

1. This chapter is adapted, with permission, from the introduction to Amos Yong and Dale Coulter, *Finding the Holy Spirit at the Christian University: Renewing Christian Higher Education* (Grand Rapids: Wm. B. Eerdmans, forthcoming).

2. See, for example, Page Smith, *Killing the Spirit: Higher Education in America* (New York: Viking Press, 1990); Dinesh D'Souza, *Illiberal Education: The Politics of Race and Sex on Campus*

A very slightly revised version of this essay was presented at the "Christian Scholarship in the Twenty-First Century Conference" at Biola University, La Mirada, California, on 19 May 2012. Thanks to Gregg Ten Elshof, Tom Crisp, Steve Porter, and Todd Vasquez of Biola University for their friendship and collegiality during the spring term of 2012, when I undertook my visiting research fellowship at their Center for Christian Thought. I am grateful also to Evan Rosa, the Center graduate assistant who helped me with my research. Finally, I appreciate also the hospitality provided while I was in town by my cousin Victor Leong and his family at their comfortable apartment; it was wonderful to renew family ties after many years.

the secular academy, in the last few decades there has been an upsurge in the popularity of the specifically Christian university — students are enrolling in such institutions in droves, leading to reflection on their whence and whither.[3] So amid those who are bemoaning the future of the university in general are another group who are frantically attempting to discern what it means to provide a Christian higher education in the globalizing and pluralistic world of the twenty-first century, particularly in light of what appears to be the winding down of at least the anti-religious processes of secularization among the historic universities of the Western world.

Into this fray I leap. Having been deeply shaped by Pentecostal and charismatic forms of Christianity, I am motivated by the possibility that perspectives on higher education from this vantage point will be of interest not only to those in institutions affiliated with this movement or tradition, but to all engaged with the Christian university regardless of ecclesial background or connection.[4] To be sure, having also worked within Pentecostal and charismatic institutions of higher education, I am under no illusion — given the challenges and realities that Pentecostal Christians face — that the following presents any kind of final or definitive template for the Christian higher educational success. Yet, as unfolded herein, I also think that Pentecostal and charismatic intuitions

---

(New York: Free Press, 1991); George M. Marsden, *The Soul of the American University: From Protestant Establishment to Established Nonbelief* (New York: Oxford University Press, 1994); Alan Kors and Harvey Silverglate, *The Shadow University: The Betrayal of Liberty on America's Campuses* (New York: Free Press, 1998); Melanie M. Morey and John J. Piderit, S.J., *Catholic Higher Education: A Culture in Crisis* (Oxford: Oxford University Press, 2006); and C. John Sommerville, *The Decline of the Secular University* (Oxford: Oxford University Press, 2006).

3. See William C. Ringenberg, *The Christian College: A History of Protestant Higher Education in America*, 2nd ed. (Grand Rapids: Baker Academic, 2006), esp. chaps. 6-7; Naomi Schaefer Riley, *God on the Quad: How Religious Colleges and the Missionary Generation Are Changing America* (Chicago: Ivan R. Dee, 2005); and Samuel Schuman, *Seeing the Light: Religious Colleges in Twenty-First-Century America* (Baltimore: Johns Hopkins University Press, 2010). For reflections on the successes experienced, see *The Christian College Phenomenon: Inside America's Fastest-Growing Institutions of Higher Learning*, ed. Samuel Joeckel and Thomas Chesnes (Abilene, Tex.: Abilene Christian University Press, 2012).

4. Pentecostal Christians have never been timid about saying what comes to mind because of their belief that the gift of the Holy Spirit empowers the witness of believers (see Acts 1:8). We are no less bashful in this regard, although we also realize that whatever we might feel about "Thus saith the Lord" will need to be argued rather than merely asserted in academic discourse, and that even if we do feel as if what we have to say is of the Lord in some respect, there is no reason why the Pauline injunction "Let two or three prophets speak, and let the others weigh what is said" (1 Cor. 14:29, NRSV) wouldn't apply in the guild — to authors writing and readers assessing — as well.

and sensibilities about the educational enterprise, especially when linked to the broader history of Christian education (as intended in my forthcoming book with Dale Coulter, of which this essay is a small part), can make a contribution to the contemporary conversation.

This essay serves as a prolegomena to such a project and does so in four sections. The first sketches the opportunities lying before renewalist and evangelical Christians[5] as they consider the task of Christian higher education, while the second examines the specific hurdles to be overcome in part because of twentieth-century renewalist instincts and habits. Section three suggests that the renewalist focus on the person and work of the Holy Spirit invites further reflection on what difference such an emphasis makes for the Christian university. The final section briefly sketches the main lines of what such a project might involve.

Global Renewal: Opportunities for Christian Higher Education

In order to appreciate that renewalist Christians, the newest arrivals on the block of Christian higher education, may have something to contribute to this discussion, let us situate the emerging Christian university within its broader historical and global context. It is no secret by now that it is only in the last century that we can talk about Christianity as a world religion.[6] There are, of course, two sides to this story. On the one hand, Christianity has always been a missionizing religion, and its literal internationalization during the twentieth

---

5. I clarify further the nomenclature of "renewal" Christianity below. What needs to be emphasized here — with Veli-Matti Kärkkäinen, "Pentecostal Theological Education in a Theological and Missiological Perspective," *Journal of the European Pentecostal Theological Association* 30, no. 1 (2010): 49-62, esp. 50-51 — is that there is not one form of Pentecostal or renewal Christianity but many. My perspective represents but one among the many, albeit one that I believe can enrich the many in turn, even the many forms of Christianities. Further, there is also a spectrum of evangelicalism, and within this range, renewalists can be understood as a subset. In this essay I use "renewal" and "evangelical" somewhat synonymously, although in certain contexts it will be obvious when I am referring to one as distinct from the other.

6. I am aware, of course, that within the religious studies guild, every "world religion" can be understood as a construction of modernity in some respect, as argued by Tomoko Masuzawa in *The Invention of World Religions: Or, How European Universalism Was Preserved in the Language of Pluralism* (Chicago: University of Chicago Press, 2005). It is beyond the scope of this essay to show that there are specific modalities of operation open to the Christian university that preserve not so much a modernist pluralism but an even more radical — that is, more biblical — account of plurality and diversity.

century can be understood in connection with its missionary impulses.[7] On the other hand, not only have the missionized been agents in their own right in constructing a form of Christianity more palatable for their own times and places, but there have been many other indigenous Christian movements that also have arisen and played roles in the emergence of the present shape of world Christianity. If the former missionaries were purveyors also of Western culture to the majority world, the latter both have transformed the gifts of the missionaries for their own purposes and, in many cases, have been motivated to return, from the "rest" to the "West," to re-evangelize the Euro-American nations of the Northern Hemisphere.[8]

On both registers — that of missionary initiatives and that of indigenous reception, mobilization, and re-engagement in reverse mission — Pentecostal and charismatic types of Christians have been arguably at the forefront. Since its appearance during the first decade of the twentieth century, Pentecostal Christianity has been intensely involved in the missionary enterprise.[9] Convinced that their empowerment of the Spirit was for the specific task of world evangelization,[10] Pentecostal Christians courageously braved hostile conditions to fulfill the Great Commission. Although for at least the first half of the century the results may have been meager, since 1970, explosive growth has occurred across the global South. Pentecostal and charismatic forms of Christianity have multiplied exponentially across Asia, Africa, and Latin America in the last forty years.[11]

Not without reason, then, the twentieth century has been dubbed "the Pen-

---

7. See, for example, Dana L. Robert, *Christian Mission: How Christianity Became a World Religion* (Malden, Mass.: Wiley-Blackwell, 2009).

8. See *Mission after Christendom: Emergent Themes in Contemporary Mission,* ed. Ogbu U. Kalu, Edmund Kee-Fook Chia, and Peter Vethanayagamony (Louisville: Westminster John Knox Press, 2010). A number of the chapters in the first part of this volume address this topic.

9. This has been documented by Allan Anderson in *Spreading Fires: The Missionary Nature of Early Pentecostalism* (Maryknoll, N.Y.: Orbis Books, 2007), and Gary B. McGee, *Miracles, Missions, and American Pentecostalism* (Maryknoll, N.Y.: Orbis Books, 2010).

10. See, for instance, James R. Goff Jr., *Fields White unto Harvest: Charles F. Parham and the Missionary Origins of Pentecostalism* (Fayetteville: University of Arkansas Press, 1988).

11. On this subject, see, for example, *Asian and Pentecostal: The Charismatic Face of Christianity in Asia,* ed. Allan Anderson and Edmond Tang (London: Regnum International, 2005); Ogbu U. Kalu, *African Pentecostalism: An Introduction* (New York: Oxford University Press, 2008); and David Stoll, *Is Latin America Turning Protestant? The Politics of Evangelical Growth* (Berkeley and Los Angeles: University of California Press, 1990). See also *The Globalization of Pentecostalism: A Religion Made to Travel,* ed. Murray W. Dempster, Byron D. Klaus, and Douglas Petersen (Irvine, Calif.: Regnum Books, 1999).

tecostal century."[12] In a very real sense, as many impartial observers have noted, the emergence of world Christianity has taken on a very real Pentecostal and charismatic shape.[13] Yet to say this is not to say that there is a homogeneous form of Pentecostalism around the world, since there isn't. Yes, there are various forms of Western Pentecostalism that continue to be "exported" around the world,[14] but in many cases, it is more accurate to talk about "Pentecostal types" rather than about Pentecostalism.[15] Further, after the charismatic renewal was initiated in the 1960s in the mainline Protestant churches and even the Roman Catholic Church, many forms of Pentecostal-charismatic spirituality have persisted across these denominations and traditions. In these cases, we can talk about a charismatization and even a Pentecostalization of these churches, but these Christians remain self-identified as evangelicals, Protestants, or Catholics.[16] Beyond the dynamic developments in the established churches, there are also many forms of indigenous churches across the majority world that have been established independently of classical Pentecostal or mainline or Catholic mission organizations, but have embraced and express an undeniable form of Pentecostal and charismatic-type spirituality. These churches look and sound Pentecostals or charismatic — in their style of worship and in the manifestations of the various spiritual gifts, especially healings, speaking in tongues, and exorcisms — but they retain neither "Pentecostal" nor "charismatic" as part of their name or self-identification.[17] In effect, this new wave of

12. See, for example, *The Century of the Holy Spirit: 100 Years of Pentecostal and Charismatic Renewal, 1901-2001,* ed. Vinson Synan (Nashville: Thomas Nelson, 2001).

13. See Harvey G. Cox, *Fire from Heaven: The Rise of Pentecostal Spirituality and the Reshaping of Religions in the Twenty-First Century* (Reading, Mass.: Addison-Wesley, 1995); David Martin, *Pentecostalism: The World Their Parish* (Malden, Mass.: Blackwell, 2002); Philip Jenkins, *The Next Christendom: The Coming of Global Christianity* (New York: Oxford University Press, 2002); and *The New Faces of Christianity: Believing the Bible in the Global South* (New York: Oxford University Press, 2006).

14. As shown by Paul Gifford, Susan D. Rose, and Steve Brouwer, *Exporting the American Gospel: Global Christian Fundamentalism* (New York: Routledge, 1996).

15. See Allan Anderson, *African Reformation: African-Initiated Christianity in the Twentieth Century* (Trenton, N.J.: Africa World Press, 2001), chap. 1.

16. See Cephas Narh Omenyo, *Pentecost outside Pentecostalism: A Study of the Development of Charismatic Renewal in the Mainline Churches in Ghana* (Zoetermeer, The Netherlands: Boekencentrum, 2006), and Edward L. Cleary, *The Rise of Charismatic Catholicism in Latin America* (Gainesville: University of Florida Press, 2006).

17. According to the *New International Dictionary of Pentecostal and Charismatic Movements,* ed. Stanley M. Burgess and Eduard M. Van der Maas (Grand Rapids: Zondervan, 2003), pp. xviii-xxi, it is this group of indigenous Pentecostal- and charismatic-type Christians that are the fastest growing across the global South; see also J. Kwabena Asamoah-Gyadu, *African*

Pentecostalized or charismatized communities of faith are at the vanguard of Christian expansion in our post-Western, post-colonial, post-denominational, and even post-Christian global landscape.[18]

It is in part because of what is happening on the ground of the world Christian movement that I have chosen to talk about "renewal Christianity" rather than to persist with either the "Pentecostal" or "charismatic" label. A recent and widely cited Pew Forum study, "Spirit and Power: A 10-Country Survey of Pentecostals" (2006), has already deployed "renewal" as the more encompassing category that includes within it Pentecostalism, Neo-Pentecostalism, charismatic renewal, and the various forms of Pentecostalized and charismatized indigenous and independent forms of Christianity around the world.[19] In this context, then, the more inclusive language of renewal and its derivatives will be more appropriate. This terminological shift will be especially important if the intent is to ground the project on a renewal-informed re-reading of select moments in the history of Christian education. Such a move is crucial precisely because much of what renewal perspectives can bring to the present discussion has already appeared in similar or related guises among charismatic or other types of renewal movements in the Christian tradition. Within this broader historical framework, it would be anachronistic to deploy especially the nomenclature of Pentecostalism, since that is now widely established as a twentieth-century phenomenon.

It ought not to be surprising, given these recent developments in world Christianity, that the work of Christian higher education has also accelerated across the international scene. According to Joel Carpenter, the director of Calvin College's Nagel Institute for the Study of World Christianity and one of the most astute observers of what is happening in the arena of global Christian higher education, not only are there at present almost six hundred identifiable Christian universities in the majority world, but there are forty-one different "evangelical Protestant degree-granting institutions of the arts, sciences, and professions that have been founded outside of North America and Western Europe since 1980."[20] Although there are only a few institutions within this

---

Charismatics: Current Developments within Independent Indigenous Pentecostalism in Ghana (Leiden: Brill, 2005).

18. See Walter Hollenweger, *Pentecostalism: Origins and Growth Worldwide* (Peabody, Mass.: Hendrickson Publishers, 1997), and Allan Anderson, *An Introduction to Pentecostalism: Global Charismatic Christianity* (Cambridge: Cambridge University Press, 2004).

19. This is available at http://pewforum.org/Christian/Evangelical-Protestant-Churches/Spirit-and-Power.aspx.

20. Joel Carpenter, "New Evangelical Universities: Cogs in a World System or Players in a New Game?" in *Interpreting Contemporary Christianity: Global Processes and Local Identities,*

group affiliated with renewal Christianity, amid the global Pentecostalizing and charismatizing trends (discussed previously), these small numbers can be deceiving to the uninitiated. Futurist demographers are clear that within the next generation, Christianity not only will increasingly become a Southern phenomenon but also will be essentially renewalist in its basic forms.[21] And as this unfolds, many students who are among the "new Christians" will be looking for a Christian education that attends to if not also explains more cogently their religious and spiritual experiences.

As it is beyond the scope of this essay to discuss these developments both within and outside of renewal Christianity in greater detail, suffice it to say for now that for the foreseeable future, Christian universities will continue to emerge,[22] and it is prudent to ask about what it would take to engage its largely renewalist constituency. True, in most cases, these schools will be struggling to meet demands in the face of insufficient public and private resources, but amid these trends and challenges, many institutions in the global South — religiously based and secular alike — will continue to look to those in the Euro-American West for guidance.[23]

Within this global scheme of things, what might renewal Christian higher educators contribute to the discussion? Even as far back as a generation ago, scholars and church leaders (such as the sociologist who worked closely with the World Council of Churches, Christian Lalive D'Epinay)[24] were calling attention to the irony that uneducated renewalist churches were flourishing while educated Methodist, Presbyterian, and other mainline Protestant churches were stagnating, and wondering who should teach whom. But even if non-renewalists might have been ready to listen then, renewalists then (and now) might not have been willing to collaborate or have anything substantive to say. Why might this have been the case?

---

ed. Ogbu U. Kalu and Alaine M. Low (Grand Rapids: Wm. B. Eerdmans, 2008), p. 152; for the list of the 579 (as of 2010) Christian universities, see Perry L. Glanzer, Joel A. Carpenter, and Nick Lantinga, "Looking for God in the University: Examining Trends in Christian Higher Education," *Higher Education* 61, no. 6 (2010): 721-55.

21. These anticipations are forecast across the *Atlas of Global Christianity, 1910-2010*, ed. Todd M. Johnson and Kenneth R. Ross (Edinburgh: Edinburgh University Press, 2009).

22. Joel A. Carpenter, "New Christian Universities and the Conversion of Cultures," *Evangelical Review of Theology* 36, no. 1 (2012): 14-30, esp. 16, talks about the processes of "massification" that are underway across international Christian higher education.

23. Philip G. Altbach, *Comparative Higher Education: Knowledge, the University, and Development* (Greenwich, Conn.: Ablex Publishing Corporation, 1998), esp. chaps. 4-5.

24. Christian Lalive D'Epinay, "Training of Pastors and Theological Education: The Case of Chile," *International Review of Mission* 56, no. 222 (April 1967): 185-92.

Hearts and Hands, but Not Heads? Challenges for Renewal Spirituality

The simple answer to the preceding question is that renewalists are well known for having warm hearts and hot hands (an affective, if not infective, spirituality and an intense commitment to mission and evangelism), but not for what is arguably at the center of the educational task, cool heads (effective minds). Indeed, renewalists, stereotypically considered, have resolutely cold heads, almost a disdain for the intellectual life. If the proposals in this chapter are going to gain any hearing, we must consider this matter in some detail.

In what is by now a classic across much of the North American evangelical intellectual world, historian Mark Noll challenged his compatriots near the end of the last century about the fact that there was not much of an evangelical mind.[25] While the causes of this were varied indeed, a few of the major culprits, in Noll's estimation, were linked to or connected directly with renewalist Christianity. In particular, Noll's analysis highlighted the roles played by the revivalist tradition of the eighteenth and nineteenth centuries, the Holiness movement's prioritizing of a dynamic spiritual life in the mid- to late nineteenth century, and the prophecy movement and its dispensationalist theological innovations of the late nineteenth and early twentieth centuries. What is interesting for our purposes here is that in Noll's assessment, these streams coincided in Pentecostalism. The revivalist focus on spiritual vitality was consistent with the Holiness call to heart piety, and both presumed the minimal importance of the intellectual life in view of their other-worldly and dispensationalist eschatology. For Pentecostal Christians, saving *souls* was much more urgent, given the apocalyptic horizon within which they discerned the signs of the times unfolding. For Noll, this dynamic web of events in the history of evangelicalism was an "intellectual disaster" that brought about the scandal of the non-existent evangelical mind.[26]

While Noll's book was working its way through to publication, Roman Catholic scholar James Burtchaell was researching and writing his book, and these labors resulted, three years later, in a massive volume on the disengagement of colleges and universities from their Christian churches, and their concomitant slow spiritual death.[27] Of the seventeen institutions of higher education studied by Burtchaell, only one — Azusa Pacific University (APU) — could

25. Mark A. Noll, *The Scandal of the Evangelical Mind* (Grand Rapids: Wm. B. Eerdmans, 1994).

26. See Noll, *The Scandal of the Evangelical Mind,* chap. 5.

27. James Tunstead Burtchaell, *The Dying of the Light: The Disengagement of Colleges and Universities from Their Christian Churches* (Grand Rapids: Wm. B. Eerdmans, 1998).

have been understood as having connections to the renewal movement, and even in that case, Pentecostal strands were only a minimal part of a multifaceted ecclesiastical cord woven into the original DNA of this school. And while in many respects developments at APU have bucked many of the secularizing trends meticulously documented elsewhere in the book, it also has been and remains assailed by various internal and external factors. In Burtchaell's appraisal, the fortunes of schools like APU were threatened by what he called "the pietist instability."[28] Beyond what Noll discusses, Burtchaell explicates various aspects of such instability. First, while historical pietism emerges oftentimes as a protest movement against an overly scholastic form of religious life, what for the protesting tradition is a simplified account of a vibrant and fervent faith in the face of a highly rationalized tradition runs the risk of devolving, for the second generation, into being merely simplistic piety. This next generation, then, is affectively engaged, but without theological substance. Faith, in this case, becomes dislodged from learning, and this in turn undermines the capacity of pietist Christians to build strong theological institutions. In the worst-case scenario, according to Burtchaell's overall thesis, such pietistic instability degenerates over time into a liberal indifferentism, with the net effect being the institutional disestablishment of and disengagement from their churches.[29]

A number of responses to these charges have emerged from the Holiness side.[30] Not unexpectedly, the rejoinders emphasize that "pietism, rightly

28. Burtchaell, *The Dying of the Light*, pp. 838-46. Pentecostal educator Jeff Hittenberger also mentions that renewal Christianity is subject to the forces of secularization due to its generally "thin ecclesiology, idiosyncratic theology, and *unstable movements*"; see Jeff Hittenberger, "The Future of Pentecostal Higher Education: The Ring, the Shire, or the Redemption of Middle Earth," in *The Future of Pentecostalism in the United States,* ed. Eric Patterson and Edmund Rybarczyk (Lanham, Md.: Lexington Books, 2007), p. 95 (italics added).

29. Lutheran theologian Robert Benne, although nowhere near as pessimistic as Burtchaell about the future of church-related institutions of higher education, agrees with his Catholic colleague that pietist traditions face additional challenges in articulating institutional identity and mission in adequate theological terms. See Robert Benne, *Quality with Soul: How Six Premier Colleges and Universities Keep Faith with Their Religious Traditions* (Grand Rapids: Wm. B. Eerdmans, 2001), pp. 36-37.

30. See the set of responses by David Bundy, Henry H. Knight III, and William Kostlevy in the *Wesleyan Theological Journal* 32 (Spring 1997). More recently, Philip W. Eaton, the president of Seattle Pacific University, a school in the Wesleyan tradition, has written *Engaging the Culture, Changing the World: The Christian University in a Post-Christian World* (Downers Grove, Ill.: IVP Academic, 2011) — although his approach is less a frontal engagement with the claims of Noll and Burtchaell than a contribution to the evangelical task of higher education from a more or less Wesleyan perspective. (Eaton speaks almost as much in his more generic "evangelical" voice as he does in a specific "Wesleyan" tone.)

understood, was not a movement opposed to reason, but one which sought to put reason in its proper context."[31] Yet rather than being a merely cognitive approach to higher education, the pietist model is integrative, requiring engagement of the whole person not only in right thinking but also in right worship, right behavior, and, indeed, right formation for all aspects of life. Thus, pietism is a "head, heart, and hands religion," and the pietist tradition "promotes an education for the head, heart, and hands — one which does not reduce the educational task to the shaping of worldviews, but emphasizes formation of the whole person."[32]

Pentecostal-Holiness educator and theologian Cheryl Bridges Johns, however, desists from either internalizing this oppressive narrative or offering a rebuttal.[33] Instead of buying into the dominant group's understanding of what the life of the mind consists of, Johns exhorts her Pentecostal colleagues to press into the scandal. Exploiting the postmodern opening to a plurality of narratives (against any hegemonic metanarrative), this approach "is a way of celebrating marginality rather than worshiping an elusive center."[34] Johns insists that Holiness and Pentecostal Christians ought to embrace precisely those aspects of their tradition that Noll, in particular, criticized as fomenting evangelicalism's intellectual disaster. So yes, "let go and let God," as the Holiness folk say, and even further, "be filled with the Holy Spirit," as Pentecostal Christians urge. To be sure, such responses represent the scandal not only of the evangelical mind but of the intellectual undertaking (or lack thereof!) as a whole. Yet, rather than leaving behind these Holiness and Pentecostal sensibilities, Johns asks her colleagues to consider what it might mean to rethink higher education in light of these commitments. How might tarrying at the altar, for instance, open up to a dimension of the mind and its operations that a purely

---

31. Kurt W. Peterson and R. J. Snell, "'Faith Forms the Intellectual Task': The Pietist Option in Christian Higher Education," in *The Pietist Impulse in Christianity,* ed. Christian T. Collins Winn, Christopher Gehrz, G. William Carlson, and Eric Holst (Eugene, Ore.: Pickwick Publications, 2011), p. 222.

32. Peterson and Snell, "'Faith Forms the Intellectual Task,'" p. 219 and p. 217, respectively.

33. Cheryl Bridges Johns, "Partners in Scandal: Wesleyan and Pentecostal Scholarship," *PNEUMA: The Journal of the Society for Pentecostal Studies* 21, no. 2 (1999): 183-97. I now realize that my original reaction to the draft version of this essay at a conference in some ways did precisely what Johns set out not to do: attempting to outdo evangelicals themselves in order to show forth "the pentecostal mind." See my responsive essay: "Whither Systematic Theology? A Systematician Chimes in on a Scandalous Conversation," *PNEUMA: The Journal of the Society for Pentecostal Studies* 20, no. 1 (Spring 1998): 85-93. Needless to say, the intervening years have made me much more sympathetic to her scandalous proposal.

34. Johns, "Partners in Scandal," p. 187.

discursive approach overlooks? Is it possible that from out of the mouths of the uneducated might come forth embarrassing words — tongues-speech, even — that reflect "a knowing which is not a grasping but a letting go . . . , [a] knowing which is not grounded in its own self presence but in the presence of the source of all knowing"?[35] Could it be that Christian higher education could develop affective modalities of knowing that could inform and even enrich the cognitive operations prized in academia, rather than dismissing Holiness and Pentecostal dispositions and practices simply because they did not meet certain standards of Enlightenment rationality?

In some respects, this project (my forthcoming book) is born out of the set of convictions represented in Johns's challenge. This does not mean that the tradition of renewal Christianity — with its antecedent and constitutive revivalist, Holiness, and Pentecostal tributaries — is beyond criticism. Not to recognize the anti-intellectualism that remains suffused throughout many segments of the movement is to be dishonest.[36] It is arguably the case that most often renewalist anti-intellectualism derives from a mistaken and indefensible dichotomizing of the spiritual and intellectual aspects of human life. This bifurcation presumes the Enlightenment dualism between mind and heart, which Holiness and Pentecostal Christians have internalized, and which Johns and others are calling to be reconsidered. So the task will necessarily involve, on the one hand, resisting the prejudices inimical to loving God with our minds; yet, on the other hand, following in the path charted out by Johns. This does not require an uncritical adoption of other forms of rationality which will only diffuse the gifts that renewal perspectives have to offer. In short, the goal is to mine resources from renewal Christianity that might reinvigorate the work of Christian higher education while being mindful of undercurrents that could in turn exacerbate whatever elements of "pietist instability" still lurk beneath the surface. Is such a *via media* possible or plausible? Perhaps not, if it is limited only to specifically twentieth-century Pentecostal resources. But what if our renewal sensibilities generated a historiographic perspective that enabled the retrieval of elements from the history of Christian education that would be important for the present task?

---

35. Johns, "Partners in Scandal," p. 197.

36. A fine exposé of this anti-intellectual strain within renewal Christianity is Rick Nañez, *Full Gospel, Fractured Minds: A Call to Use God's Gift of the Intellect* (Grand Rapids: Zondervan, 2005).

The Renewal of Christian Higher Education: What Difference Does the Holy Spirit Make?

The way forward, I am convinced, is in part to look back, and doing so helps us to discern from out of the heart of the Christian tradition a range of possibilities that can stimulate what might be called a pneumatological vision of higher education. Such an approach to Christian higher education foregrounds not necessarily the practices and ideas of a particular Christian tradition but, precisely because of the renewalist perspective, the person and work of the Holy Spirit himself, and explores that in relationship to the educational task. What difference does the Holy Spirit make to the Christian university?

Some might think this question quaint, or at best misplaced. Rhetorically, however, it is now commonplace to acknowledge the return of God to the university.[37] Best-selling books over the last two decades announced not only the "search for God at Harvard," but also that God had indeed been found, even on that most secularized of university campuses.[38] In fact, not only has God reappeared in what were presumed to be God-forsaken places; even Jesus has showed up.[39] Yet even if I believed the foregoing to be relevant also for secular universities (which I do) — in particular for Christians who find themselves laboring in such contexts — my primary focus is on the intentionally Christian form of higher educational projects. In these contexts, especially within the evangelical world, Jesus is certainly no stranger. Many evangelical institutions of higher education, especially those affiliated with (or seeking formal ties to) the Council of Christian Colleges and Universities (CCCU), are explicitly committed to advancing "the cause of *Christ-centered higher education* and to help[ing] our institutions transform lives by faithfully relating scholarship and service to biblical truth."[40] So if the work of at least the evangelical Christian university is shaped by a Christomorphic character, why would it be incredulous or out of line to ask about the person and work of the Holy Spirit in such arenas?

---

37. Trent Sheppard, *God on Campus: Sacred Causes and Global Effects* (Downers Grove, Ill.: InterVarsity Press, 2009).

38. See Ari L. Goldman, *The Search for God at Harvard* (New York: Ballantine Books, 1992), and Kelly Monroe Kullberg, *Finding God at Harvard: Spiritual Journeys of Thinking Christians* (Downers Grove, Ill.: InterVarsity Press, 2007).

39. See Harvey Cox, *When Jesus Came to Harvard: Making Moral Choices Today* (New York: Mariner Books, 2006).

40. This is the stated mission (with emphasis added) of the CCCU; see http://www.cccu .org/about.

Let us be clear that our shifting to a pneumatological axis is not intended to displace or neglect the Christ-centeredness that marks evangelical commitments. Charles Malik's clarion call to the Western university world (which came not too long ago) about re-grounding the task of higher education on its proper, Christological foundation could only have come from within an evangelical frame of reference wherein Jesus Christ is the indispensable source, criterion, and goal even of the scholarly and educational endeavor.[41] More recently, the diagnostician of the enfeebled if not absent evangelical mind turned his gaze toward probing more intentionally into what such a Christocentric life of the mind would look like.[42] If in fact Jesus Christ is the center of evangelical faith, would this not make a material difference for the Christian university?

Noll thus makes a number of fundamental Christological and, more specifically, incarnational claims that he sees as providing guidance for Christian teaching, research, and scholarship. First, the materiality, humanity, personality, and beauty of the Incarnation invites careful exploration of each of these domains of the created order, including the human realm, and this provides an explicitly theological rationale for the many disciplines of the university. Second, every "thing" has a form of double-sidedness, identified in the Chalcedonian confession of Jesus' two (divine and human) natures, which also calls for at least these dual levels — theological and non-theological — of explanatory understanding. Third, the particularity of incarnation alerts us to the relativity, contingency, and yet dignity of all created and cultural realities, including the disciplinary endeavors designed to study and understand such. Last but not least, the humiliation of the Incarnation ought to inculcate in Christians the virtue of scholarly humility.[43] Noll then goes on in the remainder of his book to elucidate how these guidelines are suggestive for Christian thinking in the anthropological, historical, and scientific disciplines.

Malik's prophetic clarity and Noll's patient enunciation of a Christ-centered educational paradigm are central for anyone interested in the distinctive character of the Christian university. An unambiguously formulated Christological vision provides a principled orientation to Christian thinking

41. Charles Malik, *A Christian Critique of the University,* 2nd ed. (Waterloo, Ont.: North Waterloo Academic Press, 1987).

42. Mark A. Noll, *Jesus Christ and the Life of the Mind* (Grand Rapids: Wm. B. Eerdmans, 2011).

43. This incarnational approach to Christian thinking and scholarship is also adopted, albeit for slightly different purposes, by Norman Klassen and Jens Zimmermann in *The Passionate Intellect: Incarnational Humanism and the Future of University Education* (Grand Rapids: Baker Academic, 2006).

that is, as Noll's work indicates, deducible in various ways from the core doctrinal commitments of historically evangelical and orthodox faith. While certainly and sufficiently Christian, Noll's proposal remains a partially articulated Trinitarian faith. While all Christians have believed in the Holy Spirit since the earliest form of the Nicene confession, the Spirit's person and work often remain minor if not entirely neglected themes with little implication or application for Christian life. After all, if Jesus is Christ only as the one anointed by the Spirit, I insist not only that Christ-centeredness needs recognition of the Spirit's work, but that apart from this a full Trinitarian Christian faith itself fails to emerge. How can we neglect the work of the Holy Spirit in sparking the imagination of Jesus, in enabling improvisation in his life and ministry, and in inspiring creativity in his words and deeds? Isn't it almost impossible to retain a vital Christocentricity apart from a vigorous pneumatology?[44]

My answer to this question is that a deeply Christomorphic vision can only be sustained by an equally expansive pneumatological imagination.[45] I thus recommend a model of the Christian university that is both Christ-centered and Spirit-filled. What, however, does the addition of the latter mean? It is not possible within the confines of this essay to fill out this claim, but I can briefly summarize what such a project would presume about the work of the Spirit. I am a theologian, but because I am writing about Christian higher education, I want to do more than just make abstract theological pronouncements in what follows.

First, I acknowledge the Holy Spirit as teacher and guide to all truth.[46] Of course, this involves illuminating the Scriptures, enabling interpersonal interaction between teachers and students (and intra-student relations as well), and invigorating the learning environment. If the Spirit teaches, we ought to want to know how we should teach — what kinds of pedagogical methods ought

44. So again, while I agree with Duane Litfin, *Conceiving a Christian College* (Grand Rapids: Wm. B. Eerdmans, 2004), chaps. 3-4, that Christ is the center of Christian faith, such Christ-centeredness does not automatically translate into Trinitarian faith; for the latter, we need an equally robust pneumatology.

45. I have written a great deal about the pneumatological imagination elsewhere — starting with *Spirit-Word-Community: Theological Hermeneutics in Trinitarian Perspective,* New Critical Thinking in Religion, Theology and Biblical Studies Series (Burlington, Vt.: Ashgate Publishing Ltd., 2002), Part II. But I do not have the space in this essay to show how this applies to the Christian university.

46. See *The Holy Spirit in Christian Education,* ed. Sylvia Lee (Springfield, Mo.: Gospel Publishing House, 1988); cf. Gary Newton, "The Holy Spirit in the Educational Process," in *Introducing Christian Education: Foundations for the Twenty-First Century,* ed. Michael J. Anthony (Grand Rapids: Baker Academic, 2001), pp. 125-29.

we to use, for instance — as those who are filled with the Spirit or aspiring to follow the Spirit's leading. Second, I recognize that the Spirit empowers life, and this includes teaching and learning. One renewal educator warns against any "domestication of the Holy Spirit," since that inevitably brings with it a form of debilitating rationalism and the "loss of spiritual power."[47] While I am also concerned about these matters, we should desire to go beyond homiletic platitudes to find out what spiritual power and spiritual life look like in the Christian university context. Do they involve what renewalists call signs, wonders, and miraculous healings? Whether or not that is the case, what does it mean to engage with these matters as teachers, researchers, and scholars? And third, of course the Spirit impassions followers of Jesus to take up his cause with zealousness and urgency.[48] And I hope my listeners and readers will be able also to sense the passion with which I am engaged in this task of Christian higher education. Such passion is important, but Burtchaell's concern also remains: that there be sufficient foundation to sustain institutions and enable not only their being passed on from one generation to the next but also their thriving. This is part of my concern as well.

In the end, such a renewalist approach to the Christian university will gain traction only if it can specify the difference the Holy Spirit makes to empowering teaching and imbuing research and scholarship with vitality. If this can be delineated, then the results ought to be relevant for all Christian — and especially evangelical — educators. How then can these renewalist "tongues" be translated into higher educational discourse?

Sketching a Renewed Vision of Christian Higher Education

There will be at least two parts to such a project. The first would involve an investigation, historiographically inflected by renewal perspectives, that revisits the history of Christian education and identifies therein the outworking of the Spirit-filled life in the formation of the Christian mind. Thus, what is interesting about historic Christian educational practices — if we were to look (as my

47. Dell Tarr, "Transcendence, Immanence, and the Emerging Pentecostal Academy," in *Pentecostalism in Context: Essays in Honor of William W. Menzies*, ed. Wonsuk Ma and Robert P. Menzies (Sheffield: Sheffield Academic Press, 1997), p. 211, p. 207.

48. See, for example, L. Grant McClung Jr., "Pentecostal/Charismatic Perspectives on Missiological Education," in *Missiological Education for the Twenty-First Century: The Book, the Circle, and the Sandals: Essays in Honor of Paul E. Pierson*, ed. J. Dudley Woodberry, Charles van Engen, and Edgar J. Elliston (Maryknoll, N.Y.: Orbis Books, 1996), pp. 57-66.

forthcoming book intends to do) at patristic *paideia,* medieval scholasticism, the monastic enterprise, Renaissance humanism, and the Reformational educational ideals — is the emphasis on divine encounter and sanctifying transformation directed towards a fully engaged spiritual, moral, and intellectual life. By and large, these goals, along with many of the attendant means to such objectives, are evident also in educational initiatives across the last century of renewalist (Pentecostal and charismatic) history, a point which will have to be further argued elsewhere.[49] The historical thesis that needs to be argued, then, is that a pneumatologically charged vision of Christian higher education will necessarily involve a fully charismatic life, one that facilitates encountering God, that cultivates the sanctified life, and that inspires a transformational engagement with the world in anticipation of the coming reign of God.

A second part to such an argument will need to build on this historical account in order to reconsider the nature of the Christian university. To be sure, the university itself is an incredibly complex phenomenon, and even the qualifier "Christian" might be understood in many different ways. The goal of such an undertaking, however, ought to be quite modest: to suggest how Christian higher education might be rejuvenated in light of perspectives derived at least in part from renewal Christianity's emphasis on the Spirit-filled life. My claim is that a charismatically oriented Christian university promises to nurture spaces that open up to transcendence (for divine encounter), to develop formative practices (for shaping the moral life), and to initiate service in the name and Spirit of the coming Christ (anticipating the impending reign of God) — all of which ought to have implications for and applications to teaching, scholarship, and Christian university life as a whole. These basic motifs ought to be articulated as the second part of the project of renewing the Christian university.

Along the way, this triadic charismatic theme will also need to be brought into conversation with other foundational theological triads, the most obvious being the basic elements of the human constitution, what pietists call (as we have seen above) the head, the heart, and the hands.[50] Each of these elements

---

49. Pentecostal educator Everett L. McKinney — quite apart from any mutual interaction between us — uses much of this language in this article: "Some Spiritual Aspects of Pentecostal Education: A Personal Journey," *Asian Journal of Pentecostal Studies* 3, no. 2 (2000): 253-79.

50. What is signaled in the triadic title of a book by Rick Ostrander — *Head, Heart, and Hand: John Brown University and Modern Evangelical Higher Education* (Fayetteville: University of Arkansas Press, 2003) — does not play any major material, formal, or theoretical role in what is essentially a rather straightforward — and very interesting — historical narrative about this evangelical university.

can be shown to unfold how charismatic encounter, the quest for the sanctified life, and missional service are directed toward realizing the truth, beauty, and goodness of Christ in a fallen world.[51] Further, following this triadic scheme, the discussions also can be organized theologically or theoretically (e.g., on thinking, feeling, and doing), imaginatively with regard to possible educational trajectories of development (i.e., related to the classroom, university life, and engagement with the world), and practically or via concrete case studies of missional applications (e.g., regarding teaching and scholarship, virtual education, and education in a global context). These should not be independent discussions of what the Gospel writers call the mind, soul, and strength; they should be intertwined.[52] Each discussion ought to presume the other two in order to ensure that a holistic vision of the Christian university is being developed.

What I hope comes through is an expression of a Christ-centered and Spirit-filled approach to the Christian university that initiates and sustains a holistic and fully Trinitarian theological vision for evangelical higher education.[53] Although renewalists have never been shy in their evangelistic mission, I am particularly sensitive about charges of triumphalism and elitism that perennially have been cast in the Pentecostal direction.[54] Hence the preceding

51. For an alternative, albeit complementary, articulation of the goals of especially theological education, see L. Gregory Jones, "Beliefs, Desires, Practices, and the Ends of Theological Education," in *Practicing Theology: Beliefs and Practices in Christian Life*, ed. Miroslav Volf and Dorothy C. Bass (Grand Rapids: Wm. B. Eerdmans, 2002), pp. 185-205. See also Mark R. Schwehn, "A Christian University: Defining the Difference," *First Things* (May 1999): 25-31, esp. 29; he talks about one of the objectives of Christian higher education as seeking to transmit "a particular tradition of thought, feeling, and practice."

52. J. P. Moreland, *Kingdom Triangle: Recover the Christian Mind, Renovate the Soul, Restore the Spirit's Power* (Grand Rapids: Zondervan, 2007), also has a triadic structure and an argument that are close to what I am suggesting, except that for him, the spiritual dimension (of power) is distinct from that of the mind and the heart, whereas I prefer an overarching pneumatological and Trinitarian framework within which to understand the relationality of heads, hearts, and hands.

53. This would go far beyond what is embryonically suggested in Marjorie Suchocki, "John Cobb's Trinity: Implications for the University," in *Theology and the University: Essays in Honor of John B. Cobb Jr.*, ed. David Ray Griffin and Joseph C. Hough Jr. (Albany: State University of New York Press, 1991), pp. 147-65. This essay simply iterates a Christological form and a pneumatological dynamic empowering trans-*form*-ative achievement of the Christ-form.

54. Howard K. Gregory, "A Response," in *Towards Viable Theological Education: Ecumenical Imperative, Catalyst of Renewal*, ed. John S. Pobee (Geneva: WCC Publications, 1997), pp. 151-57, has even hinted that the emerging renewalist paradigm, shaped by Pentecostal and Neo-Pentecostal commitments, is in danger of morphing into a new form of postmodern Pentecostal imperialism. I will need to be careful to avoid falling into that trap.

ideas are offered not as if they were something new that youthful renewal up-starts — at least to the business of higher education in general, if not Christian higher education in particular — have to offer to those who have up to now been their teachers. Indeed, as the Preacher said of old, "There is nothing new under the sun" (Eccles. 1:9). Rather, all I am calling for is a revisitation of the wisdom of the ancients and those others who have gone before us — a retrieval from the rich heritage of the church — and then a retrieval and an application of their insights and achievements to our own newly emerging global context. If there is anything of value in what emerges, it will consist of making new connections with old ideas, in part involving a discernment of the signs of our present times. What emerges might be nothing more than seeing how Christ and the Spirit are present and active today, even in the task of constructing, maintaining, and growing a Christian university.

Barth on What It Means to Be Human:
A Christian Scholar Confronts the Options

George Hunsinger

Christian theologians must address a number of questions about what it means to be human. Among them are the following:

How should we understand human nature from a theological standpoint?

If we develop a theological account of human nature — a theological anthropology — how might secular or non-Christian alternatives stack up against it?

Finally, within the range of specifically Christian proposals, what would a theologically adequate account of human nature look like as opposed to one that was below par?

These are some of the questions tackled by Karl Barth in *Church Dogmatics*, vol. III, part 2.[1] It is the treatise where he develops his theological anthropology from within the context of the doctrine of creation. With regard to God the Creator, Barth defines human nature in terms of a basic God-relationship. Fundamental to our being as creatures is that we are bound to God because God our Creator has bound himself to us. With this basic anthropological premise as his yardstick, which he will elaborate at considerable length, Barth

---

1. Karl Barth, *Church Dogmatics*, 4 vols., ed. Thomas F. Torrance, trans. Geoffrey W. Bromiley (Edinburgh: T&T Clark, 1936-69), vol. III, part 2. This work will be cited parenthetically in the text; occasionally the author has made slight revisions to these citations.

proceeds to consider several competing views of what it means to be human. Where no reference exists to God the Creator as revealed in Holy Scripture, Barth wonders, can the nature and meaning of human existence be captured at all?

Barth's answer to this question is at once simple and complex. It hinges on a basic distinction between the real and the phenomenal. Let us consider first the idea of the real. The real human being is the one who exists in relationship to God. Human beings have no reality apart from this relationship. Their central purpose as creatures is to know, love, and glorify God forever. There is therefore no such thing as a godless human being, because no human being exists apart from this basic God-relationship. By the same token, there is no such thing, so to speak, as a God without humanity or a "humanless" God. As revealed in Jesus Christ, God does not will to be God without us. The real God exists in relationship to humanity, and the real human being exists in relationship to God.

The reality of what it means to be human cannot be known where this relatedness to God is not known. Does that mean, then, that non-theological anthropologies can grasp nothing true about human existence? Barth, who finds much to commend in non-theological anthropologies, thinks that this conclusion would be premature. Certainly, by leaving God out of the picture, non-theological or philosophical anthropologies cannot know the real human being or human nature as it really is. Nevertheless, these anthropologies can and actually do discover genuine aspects of human nature. Barth calls these genuine aspects "symptoms" or "phenomena." Reason alone cannot know humanity as it really is in relation to God, but it can know phenomena of the human. A Christian theological anthropology needs to respect and learn from these phenomena.

My procedure in this essay will be as follows. First, I will set forth the basic criteria that Barth develops for establishing a theological anthropology. His criteria are remarkable, not least because he derives them from a Christological center, even though he is describing human nature from the standpoint of the doctrine of creation. I will then show how Barth uses these criteria to assess four alternative types of anthropology that he finds instructive but finally deficient. For the sake of convenience I will call these alternatives naturalism, idealism, existentialism, and neo-orthodoxy. In conclusion I will comment on the kind of Christian scholarship that Barth practices in dealing with views that he at once commends and yet pointedly critiques.

Real Human Existence Means Being towards God
in a Particular History Determined by Jesus

Barth picks out six attributes that define a theologically adequate anthropology. Although they exist at the level of general presuppositions, he sees them as material attributes, not just formal features. They are therefore sufficient for distinguishing a Christian anthropology from other anthropologies. They sketch a theological definition of human existence, which can be used for distinguishing what is real from what is merely phenomenal.

The first feature mentioned by Barth has to do with the idea of divine presence. God is not just present to human creatures in a general way, but most especially in and through Jesus. Jesus is God with us, fully God and fully human. He is the incarnation of the eternal Word of God. Human creatures must be seen as conditioned by him. In and through the humanity of Jesus, they have to do immediately with the divine presence. Jesus' humanity is the medium of communication through which God is made present to them and they are made present to God. In and through Jesus they belong to God as those created for the sake of fellowship with God. For the sake of this fellowship, God becomes present to them in and through Jesus. Being determined for fellowship through God's presence in Jesus is a distinctive feature of human existence (III/2, 68, 73).

Barth's second feature has to do with the idea of history. God exists for the human creature only in a certain history. It is a history of deliverance in which God becomes present to the human creature through the covenant fulfilled in Jesus. Human beings are conditioned by the fact that this deliverance takes place for them. All of them exist in God's history of deliverance in such a way that their being as creatures is inseparable from it. In this history their Creator takes on the role of a Savior. Human beings are included in a history of deliverance as fulfilled in Jesus, and their inclusion is another distinctive feature of what it means to be human (III/2, 68-69, 73).

Along with the ideas of presence and history, Barth's third feature of being human involves the idea of divine glory. When God becomes present to human beings in Jesus by including them in a history of deliverance, God's deity is not compromised. God's deity is not lost in Jesus' humanity despite being completely present and revealed in it. God remains entirely God. Certainly, God's act of deliverance is an act of self-humiliation. It is God's total immersion into human frailty, sin and death — an immersion, finally, into total disgrace. But this immersion is not only an act of divine love. It is also an act of divine freedom. In it God confirms who God is and triumphs as the Creator. God is never more glorious than when hidden in Jesus as he died ingloriously on the cross. In and through Jesus the being of every human creature is included in the glory of God's self-humiliation. Because humans are included in it, their being is not an end in itself. It is a being in and for God's glory. Their existence for the sake of God's glory is another distinctive characteristic of what it means to be human (III/2, 69, 74).

The idea of God's sovereignty is the fourth factor singled out by Barth as determining human existence. God's sovereignty is seen most supremely in the history of deliverance fulfilled in Jesus. Jesus exists not outside God's sovereignty but within it. Jesus' weakness embodies what it reveals — the sovereignty of God, and this sovereignty is the power of salvation. In the person of Jesus the humanity of all others is posited, contained, and included. Because of the crucified Jesus, in whom God's lordship is present and revealed, all other human beings also exist under that lordship, and not otherwise. They are all determined by the lordship of God as enacted, fulfilled, and mediated in Jesus. Being determined by God's lordship in Jesus is another distinctive feature of what it means to be human (III/2, 69-70, 74).

The idea of freedom is the fifth factor singled out by Barth as an important feature of what it means to be human. Divine sovereignty and human freedom cannot be separated, Barth urges, nor can they be placed in competition. Whatever human freedom may mean, it cannot consist in the freedom to escape God's lordship. "Freedom" is an ambiguous term with at least two meanings. Freedom in the substantive sense of proper fulfillment must be distinguished from mere freedom of choice. As in Jesus so also in us, substantive freedom is strictly the freedom to decide for God, and not otherwise. Freedom is therefore not something neutral. Nor is it something independent of grace or outside it. Freedom in the substantive sense does not include the possibility of rejecting grace, because when grace is rejected, freedom contradicts itself and is lost. It enters into the bondage of sin and death. The rejection of grace is not an act of freedom; it is an act of self-negation. Human freedom is free, furthermore, only as it depends on divine grace. Because Jesus was free for God in this substantive way, our freedom shares the same conditions. Freedom for God in dependence on grace, as manifested in Jesus, is a distinctive characteristic of human existence (III/2, 70, 74, 109).

The sixth and final factor in Barth's sketch of theological anthropology concerns the idea of service. Human beings exist not for themselves but for the sake of serving God. God is served when they give thanks for the history of their deliverance through God's presence in the person of Jesus. God is served when human beings bow to God's lordship, glory, grace, and love. And God is served when they freely bear witness to what God has done for them in Jesus, corresponding to it with their lives. Although only Jesus has ever served God and lived for God fully in this way, all others are called to a corresponding form of service in him. The vocation of service to God is a distinctive feature of human existence (III/2, 71, 74).

Let me sum up. As set forth by Barth, real human existence means existence in relationship to God. It cannot be understood apart from the ideas of presence, history, glory, lordship, freedom, and service. God is present to human beings in and through a particular history, a history of deliverance as fulfilled in Jesus. In this history God is hidden and revealed in glory under the form of the cross and manifest as the Lord of all. At the same time, human creatures are posited, contained, and included in the person of Jesus. They are embraced in the history of deliverance as centered in him so that they have no real being apart from it. The freedom given to them is freedom for God under the lordship of God. By grace they are made free to serve God as present and known in Jesus. These are some distinctive features of human existence from the standpoint of theological anthropology.

Phenomena of the Human

Although a theological anthropology would involve more than these six distinctive features, they constitute a kind of irreducible minimum. Other proposals about human nature must be examined in light of these distinctives. They serve as criteria by which both positive and negative assessments can be made. No definition of human nature can be adequate, however, if it disregards divine revelation. Proposals derived from general experience will always result in a vicious circle in which we will never attain to real human existence. How can we expect to grasp what human nature really is if we disregard the fact that we belong to God, that we exist in relationship to the work of God, and that we live for the glory, under the lordship, and in the service of God? What kind of human beings are we, Barth asks, if we think we can disregard all this? Those who know the reality of human existence cannot disregard it. Only phantom human beings would think we can know what human nature is without first taking God into account (III/2, 75).

On this basis, Barth proceeds to interrogate four types of anthropology: naturalism, idealism, existentialism, and neo-orthodoxy. When measured against his six criteria, while each has something to be said for it, each is finally deficient. Each grasps phenomena of the human without comprehending the reality.

Naturalism

Barth begins with a reflection on the familiar Aristotelian idea that the human being is a "rational animal." This definition was sometimes adopted by Protestant theologians in the seventeenth century who had impeccable credentials with regard to theological orthodoxy. Adopting this definition had an unfortunate consequence, however. For as time went on it suggested that a theological interpretation of human existence "could be regarded as an appendix or even ignored" (III/2, 77). Barth observes, "If we start with the idea of the human being as an animal endowed with reason, we are not led by any necessary inference to God, and therefore not to the human being as a being essentially related to God. If the interpretation is to be valid, the definition must include the truth that our relation to God as humans is an essential part of our being" (III/2, 77 revised).

If we construct a general definition before bringing in our relatedness to God, we are in danger, Barth cautions, of making it seem optional or superfluous. But the most particular thing about us is also the most truly universal and decisive, namely, that we exist in a history determined by God's attitude toward us. Our God-relationship is not simply one fact among others. If we try to make some other idea general and universal, as if our God-relationship were somehow secondary, we will end up pointing into the void, not to human existence as it really is (III/2, 77).

Barth then turns to evolutionary biology and theological attempts to interpret it. Late nineteenth- and early twentieth-century apologists tried to confront evolutionary naturalism with the necessary "No and Yes of Christian faith, insight, and confession." In opposing the leveling down of the human being as threatened by evolutionary views, these apologists did what was essential: "They made a serious effort to put up the necessary resistance." Unfortunately, they did not always do so in the most fortunate way. Something else must be said in favor of these apologists, however. "They were," Barth notes with approval, "prepared to learn both externally and intensively from the science of their time." According to Barth, the insights of evolutionary biology, which are manifold and rich, deserve to be welcomed, as far as they go, with gratitude (III/2, 84, 85).

Writing in 1948, Barth next devotes extensive attention to the views of Adolf Portmann, a zoologist who published a work on evolutionary biology in

1944 with no noticeable theological concern. Portmann, whom Barth praises for his moderation, represents a point of view that is perhaps anticipatory of a work published in 2007 called *The Evolution Controversy: A Survey of Competing Theories* by Thomas B. Fowler and Daniel Kuebler.[2] Like Portmann, Fowler and Kuebler are scientists who attempt to offer a balanced and critical assessment of the current state of evolutionary biology for non-scientists.

What Barth says about Portmann would apply equally well to Fowler and Kuebler. When it comes to our knowledge of ourselves as human beings, evolutionary biology "can offer us only modest, i.e., limited, conditioned, and relative certainty, and definitely not the certainty which life demands of us as human beings." Furthermore, when we have examined the findings of evolutionary biology, we have encountered only phenomena of the human, not the reality of human existence. The true significance of these natural phenomena "is not itself a phenomenon but the subject of a judgment that has not the slightest connection with the observation of the facts" (III/2, 88).

Unless we already know the reality of human existence in its essential relatedness to God, Barth contends, we will not be able to evaluate properly the findings of evolutionary biology. We will be inclined to think that our reality as human beings consists in what we have in common with the animal kingdom and the rest of creation generally. We will be blind even though we see. We will mistake the part for the whole (III/2, 90).

Here again, as with the definition of human beings as rational animals, the fatal mistake must not be made of allowing our opponents to determine the form of the question. We must not proceed on the assumption that as human beings we are only animals, a higher form of mammals, before trying to speak theologically. Furthermore, even apart from divine revelation, we can see that naturalism cannot account for certain attributes like human consciousness and human freedom. In order to account for these attributes, we must enter into another sphere of discourse (III/2, 91-93).

Idealism

In considering idealist proposals about what it means to be human, Barth makes a kind of double move. He considers what can be known by reason alone while at the same time allowing his perceptions to be informed by divine

---

2. Thomas B. Fowler and Daniel Kuebler, *The Evolution Controversy: A Survey of Competing Theories* (Grand Rapids: Baker, 2001).

revelation. In particular, the phenomenon of human freedom must be taken seriously, even though idealism finally falls short in dealing with it.

On the basis of reason alone it can be seen that human beings exist in connection with their environment and yet also in freedom from it. Human beings must therefore see themselves as having an identity in two spheres. In their knowledge of themselves, they can see that they are in some sense causally determined while yet also being more than beings who are causally determined. They exist, so to speak, in two spheres: the sphere of natural causation and the sphere of freedom. On the one hand, they are causally determined, while on the other hand, they are the conscious subjects of free decisions (III/2, 94).

The central example Barth takes to represent idealist views of human nature is Johann Gottlieb Fichte.[3] Fichte was an exponent of the kind of high German idealism in the nineteenth century that placed a premium on the freedom of the human subject over and above all natural or causal determinism. What Barth observes about Fichte, however, might also have some bearing on the views of other philosophers more familiar to us today. I think in particular of John Searle and Thomas Nagel.

Although Searle and Nagel are very far from Fichte in many ways, they share at least one point in common with him. Like Fichte, both Searle and Nagel (and each in his own way) seek to resist naturalistic forms of reductionism in their views of human nature. They both adopt a kind of double perspective that will allow them to accept the full findings of the natural and biological sciences while still seeking to preserve a place for an irreducible human consciousness and freedom.

Searle holds that two things are true at the same time: consciousness is a real subjective experience, and yet it is also caused by physical processes of the brain. Consciousness is both real and yet a mystery.[4] Nagel, similarly, argues for the validity of two viewpoints: a third-person perspective which is objective and causal along with a first-person perspective that is subjective and transcendent. Finding no way to reconcile these two perspectives, Nagel recommends moving back and forth between the two.[5]

It is the irreducibly subjective element of human experience that offers a point of contact between Searle and Nagel, on the one hand, and Fichte on the

3. Johann Gottlieb Fichte, *Die Bestimmung des Menschen* (Berlin: Vossischen Buchhandlung, 1800); English translation: *The Vocation of Man*, translated, with introduction and notes, by Peter Preuss (Indianapolis: Hackett Publishing Co., 1987).

4. See John R. Searle, *The Rediscovery of the Mind* (Cambridge, Mass.: MIT Press, 1992), and *The Mystery of Consciousness* (New York: The New York Review of Books, 1999).

5. Thomas Nagel, *The View from Nowhere* (New York: Oxford University Press, 1989).

other. The divergences, of course, are also great. We might say that while Fichte operates, so to speak, with an idealism that veers toward naturalism, Searle and Nagel operate with a basic naturalism that gestures toward idealism. In any case, all three philosophers take the subjective element seriously, and all three propose to grasp the reality of human nature on the basis of reason alone.

Barth subjects Fichte to an internal critique before he proceeds to an external critique. He sets forth Fichte on his own terms as extensively as he did the evolutionary biologists. Barth is then in a position to press Fichte on the coherence of holding to both human freedom and natural determinism at the same time. We might wonder much the same about Searle and Nagel, though they at least have the virtue of owning up to the perplexity in a way that is less evident in Fichte.

What Barth finds of value in Fichte is that on the basis of mere reason he discovers what Barth calls "the phenomenon of the human in its ethical aspect" (III/2, 107). For Barth this is no small achievement, since it describes from the philosophical side something of great importance about the reality of human existence from the theological side. Yet the idea of the ethical subject in Fichte's philosophy is judged finally to be both unstable and inflated. Fichte glimpses something that he cannot sustain.

Barth concludes by reverting to his six criteria:

A God to whom human beings belong as to another; a God who can act in relation to them and become their Savior; a God who has his own glory in which the essential concern of humanity is to be seen; a God who reigns; a God in relation to whom human beings gain their freedom and whom they must serve in their freedom; a God who confronts and limits them and is thus their true determination, is for Fichte nonexistent. Fichte's god is Fichte's man, and Fichte's man is Fichte's god. And it is because God is non-existent that Fichte has had to conceive the idea of absolutely autarchic and subjective being, to ascribe this being to humankind, and to regard the resultant figure as the real human being. (III/2, 108-109, revised)

While this external critique would not fully apply to Searle and Nagel, Barth's final word to Fichte might also pertain, with modifications, to them. For Barth suggests that naturalism cannot finally be overcome by a higher idealism without referring to God:

If the aim [writes Barth of Fichte] was to provide a philosophy of freedom, it would have been better not to regard God as non-existent, and therefore to become blind even to the phenomenon of what it means to be human. This is the warning which we are finally given by this stimulating example. (III/2, 109, revised)

Existentialism

The views that Barth has considered so far — anthropological naturalism and anthropological idealism — both seem to have something in common. Both in various ways seem to regard human nature — whether as determined by natural forces or as self-determining — as something ahistorical and self-contained. In turning to anthropological existentialism, as seen in the philosophy of Karl Jaspers, the discussion moves to a new level.[6] Human existence is now seen as a history that is open to the transcendent, and this transcendent other, while remaining nameless and impersonal, is nonetheless necessary for human self-knowledge and human self-fulfillment.

The idea of an unthinkable and inexpressible transcendence has appeared more recently in the philosophies of Emmanuel Levinas[7] and Jacques Derrida.[8] Barth's reflections on Jaspers might to that extent pertain, with proper qualifications, also to them. Like Jaspers, Levinas and Derrida allow for a transcendent God who remains nameless but who allows himself to be gestured at by human words. Levinas, with his strong emphasis on the ethical subject, is perhaps closer than the others to idealism. He argues for a deliberate separation from God after the Holocaust so as to encounter the face of the human other as absolutely other. The human other is to be honored and respected in its otherness. Derrida, on the other hand, also traumatized by the Holocaust, opts for a view that might be called "mystical atheism." He presents himself as a kind of atheist for the sake of God, waiting painfully for an ineffable transcendence that he never expects to appear.

Neither Levinas nor Derrida, however, would be as interesting to Barth as Jaspers. What Barth appreciates in his Basel colleague is the way he combines two key aspects: the historicity of human existence, on the one hand, and an openness to transcendence on the other. A living relation to this transcendence is thought to be indispensable for the actualization of human existence. Look-

---

6. Karl Jaspers, *Philosophy,* 3 vols. (Chicago: University of Chicago Press, 1969).

7. Emmanuel Levinas, *God, Death, and Time* (Stanford, Calif.: Stanford University Press, 2000).

8. Jacques Derrida, *Acts of Religion* (London: Routledge, 2002).

ing back from his core idea that real human existence means being towards God, Barth is prepared to grant that Jaspers, by means of reason alone, has grasped a genuine phenomenon, though of course not the reality, of what it means to be human. Jaspers has the advantage of understanding that human existence, rather than being self-grounded, self-resting, and self-moving, is dynamically open to and dependent on an encounter with the transcendent other (III/2, 113-14).

Nevertheless, Barth departs from Jaspers when Jaspers argues that the way transcendence breaks in on human existence is through the negative experiences of the boundary situation. Barth grants that human beings are continually involved in the "boundary situations" of suffering and death, conflict and guilt. "But it is far from obvious," Barth writes, "nor is there any compelling reason to suppose, that it is such crises which really bring human beings into relation with the [transcendent] wholly other, and lead them into an existence which embodies the meaning of this relation" (III/2, 114).

Barth expresses doubt that boundary situations are "saturated with transcendence" (III/2, 117). He is also skeptical that human beings are capable of themselves of fulfilling the condition of living by transcendence, as Jaspers supposes they are (III/2, 118). We are still confronted, Barth concludes, with the picture of a self-enclosed human reality beyond which there is finally nothing to confront it other than itself. Jaspers has no true concept of a phenomenon that might be "identified with the God who is distinct from humanity and the world, superior to both" (III/2, 119).

The reality of human existence, Barth concludes, cannot be known on the basis of autonomous human self-understanding. Unlike naturalistic, ethical, and existentialist views, theological anthropology cannot recognize the real human being in a figure who is neutral, indefinite, or obscure regarding God's attitude towards it and its own attitude to God.

Barth therefore subjects Jaspers to both an internal and an external critique. His internal critique is that Jaspers cannot convincingly establish the transcendent as a reality independent of human existence. His external critique, on the other hand, appeals once again to his six points. Barth writes,

> On a very definite ground, that of the picture of the human Jesus which is normative for Christian theology, we have postulated that real human beings must in any event be beings who as such belong to God, to whom God turns as Savior, the determination of whom is God's glory, who exist under the lordship of God and are set in the service of God. We were warned at the outset not to seek real human existence elsewhere than in this history

between God and humanity, and to recognize as the essence of real human existence none other than its existence in this history. (III/2, 121, revised)

Despite their laudable appeals to the transcendent, neither Jaspers, on the one hand, nor Levinas and Derrida on the other manage to capture very much in the way of phenomenal expressions of this core human reality.

Neo-Orthodoxy

The naturalistic, ethical, and existentialist views of what it means to be human are seen by Barth as the most important stages on the way to an autonomous human self-understanding. He does not reject these views out of hand. They each capture something important about the phenomenon of human existence as it can be known apart from revelation. Taken in sequence, these views represent "a progressively more penetrating analysis" of the picture that can be gained about humanity by reason alone. But at best this picture leaves us with mere abstract phenomena, not with the concrete reality of human existence (III/2, 121).

By turning in conclusion to Emil Brunner's theological anthropology,[9] Barth seeks for a way to break out of the "closed circle" of existentialist anthropology (III/2, 129). A proper theological anthropology, Barth contends, will be not abstract but concrete, not neutral but affirmative, not formal but substantive, not indefinite but specific, not obscure but well-defined. It will move not from general anthropological possibilities to actualities, but from concrete actualities to the conditions for their possibility. It will start from real human existence as first of all instantiated and defined by Jesus. It will ground itself in the concrete reality of our being towards God.

What Barth has to say about Brunner would also apply in some ways to Reinhold Niebuhr[10] and his brother, H. Richard Niebuhr,[11] though certainly in rather different respects. To be sure, Brunner's theology was more Christocentric, more Trinitarian, and more oriented toward the Word of God than

9. Emil Brunner, *Man in Revolt: A Christian Anthropology* (Philadelphia: Westminster Press, 1947).

10. Reinhold Niebuhr, *The Nature and Destiny of Man,* 2 vols. (New York: Charles Scribner's Sons, 1941-43).

11. H. Richard Niebuhr, *The Meaning of Revelation* (New York: Macmillan, 1941), *The Responsible Self* (New York: Harper & Row, 1963), and *Radical Monotheism and Western Civilization* (Lincoln: University of Nebraska Press, 1960).

anything to be found in either of the Niebuhrs. Nevertheless, Reinhold Niebuhr drew heavily upon Brunner's theological anthropology, and H. Richard Niebuhr arguably shared with Brunner a certain penchant for the abstract and the general over the concrete and the particular. It is this latter tendency that worried Barth.

Although the concept of freedom is finally the focus of what Barth has to say about Brunner's anthropology, Barth first introduces a number of new ideas into the mix. These ideas are listed at one point as "rationality, responsibility, personality, historicity, and capacity for decision" (III/2, 130). For Barth, theological anthropology must understand what these ideas indicate not as abstract possibilities but as concrete actualities, not as innate attributes but as events in the history of God with humanity and of humanity with God. They must therefore be understood not in a formal and neutral way, but rather in a way that is substantive and determined by grace.

Here we must restrict ourselves to considering the concept of freedom. Barth's question to Brunner hinges on the distinction between formal freedom and substantive freedom. Recall that formal freedom would simply be freedom of choice. Substantive freedom, on the other hand, would be freedom as given and fulfilled by grace. It would be freedom as it is properly enacted in the course of the actual history in which humans have their being with God and towards God. Humans have their real being in the history of God's gracious covenant as determined and fulfilled in Jesus. Barth's quarrel with Brunner is that his anthropology is ambiguous about the meaning of freedom. Indeed, it is finally more than ambiguous, since it tilts towards neutrality and abstraction in its idea of freedom as merely freedom of choice.

For Barth, real human existence is existence as fulfilled in relationship to God. In this relationship human freedom is not something neutral and formal. Sin in particular is not to be regarded as "one of the possibilities given in human creatureliness" (III/2, 130). It is rather to be seen as a self-contradiction of freedom that leads to destruction of creatureliness. Unlike Brunner and the Niebuhrs, the operative distinction for Barth is not between the ideal and the real, but rather between the real and the unreal. Sin is a possibility alien to our true creaturely being, not one that is integral to it (III/2, 131). It threatens to plunge the human creature into annihilation and nothingness. By sinning the creature loses its being towards God and plummets into a being towards death. Sin can be described only paradoxically as "the impossible possibility" and "the unreal reality."

For Barth, however, the real is defined not by sin but by grace. The human nosedive into sin is arrested by God's intervention for the human race in Jesus. It is blocked and reversed in the history of God's covenant as fulfilled in him.

The history of our deliverance is the history in which our real being as humans is to be found, despite our sin. Our being as humans can be described only in concrete, actual, and particular terms. It has no reality apart from the history fulfilled in Jesus, in which we are objectively included by grace and which we are called to acknowledge and receive by faith.

We may return to Barth's six points one last time. Here they are stated most explicitly with reference to the human Jesus:

> The ontological determination of humanity is grounded in the fact that one man among all others is the man Jesus. So long as we select any other starting point for our study, we shall reach only the phenomena of the human. We are condemned to abstractions so long as our attention is riveted as it were on other human beings, or rather on humanity in general, as if we could learn about real human existence from a study of humanity in general, and in abstraction from the fact that one man among all others is the man Jesus. In this case we miss the one Archimedean point given us beyond humanity, and therefore the one possibility of discovering the ontological determination of human existence. Theological anthropology has no choice in this matter. It is not yet or no longer theological anthropology if it tries to pose and answer the question of the true being of human existence from any other angle.
>
> We remember who and what the man Jesus is. As we have seen, he is the one creaturely being in whose existence we have to do immediately and directly with the being of God also. Again, he is the creaturely being in whose existence God's act of deliverance has taken place for all other human beings. He is the creaturely being in whom God as the Savior of all human beings also reveals and affirms his own glory as the Creator. He is the creaturely being who as such embodies the sovereignty of God, or conversely the sovereignty of God which as such actualizes this creaturely being. He is the creaturely being whose existence consists in his fulfillment of the will of God. And finally he is the creaturely being who as such not only exists from God and in God but absolutely for God instead of for himself. (III/2, 132-33, revised)

Conclusion

Three quick lessons may be drawn from Barth's discussion of theological anthropology:

Before he turns to examine alternative views of human nature — whether naturalist, idealist, existentialist, or neo-orthodox — Barth develops a set of normative criteria based on scriptural revelation. These criteria enable him to distinguish the phenomenal from the real, the abstract from the concrete, and the merely formal from the substantive. They also enable him to set the terms of discussion rather than allowing competing views to assume that role, a move that he believes is always fatal.

Barth always engages in descriptive criticism before he turns to evaluative criticism. He presents alternative views carefully and fairly before attempting an assessment. Sometimes he offers an internal critique based on conceptual problems inherent in the view he is considering. At other times he develops an external critique based on his normative theological criteria. The criteria enable him to find points of value in alternative views even when they are finally deficient.

Finally, Barth thinks everything through from a center in Christ. It is Jesus Christ who determines what is real and what is merely phenomenal. It is he who conditions our lives as human beings. It is he in relation to whom we live and move and have our being. Our real existence as humans is our being for God in and through him.

This method of inquiry would seem to be highly suggestive for those after Barth who wish to pursue Christian scholarship in the twenty-first century.

List of Contributors

EDITORS

Thomas M. Crisp is Associate Professor of Philosophy, Biola University.

Steve L. Porter is Associate Professor of Theology, Spiritual Formation, and Philosophy, Biola University.

Gregg A. Ten Elshof is Professor of Philosophy, Biola University.

ESSAYISTS

Jonathan A. Anderson is Associate Professor of Art, Biola University.

Dariusz M. Bryćko is College Minister, First Presbyterian Church in Columbia, South Carolina, and President of Tolle Lege Institute.

Natasha Duquette is Associate Dean, Tyndale University College & Seminary.

M. Elizabeth Lewis Hall is Professor of Psychology, Biola University.

George Hunsinger is Hazel Thompson McCord Professor of Systematic Theology, Princeton Theological Seminary.

Paul K. Moser is Professor of Philosophy, Loyola University Chicago.

Alvin Plantinga is John A. O'Brien Professor of Philosophy Emeritus, University of Notre Dame.

Craig J. Slane is Frances Owen Distinguished Professor of Theology, Simpson University.

Nicholas Wolterstorff is Noah Porter Professor Emeritus of Philosophical Theology, Yale University.

Amos Yong is Professor of Theology and Mission, and Director of Center for Missiological Research, Fuller Theological Seminary.